TWO STEPS FORWARD
ONE STEP BACK
MY LIFE IN THE MUSIC BUSINESS

MILES A. COPELAND III

TWO STEPS FORWARD, ONE STEP BACK
MY LIFE IN THE MUSIC BUSINESS
MILES A. COPELAND III

A JAWBONE BOOK
Published in the UK and the USA
by Jawbone Press
Office G1
141–157 Acre Lane
London SW2 5UA
England
www.jawbonepress.com

ISBN 978-1-911036-77-7

Printed in the Czech Republic by PRtisk

1 2 3 4 5 25 24 23 22 21

CONTENTS

I dedicate this book to my three sons, Miles 4th, Aeson, and Axton, who will at some point be interested in what their father did, where he succeeded, where he screwed up, so that they may learn and hopefully may even be inspired. At least they might be entertained. It took me a while to appreciate my own father, which in the end I did. Believe me, reading his memoirs and prolific writings, I certainly was entertained! I also dedicate it to my wife Adriana, who has put up with me and all the crazy people I had to deal with. Of course, I dedicate it as well to all those crazy people who have made my story, so . . . well, let's just say 'colorful.' **You know who you are.**

PREFACE

August 18, 1983. I am standing centerstage at Shea Stadium, New York—the ballpark made famous as a music venue two decades earlier by The Beatles—making the introductions, as my brother Stewart and his bandmates, Sting and Andy Summers, prepare to take the stage.

'LADIES AND GENTELMEN
IT'S TIME FOR … THE POLICE!'

Moments later, I am watching from the side of the stage with my mother and father. Who could have imagined they would be standing here in front of eighty thousand people, to see their sons bask in the glory of the biggest rock'n'roll band in the world?

ço

The story of my career in the music business is filled with moments like these. But my real story starts with a disaster, an unmitigated, pull-the-rug-from-under-you, clean-out-the-bank-account disaster. A disaster that led me so close to the edge of bankruptcy that I still don't know how I survived to fight another day.

It was a disaster that, if it had not happened, The Police most likely would never have existed, and they certainly would have never risen to become the biggest rock band in the world. Jools Holland would not have become a TV fixture in the UK; The Bangles, The Go-Go's, R.E.M., and many other music stars might never have made it either.

It's strange how a fluke, a disaster, an unlikely event, can lead to incredible results. But that is in essence what happened to me.

That disaster was StarTruckin' 75, a kind of traveling music festival— probably the first of its kind in Europe, and maybe anywhere. The idea was to bring together my management clients—Wishbone Ash, Renaissance, The Climax Blues Band, and others—with acts like Lou Reed and Mahavishnu Orchestra. It was 'greatness by association,' hoping their fame would splash on my artists.

We chartered two planes to take the acts around Europe—thirteen dates in six countries, beginning in Copenhagen, Denmark, on August 5, 1975. I quickly learned that if you take one band out on the road, you only have one set of problems to deal with, but if you take eight bands, you know someone's going to screw up.

The big problem was Lou Reed. *Where was Lou Reed?* Nobody knew. The shows were happening, but there was no sign of Lou. Eventually I tracked him down to a hotel bathroom in New Zealand: 'He's been in there a day already, and I don't see him coming out for another week.'

We had to scamper around to find out who might be available to replace him at short notice. In the end we got Ike & Tina Turner, who gave us a great show, but it was last-minute, so the agent had the opportunity to hit us with a big bill. Financially it was a complete disaster. With each show we were losing more and more money, and that just pulled the rug out from under the tour. It was a financial fiasco that took me to the brink of bankruptcy. The bailiffs closed my London office, and the New York office disappeared too, leaving my brother Ian stranded. The booking agent I had worked with for so long and so successfully in the USA was telling people, 'Miles Copeland is over.' And for much of the music world that I had been dealing with up to then, that pretty much summed it up.

It never occurred to me that I would be going too far or doing too much. I had never been in a position where I had failed to do what I said I'd do. But this was also the key turning point in my life. It firmly ended one era and set me on a course to a new one. If it had not happened, my morphing into the punk world and everything that followed might never have happened either. Perhaps the whole punk-to-new-wave revolution might have been very different.

Maybe StarTruckin' was an idea ahead of its time. There were big lessons to learn from that tour, but more than anything, the scale of the disaster forced me to look in places I might not have. I owe a lot to that disaster. Without it, none of the rest of this would have happened.

෴

For several years I dabbled at writing a book, first from a motivational approach, like: *This is what I did, what I learned, and what you might learn from too.* My intent was not to boast about my accomplishments or trivialize my failures. Rather, to offer them as lessons one can learn from, and that might apply to many endeavors beyond the narrow confines of the entertainment business.

As my children are about as interested in my musical tastes as I was in my father's, I figured if they were going to read anything I wrote, the more universal I could make the lessons, the better. And, of course, put in plenty of funny and crazy stories to hold their attention along the way. Believe me, there are plenty to tell.

My father, a notorious CIA operative involved in various stories of skullduggery both real and perceived, used to have fun writing about his children. He liked to mix up known theories with ones he made up, but he always managed to keep a grain of truth in the many letters he sent me and the stories he created around my brothers, Ian and Stewart, The Police, and even Sting and Andy Summers.

The high-profile success of his kids in the music business and the propensity for 'hype' in the entertainment world gave him license to write in ways he could not do when describing his own exploits in the CIA in the books he published (*Game Of Nations, Real Spy World, Without Cloak And Dagger, The Game Player*).

One of his favorite Copeland family stories was this:

> Miles, we like to say, Thinks Big Upwards—in geography, dollars, economic whammy, and political power. Stewart, on the other hand, is Breadth. Students of the Copeland phenomenon have marveled at how Miles III is able to 'conceptualize beyond horizons' (*New York Times*, January 12, 1976). Stewart's concepts START at the horizons. As you know, it has been a family routine to have each of

the kids tested by CIA psychologists upon reaching his or her twelfth birthday. The results of Miles, his sister Lennie, and brother Ian were 'positively astounding,' as an agency's director of personnel wrote in a memorandum to the recruiting office in 1962, when the whole family, as such, was being considered for 'certain community duties' in Beirut, Lebanon. On the second day of Stewart's sessions, however, somewhere out in Virginia, an hour's drive from Washington, the psychologists gave up on him, with remarks on his test report to the effect that his kind of intelligence 'simply isn't relevant and is therefore immeasurable.' Isn't RELEVANT? What the hell does that mean? 'It means,' explained the patronizing little shit who headed the testing unit, 'that we've all got one kind of intelligence and Stewart has quite another, and we can only measure the first kind.'

I can assure the reader that I have tried to avoid my father's oft-quoted rule, 'Never let the truth stand in the way of a good story.' As far as I know, I have made no claims that are untrue, as I have tried to be as accurate as humanly possible.

Some important players, like my brother Ian and my partner Kim Turner, are no longer with us, so I could not benefit from their help. In the end, I hope my experiences and lessons learned will entertain but, more than that, will offer insights and inspiration for others, no matter what walk of life one has chosen.

CHAPTER 1

ROAD TO DAMASCUS

· · · · · · · ·

I like to joke that I was born under a bright star, but no one was sure what star it was. In fact, I doubt if anyone was looking skyward that night, unless they were in London, watching for the German buzz bombs that were about to fall on the city—or the Germans looking skyward, to see if the allied planes were bombing them that night. It was a year before the end of World War II, and bad things were happening in most of the world. Of course, I knew nothing about any of this, as I was just a tiny baby. But had that war not happened, I would not have existed either, and I would not be here to tell this story.

You see, my father was a jazz trumpet player from Birmingham, Alabama. My mother was a secretary in London, England. Neither knew of the other's existence in 1942. Neither had any idea where their lives would lead, and certainly no idea that I, my brothers Ian and Stewart, and my sister Lennie would be part of it.

I recently discovered a piece my father wrote back in 1982, when he must have been thinking about his children. He had a pretty good idea who we were, even if he was prone to embellish somewhat. This is what he wrote:

> The real history of the Copeland family begins with Miles III. Lorraine and I cannot entirely take credit, as parents, for the fairly remarkable development of him, because our child-rearing policy, although it turns out to have been a wise one, was born partly out of sheer laziness

and out of pre-occupation with distracting professional pursuits. After the war was over, I was employed by the OSS's successor organization, the Central Intelligence Agency, and became a specialist in what we called 'political action'—you know, rigging elections, laying on coups d'état, inciting riots. That sort of thing. Miles was born in London in the middle of the war, but as he was growing up the family was living, successively, in Syria (where Ian was born), Egypt (where we moved just after Stewart was born), and Lebanon, and while they were in the process of becoming conscious of the world about them, I was making 'adjustments' in the governments of those places, and trying to guide Egypt's President Nasser, to whom I was political advisor, into modes of behavior acceptable to the United States.

Lorraine, mother of my children, once complained that we weren't sufficiently conscientious in our child-rearing. I heard myself replying, 'Us rear them? They can damn well rear themselves!' Now, I said this without thinking. But later, as I thought about it, I realized that such an attitude made sense. Parents can GUIDE their kids; they can inspire them and stimulate their interest in worthwhile pursuits—or, rather, they can place them in environments which inspire and stimulate, but the central phenomenon of an individual's development is not his BEING TAUGHT, it's his LEARNING. To put it another way, instead of parents taking upon themselves the burden of teaching, they must place on their children the burden to learn. They must discover their children's special talents and propensities, then show them the advantages which will accrue from developing them. After that, their role is that of consultants, i.e., they give advice only when it is asked for. To my way of thinking, the 'uncommon man' is one who makes and lives by his own disciplines. By supplying the right intellectual and moral environment, a parent guides his children into a proper realization of what those disciplines have to be. From then on, they're on their own.

Well, not quite. The phrase 'supplying the right intellectual and moral environment' and the word 'guiding' comprise a very large mouthful. They must result in a kind of concentration we in the Copeland family call 'targeting.' The 'uncommon man' sets his sights on some particular interest and becomes obsessed with it—deeply, not dilettantishly. The interest—the 'obsession' must be something outside himself, something on which he can become an authority, an expert, a master. As I said, the parent's task is to discover their offspring's special talents and propensities, and THEN stimulate interests which will make the most of them. Miles, when he was making only slightly above-average grades in school, continually demonstrated that underrated quality, 'sound judgement,' to the detriment of his relations with his teachers because it caused him to resist 'being taught.' Example: an examination question is, 'Give three reasons for the fall of the Roman Empire,' and he would answer something like, 'Well, the guy who wrote the book says it was drink, sex, and general profligacy, but that's just HIS idea.' Then he would proceed to explain how things might have been different had HE been living back in Roman times so that he could have taken over. Like that.

Well, Miles's first obsession was Japanese martial arts and the philosophy that goes with them—the main feature of which is FLEXIBILITY of decision. You see, every successful person in the Western tradition opines that 'if you don't know where you are going you aren't going anywhere,' and 'the world belongs to those who plan for it.' But Japanese phenomenology adds a special twist: how can you plan for an unpredictable future? How can you know where you are going when you don't yet know where there is to go? How could John Glenn have set his sights on becoming an astronaut when, as a boy, he had no practical way of knowing such a profession would exist? Japanese teleology doesn't rule out goals, as we Westerners see them, it only emphasizes their subjectivity. As understood by Miles, having a precisely defined goal was less important than living according to a fixed purpose. 'Goal' implies a definite place, position or status such as it can be comprehended now, without regard for changes in environment such as may occur en route to it. 'Purpose' implies FUNCTION, and function of a sort that will fit ANY environment. Thus, in Miles III's adaptation of Japanese philosophy, a 'target' is something to be shot at just ahead—a STEP, in other words. But there must be FLEXIBILITY. In Judo, you delay your decision until the last micro-second, keeping yourself equally capable of throwing your opponent in either direction, depending on whatever his vulnerability happens to be at the moment of action. Translated to the world of general living, it means keeping ever alert to changes in what military strategists call 'the situation,' and being forever prepared to adjust to them—without, of course, abandoning long-range objectives or the 'obsession' which keeps one driving towards them.

Miles got into all this in the summer of 1958, when the Lebanese Christians and Muslims began shooting at one another, and our family had to be evacuated to London, leaving me in Beirut to sort it all out (see *Game Of Nations*). On a quick visit to London, I introduced Miles to the Budokwai, Britain's leading judo club, and, as I predicted, his particular kind of mental attitude fitted right in. That started him up the ladder to wearing the prized black belt—only a Lebanese one, but enough to have the local television station have him demonstrate his proficiency to an admiring audience.

こと

Now that I am older than I care to mention, and frankly a bit of a history buff, I can look back on the past and reflect on this unlikely story. Throughout history, most families lived a linear life: son followed father, father followed his father. Farmers expected their children to carry on with the farm as they had carried on from their parents. Many societies are set up to perpetuate this fact. The class system, caste system, pressure to marry within your close group or religion. Social mobility has been largely a recent phenomenon. Most Americans have never stepped outside the United States, and many of those never even stepped outside their state. I know people in England who have never been to London, let alone outside the country. It seems the linear and predictable life remains the norm, even today.

The story of my family was anything but that. Starting with my father, the son of a doctor in Birmingham, Alabama, who took up the trumpet and became a professional trumpet player in a jazz band—already an unlikely career choice for a white kid from the South. When World War II started, he joined the army and ended up in Washington, DC, where he joined the new OSS (Organization of Strategic Services) as a counterintelligence operative. That led to his transfer to England, where he met my mother, Lorraine Adie, a Scot who worked in the SOE (Special Operations Executive) for British Intelligence in London. They were married in July 1943, and I was born on May 2, 1944.

At the end of the war, my father was ordered back to Washington, where he joined other OSS operatives tasked with the job of creating a central intelligence-gathering agency. That made him officially a founder of the Central Intelligence Agency or CIA. Once that job was completed in 1948, he was sent to Damascus, Syria, to be installed as the CIA station chief there, with the cover of 'cultural attaché.' The family was there from 1948 to 1950.

This was already an unlikely path, as most people in Alabama even now cannot tell you where Damascus is. In 1962, when I started my first year at Birmingham Southern College, having just come from Beirut, Lebanon, where I spent all my high-school years, people were surprised that I could drive a car.

'Don't yawl ride camels over thar?'

I will always remember the look on my history professor's face when he realized most of his class had no idea which countries of Europe were which. Professor Timothy Hornsby, fresh from the prestigious Oxford University in England, was teaching European History 101. On the second day he decided to get an idea of what his students knew, so he passed out a map of Europe with borders and capital cites noted with blanks. At the bottom of the page the countries and cities were listed. The point was to connect the cities and countries to the map at the top of the page. I was not sure of Bucharest or Budapest, but obviously London was the capital of England, the little island at the top left of the page, Madrid—Spain, etc. At the end of the class, he collected the papers.

The next day, Professor Hornsby came into the class with a look of complete dismay, saying he was so taken aback at reading all the forms that he wanted to pass them along so us students could see just how little we knew. Of all the papers that passed before me, only two were reasonably correct. One was mine (I did mix up Bucharest and Budapest); the rest were, at best, random choice. These were not stupid students, but London was in Moscow, Moscow was in Belgium, England was Italy,

France was Norway, and so on. Professor Hornsby was not the only one who was shocked. It was a graphic education for just how isolationist the USA really is.

My first real recollections of my childhood are of Damascus, Syria, around 1948–49. I remember the farmer in the *mish mish* (apricot) field behind our house poisoned our dog, Pickles, apparently because it yapped too much. I remember playing with the local Syrian kids and speaking fluent Arabic as well as English—in fact, I became the chief translator for my sister Lennie, who spoke only Arabic at the time. I guess that was because she spent much more time with the Syrian nanny than with my parents.

'Miles, tell your sister to eat her spinach,' my mother would say. 'Lennie says she does not like spinach,' would be the reply.

My mother recounted the family's time in Syria in a letter she wrote to Prof. Hugh Wilford, who wrote *America's Great Game*, telling the exploits of my father and the two Roosevelts, Kermit and Archie, who between the three of them he says formed the bulk of American foreign policy towards the Middle East for half a century. My mother wrote:

> It was a wonderful period in our lives. Miles (father) was enthusiastic about his job (at the start of the Cold War), his first idea, on hearing that the Russians were about to move into a new Embassy building, was to propose to bug the new building. Shocked, Head Office turned this down. We lived in a modern villa in the Ghouta 'garden suburb,' with a cook, nannie and maid from Christian villages. It was a cocooned, privileged existence quite separate from the lives of the local Syrian populace. But in those days Americans were loved and admired, and we spent much time going on touristic trips into the countryside, and to adjacent countries, or just for picnics when we went into a village, they all (including the bedridden, bed and all), came out to gawp at the 'aliens,' and we were invited to drinks and meals with typical Arab hospitality.

The one major incident I remember vividly was being told that we were leaving the house to stay in a hotel in the mountains—no explanation, just hurry up, we are going: Mom, me, sister Lennie, and baby Ian. It must have been early in 1949. When we returned, a day or so later, the house had been shot up. We went to see the bomb damage at the American legation, which turned out to be merely a hole in the garden and some blown-out windows. I was five.

Later, I learned that some soldiers had come to the house and started shooting while my father and the US military attaché, Col. Steve Meade, were in the house, defending it. The soldiers were supposed to use blanks but typically there were none to be found, so they had to use live ammunition. Around the same time, a bomb was set off harmlessly in the US legation: all a setup to validate the coup d'état of General Husni al-Za'im later that day. Apparently, the general had decided to take over the government one night while playing cards with my father and Steve Meade.

It had started innocently enough, with the general inquiring, 'philosophically,' about what steps one would take to overthrow a government. As my father used to tell it, neither he nor Steve Meade took it seriously; discussing the topic, they decided that first you would create a reason for the overthrow, then you have troops in place and take over the radio station, etc. Then they noticed the general had stopped drinking, and to their horror said, 'We can do this!' Thinking it would blow over after a good night's sleep, they soon found out that the general was deadly serious, *and* he insisted on American help to pull it off. Cables went back and forth with the CIA in Washington saying no, but when al-Za'im finally said, 'Either America helps or I go to the Russians,' a cable came back that basically said, 'Do what you have to do.' The shoot-up of the family house and the bomb at the legation were then planned and executed, and General Husni al-Za'im installed himself as president of Syria. So, as inadvertent and unplanned as it was, my father could rightly claim to have aided the overthrow of a foreign government by covert means—the first such action by the new CIA.

I don't know what impact these events had on my psyche, other than becoming an interesting and quite unique part of the family history. However, the events in Syria and all the other events in my many years living in and out of the Middle East must have given me a perspective on the region and America's policy towards it that most Americans could never have.

In mid-1950, the family moved back to the USA, moving three times around Washington, DC. The only things that I would say about this period are that my youngest brother Stewart was born, and I forgot much of my Arabic.

Meanwhile, things were heating up in Egypt, and the CIA was in the middle of it. The most knowledgeable CIA operatives of the region were my father and the two Roosevelts, Kermit and Archie. So, in July of 1953, the family went back to the Middle East, this time to be stationed in Cairo, Egypt. My father, under the cover of a business consultancy with Booz Allen Hamilton, was actually there to help President Nasser build the Mukabarat—Nasser's version of the CIA.

We lived just outside of Cairo, in the suburb of Ma'adi, where many of the expats lived. The Cairo American School, where I attended third and fourth grade, was a few blocks away from our house. We were members of the Ma'adi Club, where my siblings and I learned to swim and ride horses. I used to walk to school and bicycle to the club, which was on the edge of the desert, about half a mile from our house. On many weekends we went to picnics at the pyramids, and my mother and I searched the rubble to find ancient Egyptian trinkets. In some ways, I could honestly say I started life as a graverobber—graves 3,000 BC and beyond. I even climbed the Great Pyramid and carved my name at the top.

Our next-door neighbor was Hussan Tuhami, who was President Nasser's bodyguard. I used to sneak under the fence separating our house from his, and he would show off his gun collection. He turned out to be a valuable contact for the future when he came to The Police's rescue for our concert at the American University in 1980.

Life for Americans in Cairo at that time was pretty idyllic. As my mother explained:

> Our next posting was to Cairo, with Miles working for the consultant firm Booz Allen Hamilton. I think their job was to reorganize the Ministry of the Interior, which was chaotic. But there was a large CIA team in Cairo then, some under embassy cover, others not. We lived in a splendid country villa on the banks of the Nile in the village of Ma'adi, about a thirty-minute drive through timeless Egyptian

farmland with farmers tending crops and buffalos wallowing in the canals. Our period in Egypt was exciting and enriching. Once more it was a cocooned life, supported by privileges such as access to the PX (post exchange). We had the leisure due to a full staff, to go to all the antiquities, the pyramids, Sphinx, the complex at Saqqara, where we had many Sunday picnics. With our colleagues we went on excursions further afield (Alexandria; Luxor). Us wives lived on a different plane to that of our husbands, whose work we knew little about. However, real life impinged when we had Nasser to dinner a couple of times. He roared up with a motor-cycle escort and an entourage. Our suffragi was terrified in case he poured the soup down Nasser's front while serving him.

The 'full staff,' by the way, was a chauffeur, two nannies, five gardeners, a chief cook, an assistant cook, and several maids. Probably cost us a few dollars a week.

At the end of 1955, the family moved back to the States via Holland and England. Arrival in Amsterdam gave us the unbelievable luxury of having cow's milk again, real ice cream, and butter for the first time in almost three years. In Egypt it had been gamoos milk—a kind of water buffalo—or powdered milk. Amsterdam was clean and orderly—it was like arriving back in a civilization that we had almost forgotten about.

Back in the USA, my father was still in the CIA, so the family settled in nearby Virginia, just outside of Washington, DC. For my mother it was a jolt to no longer have any servants. For us kids it was a time of fitting in with people who had lived there all their lives and had established relationships. Of course, by the time we were comfortable in the USA, had made friends, and were once again 'typical Americans,' it was time for the family to move back overseas.

CHAPTER 2

BEIRUT

. . . .

In 1958, we were off again to the Middle East. My father had officially resigned from the CIA in 1957 and, together with some ex-CIA buddies, set up his own private CIA to help companies maneuver through the complicated politics of the region. The best place to do that was Lebanon, so that's where we went. Our first few weeks in Beirut were at the Riviera Hotel, right on the Mediterranean seafront. What I remember most was the dreaded effect of eating the local food and spending a week near a toilet. Eventually, we moved into an apartment building called the Gamerian, near Pigeon Rocks, with a great view of the sea about half a kilometer away.

Beirut is where most of my teenage memories come from. I started in the eighth grade there, and, except for a semester in London, all my high-school years were at the American Community School (ACS), where I graduated in 1966. Lebanon was culturally more advanced than Egypt, and the more well-to-do Lebanese actually fancied themselves more like Europeans than Arabs. Donkeys were not a major means of transport, and we rarely saw camels. Most of the people wore Western clothes, and you could even get a decent hamburger.

Beirut was known as the Paris of the Middle East. As half Christian and half Muslim, the country was far more liberal than the other Arab states, so it became the natural haunt for Arabs from nearby countries to come and let their hair down and spend a lot of money.

Beirut was also the natural center of the area's political intrigue, and you couldn't help but pick up on the confused politics just by being there. One day, as our chauffeur was driving us kids to school, he said he liked the last president, Camille Chamoun, who I knew as a crook, like most of the politicians there. When I asked why, he said, 'He give me amnesty and let me out of jail.'

'Jail? What did you do?'

'I kill a man,' he said, like he had swatted a fly.

'Killed a man! Why, were you attacked, defending your family?'

'He was a Muslim.'

That was it: no more explanation needed. It was that kind of thinking that finally made me quit the Middle East. Needless to say, it was a shock to see the same thing in Alabama several years later. In Beirut it was religion, in Alabama it was race—but for both it was really the same thing.

The life of an American teenager in Lebanon at that time was pretty carefree. There were no fears of kidnapping or other dangers that exist now. Summers were spent at the beach or in the mountains, where it was cool. The American School was much like the ones in the USA, except all the kids were from at least middle-class families. Most of my friends were Americans who I went to school with. The only exception was Amr Ghaleb, son of the Egyptian ambassador, who also went to the American school and spoke English as well as he did Arabic. We became good friends. My best friend was Tal Brooke, son of the head of the USIA (United States Information Service) office in Lebanon. He had some strange ideas but was very bright. There was a rumor about him that he slept in a coffin at night, which I told any student that asked was untrue. At least I never saw a coffin.

Weekends were spent visiting medieval castles and Roman ruins. The most popular hangout was Uncle Sam's, the local hamburger joint, across the street from the American University. Movies could be seen in English. Occasionally, the family would travel up the mountain and down to Zah'le in the Beqaa Valley, to eat at one of the many restaurants along the river. Lebanon boasts one of the world's great cuisines. You could eat very well there.

In 1960, the family moved out of town about a half-hour drive to a great house called Villa Tarrazi in an area called Fiyadiye. It had a big garden with olive groves behind it. It was about this time that the weekend sightseeing trips became more elaborate, and a British journalist by the name of Kim Philby, sometimes alone or with his family, began to be at all of them.

Philby was with a big English newspaper, so he was a natural person for my father to know. The job of the journalist, after all, is to find out what's going on. That was pretty much what my father's job was, too, except he was also given to 'influence' what was going on. Philby stuttered and drank a lot, so I did not warm to him, and as a typical American kid I did not really like his British kids, either. When I suggested to my father that we *not* spend so much time with the Philbys, my father told me to shut up, which was abnormally blunt.

After January 1963, none of us ever saw Kim Philby again—he had defected to Moscow as one of the most important Soviet spies ever. I then was told the whole story. My father's buddies from the CIA had asked him to 'keep an eye on Philby,' as they had serious suspicions that he was a Soviet agent and must be up to something. The CIA had in fact earlier forced the British to fire him from MI5, the UK's equivalent of the CIA, right before he was due to become the head of the organization. The British refused to believe he was a spy, but the CIA insisted. So Philby ended up working as a journalist in Beirut. He must have been very good at hiding his real beliefs because my father was also not sure he really was a spy, and he quite liked him. He was apparently an engaging chap, a bit of a ladies' man, and well-liked by everyone except me. In any case, my father's way of keeping an eye on Philby was to invite him to all the family parties, boat trips, and picnics, and send the bill to the CIA. His defection definitely put a dent in future family entertainment. No more boat, that's for sure.

My senior year at the American Community School was perhaps the most eventful. I am not sure how, but I got elected president of the senior class. I was not the greatest student, but I did manage to keep my grades above a C average. My brother Ian was also elected president of his class. That was no mystery, because he definitely was the most popular kid in school. Alas, his grades were not so good, so he had to give up the position. I am sure that added to his development as a rebel.

After school I taught judo at a local wrestling club. Khaleal, the owner of the club, was the Lebanese champion of the Greco-Roman style of wrestling called 'catch.' He was a pretty big deal in Lebanon. When Lebanese TV filmed a program on the club, I got roped in to do a judo demonstration and was given a catch wrestler to be my sparring partner. He got the idea that it was a show and virtually threw himself before I could. I had to keep telling him in my broken Arabic that I did not need his help to throw him. I don't know how convincing my part was, but it was my first time on TV, and my father decided to get one of his contacts in the Lebanese army to see it. The next thing I knew, I received a centrifugate appointing me as an instructor to the Lebanese army in the art of self-defense. I guess that was a pretty unique honor. I also got a serious case of the crabs from that gym.

My father did a lot of traveling during the latter part of my high-school years in Beirut. I know he went to Ghana to meet a general who was considering overthrowing the government, and he also went to the Congo at the behest of the CIA. Though he was no longer an official employee of the CIA, it seemed that once you were on the team, you never really left. The good news for me was that it took him to Washington several times a year, so he could bring back the latest hit records. From what he told me, he would go to a record store and ask for the current Top 10 singles. On one trip, he came back with Jerry Lee Lewis's 'Great Balls Of Fire' and 'Purple People Eater.' It was a great moment when he returned and opened his suitcase. I was a very popular guy at school for a few weeks after.

The reality of growing up in places like Lebanon is the exposure to 'other' ways of thinking one would not normally be exposed to, living in the West. Some concepts we assume are fact are not the same to people of the Third World. When we moved to Villa Tarrazi, we had a chauffeur by the name of Georges Yasmin who was also the leader of one of the local chauffeur unions, and as such he was often recruited to help this 'deputy' or that run for office. A deputy was the Lebanese equivalent of a congressman. One day he came into the kitchen declaring he had just met the most honest man he had ever seen. He explained how important the man was: he was the town's priest, and apparently so votes the priest, so votes the rest of the townsfolk. He had to get the priest's vote. 'I offer £50 for his vote—he say no. I offer £100—he say NO—Yeye, he so honest!

I offer £150, NO! £200, £250. It took me £400 to buy his vote! Yeye, how honest was this man!' Another important lesson in the reality of how different morality can be.

George turned out to be just the type of character you need to learn the ins and outs of how to get things done in Lebanon. In my senior year, turning eighteen, it was time to get a driver's license. The Lebanese driver's test was known to be super-difficult, and one was advised to take it in a Jeep. I figured, *How difficult could it be?* and took it in the family car. I went with George to the test site, and I was doing pretty well until the instructor asked me to back up the hill between the white lines at forty miles an hour. I quickly realized the test was fixed to make people fail, which, of course, I did. Dejected, I reported the result to George, who said, 'Give me £75 and wait here.' He disappeared into the testing office and came out twenty minutes later with my driver's license. I was so happy, I never asked him how much his take was. I presume he paid £50 for the license and pocketed the £25 himself. That was the way things were done in Lebanon.

After my high-school graduation, my father sat me down and said I was now going to have to follow the family tradition (which he had invented some years earlier) and travel to Tehran on my own, with no passport. That was to *make a man of me.* He was half-serious, but while it might have been possible to do so in the early 50s, in 1962 it would be extremely difficult. As it was, I agreed to go to Amman, Jordan, to visit my girlfriend—and to try to do it with no passport.

I took a service taxi from Beirut to Damascus, and I managed to get through the Lebanese–Syrian border with no problem. The service taxi is basically a taxi where all five passengers pay a fee, like on a bus. Not the most comfortable way to travel, I can tell you. From Damascus, I took another service taxi to Amman, and at the Jordanian border side, with a machine gun pointing at me, I had to produce my passport or risk arrest. Times had changed from the days when my father first imagined that traveling with no passport would make a man of his sons. His supposed Copeland tradition stopped with me.

CHAPTER 3

TO ALABAMA
AND BACK AGAIN

. . . .

At the end of the summer of 1962, I left Beirut for the USA and college in Birmingham, Alabama, where my grandmother and cousins lived, and where my father had grown up. I had been accepted to New York University, but my parents thought New York City would be too tempting. They said I should experience the 'real' America and get to know my grandmother and relatives.

No point in dwelling too much on those years in Alabama. Suffice it to say, I learned about racism, started to say 'yawl,' joined a fraternity (SAE), bought my first car (a 1957 Ford convertible, which had holes in the floorboard), and I did get to know my grandmother and various aunts and cousins.

It was 1962, so I arrived in Alabama just in time for the race riots, Selma, Bull Connor, George Wallace, and the like. One of my fraternity brothers was a rabid racist, but for the most part the college and the students I mixed with were relatively isolated from all those goings on, though we read about them in the newspapers. In my senior year, Birmingham Southern College was integrated. Thankfully, there were no problems I could see. I do remember, however, a lengthy debate in the SAE fraternity house over whether to admit Jews into the fraternity. Some were for, some were against. One argument was that they already had their own fraternity on campus, like that meant they were not being discriminated against. To me, it was more of the same as I'd experienced in Lebanon.

People seemed dedicated to finding ways to separate themselves from 'the other.' What was surprising was how open the prejudice was—like it was perfectly normal. This definitely was not a time of political correctness.

It made me think of the time my father told me of his conversation with Zakaria Mohieddin, Vice President of Egypt, back in 1953. After my father stated that it was US policy *not* to discriminate against people because of race, creed, or color, a perplexed Zakaria said, 'If you don't discriminate for any of those reasons—then how do you discriminate?'

As the drinking age in Alabama was eighteen, peer pressure pushed me into drink. Unfortunately, or rather fortunately, I tried gin and promptly vomited, and then vodka with the same result, until I had gone through all options and decided alcohol and my body did not get on. After that, in later years, the most I could deal with was a couple glasses of wine. Thankfully, at that time, drugs were not part of the college scene.

As far as girls went, it was a bit of a wasteland, largely because it seemed that marriage was the main objective for every female attending the college. One explained that if a girl was not engaged by senior year, it was panic time: that girl was destined to be an 'old maid.' This further educated me about the insularity of much of America.

I also saw my first rock concert: a stadium show with The Rolling Stones, The Beach Boys, Cannibal & The Headhunters, and Petula Clark. Each act played twenty-five minutes. My second concert was in a small theatre, with Herb Alpert & The Tijuana Brass. Little did I know at the time that, fourteen years later, his company would play a big part in my life.

Given the business that I eventually went into, I should be embarrassed that the worst grade I got was a D in music. I should have gotten an F, but the teacher took pity on me when I argued that most of the music taught had little relevance to what I thought my future would be somewhere in the Middle East. Why would I ever need to be able to identify the parts of Beethoven's Fifth? On the positive side, the best grade I got was an A in philosophy.

By my senior year, I had had it with Alabama. I didn't even stay for graduation. I headed back to Lebanon, where in 1966 I enrolled at the American University of Beirut (AUB) for my MA degree. In many ways, even though I was a foreigner, I felt more at home in Beirut than I had in

Birmingham. At least in Beirut I knew who I was—I was an American, pure and simple. In Birmingham, I was white, not black, and not from there.

At the point of entering AUB, I still had not focused on what career I was to aim for. So far, I was following the line of least resistance. My father had already convinced me that the CIA would be a bad option—not because he objected to it in principle, but because he objected to where the organization was heading. His words to me were, 'You would hate it.' The message was, I would be dealing with ignorant people who didn't know what they were talking about, and I would not put up with the stupidity I would inevitably find. So, I assumed my direction would be business in the Middle East, though what type of business I had no idea.

That first year in Beirut was typical of most first-year students going into an MA degree. Figuring out what the end-of-degree thesis would be, choosing classes, and the like. My major was based around economics of nations and economics of business, with more emphasis on countries than businesses. The idea, loosely, was to figure out how to take a Third World country and help guide it into the twentieth century. To tell the truth, I don't know if I actually learned anything from this. What I do know is that, by the time I left the university, my basic conclusion was that unless there was a lot of money, like oil revenues or huge foreign aid, there was little hope any of these countries would ever be successful on terms we would consider successful in Europe or the USA. Without such funding, they would all likely be the 'shithole' countries Donald Trump likes to call them.

By September 1966, my family had relocated fully to London, leaving me to set up in my own apartment across the street from AUB with the family mastiff, Ozzie. The period from 1966 to 1969 was educational in many ways that had nothing to do with my studies at the university. My father liked to say his book *Game Of Nations*, though it was based on what happened in Egypt, was really a lesson on how *any* country of the Third World worked, and more specifically the type of thinking *any* leader of a Third World country was likely to think. Likewise, my time in Beirut during this period became *my* lesson in how much of the world thinks, and how different that is from what I would think had I grown up in Des Moines, Iowa, or indeed Birmingham, Alabama.

It was during the second year of my time at the university, just before the June 1967 war between Israel and the surrounding Arab countries, that my father asked me to meet him in Cairo, where he kept an apartment that once belonged to Omar Sharif. Something was going on vis-à-vis Egypt and Israel, but it was more show by Nasser than any real intention to do anything. Nasser wanted my father to assure the powers that be in the USA that it was really a show, and to make sure the Israelis knew it, too. The Egyptian army was in no state to fight a shooting war, and that was pretty well known, even to the Israelis. It used to be a joke in Egypt that the 'idiot light' that went on when the oil was low in a truck or tank was easily solved simply by removing the light. Nasser was no dummy: he knew the state of his army, and he had no intention of going to war with an army like Israel's. At the same time, he had to look good to his people; rattling sabers would work, as long as the other side did not misinterpret his intentions. I got the gist of this from my father and the few government types we met at his apartment. And, by then, I had learned to read between the lines of the newspapers, so I was not that worried that there would be a bad outcome. Just the usual hot air, I thought.

A few months later, that hot air became *hot*, but it was not air. Nasser miscalculated. His attempt to enhance his position with the Arab people, and especially the Egyptian public, offered too much temptation to the Israelis. They had built enough support within the United States Congress that they calculated they could get away with jumping on that temptation and the USA would not stop them as it had during the Suez Crisis in 1956. They were right.

On the morning of June 5, 1967, I went with my old friend Amr to Khalea's Gym and soon heard news that war had broken out between Israel and the Arab countries. We rushed first to the Egyptian embassy, where Amr's older brother was excitedly screaming, 'This is it, this is it!' From the news he told us, it sounded like many Israeli planes had been shot down. Then we went to AUB, to see if our classes would be affected. There we found a carnival atmosphere. Martial music bellowed from the many transistor radios tuned to Radio Damascus and Radio Cairo. The many students mixing about with smiling faces seemed to be happy but slightly disbelieving. Most of them had dreamed of this day for twenty years, and now it was becoming a reality.

Radio Damascus was by far the most popular station, and every few minutes it would announce that another large number of Israeli planes had been downed. Each announcement brought jubilant cheers from the crowd. It was not long before the planes claimed to have been shot down exceeded the total number in the Israeli Air Force—and with very few Arab losses. It was a great lesson in truth—or rather the lack of it. None of those students would have ever listened to Radio Damascus and certainly never believed such wild claims before. Now they *wanted* to believe, and they tuned to the station that told them what they wanted to hear. If they had tuned to the BBC, they would have heard an entirely different story. In fact, the Israelis had virtually eliminated all the Arab air forces in the first few hours of the war.

My first concern was the possibility of US intervention, which could mean evacuation for American citizens like me. I prepared for that eventuality by organizing someone to look after my dog, Ozzie, but I hoped I could stay and finish out the college year. Meanwhile, Amr insisted I stay in the apartment: 'Close your shutters and stay off the streets.' When I finally had to walk the dog late at night, the streets were totally dark. Lebanon had instituted a blackout.

The next afternoon, I was told that all the American girls in the university dormitories were scheduled to be evacuated to Rome. The news was getting worse, and the Arabs came to believe that American planes were helping Israel, so naturally people were becoming hostile to anything American. An urgent call at midnight on Tuesday made me change my mind about staying. 'All Americans are to be out of the country by 9:00 Wednesday morning.' So, with thousands of other rather confused Americans, I gathered at the staging center at 5am to await instructions. A bunch of us were soon assigned to an American freighter bound for Cyprus and herded into open-air trucks to take us to the port of Beirut. Crowds jeered at us along the way as we drove through some of the more unsavory parts of the city. I and several of my friends, along with around three hundred other Americans, boarded the ship at 7am, and we were on our way a little later. In Cyprus, the American embassy organized a flight to Greece, and from there I flew to London, where I met up with my family.

CHAPTER 4

BACK IN
BEIRUT

. . . .

By September '67, I was back in Beirut and attending classes at the university again. Things had settled down, so for the most part it seemed reasonably safe. Lebanon, after all, had not participated in the war. Still, I found myself being a lot more careful than I had been before the June war. Looking over one's shoulder became a habit.

My mother and Stewart came to Beirut to visit around Christmas 1967. That turned out to be more important to my future, and indeed Stewart's, than either of us could know at the time. Some of his high-school friends from the American Community School had organized a rock band they called the Wichita Vortex Sutra, and their drummer had gone to America for Christmas. They had managed to get a gig at a club, needed a drummer, and asked Stewart to take his place. My friend Amr and I went to see the show.

What I remember is a fairly empty club, but seeing my brother up there, playing drums in a rock band, must have done something to my brain. It must have transformed me from the person I had been up to that time—looking at music from the outside, like any fan—to a person who could be inside the music, as a participant. At least it must have planted a seed.

Around this time, my brother Ian showed up in Beirut. He was the wild brother that neither my mother nor father could figure out how to deal with, so my father told me, as the oldest son, to take on that responsibility. Ian once said to me, 'Stewart is the youngest, you are the oldest, Lennie is the girl, so where does that leave me?' I guess you could call it the classic 'middle child syndrome.'

Ian was hanging out with some unsavory types in north Beirut—from what I heard, a motorcycle gang headed by an Armenian guy they called the King of Death. When Ian came to me for money, I refused to give him any unless he committed to do something with his life. Hanging around those motorcycle guys was not it. We had a huge argument, after which I said he should join the US Army—that would sort him out. To my surprise, he agreed. I got him a plane ticket back to the States, and the next thing we knew he was in Vietnam with the Big Red One.

In February of 1968, Amr's father was promoted to a high position in the Egyptian Ministry of Foreign Affairs back in Cairo, leaving Amr in Beirut at the university. I figured that could be great for me, to help pay for the apartment, so I talked him into becoming my roommate. Amr moved in while his family was preparing to move to Egypt. We soon began pissing off the upstairs neighbor, who we shared a telephone with—it was a 'party line' that would ring in both of our apartments.

Jack Dagilatus was American and worked as some sort of professor at one of the local colleges. Amr and I thought it was funny to answer the phone, 'CIA, how can we help you?' Jack thought this was not at all funny, and he kept asking us to stop. It did stop when a knock at the door produced the local CIA station chief, who came to see if he was being fired, thinking I really was something to do with the CIA. When he realized this was just a couple of college kids fooling around, he told us we had better stop if we knew what was good for us. When he left, Amr and I had a good laugh about it . . . until an hour or so later, when his father called and said come to the Egyptian embassy residence immediately.

Amr's father was not happy, and in the sternest tone we were told that such a prank could land us in jail: 'The sons of an Egyptian ambassador and a known CIA operative, what were you thinking? You do not want to end up in a Lebanese jail and if you do, I soon won't be around to get you out. Both of us knew that you *don't* want to be in a Lebanese jail.' That stopped our prank dead.

Meanwhile, at the university, I ended up with time on my hands when students learned that political upheaval could be used to their advantage.

When it came close to exam time, some students evidently were not ready, so they planted notes saying there was a bomb on campus. The ensuing lockdown lasted several days and gave the students the extra days they needed to study. The problem was, it kept happening, so school was more off than on. This lasted all the way until I finally left Beirut in mid-1969. It did, however, launch me into other pursuits that ended up changing my life.

Most significantly, I got to be known for giving wild parties. These were not wild parties like I came to experience in the music business years later, but for Beirut at that time I guess they qualified. My parents had left me with a movie projector, several films, and a great stereo setup. I bought some black lights from somewhere, and I had built a nice record collection: The Doors, Jefferson Airplane, Big Brother & The Holding Company, Moby Grape, the Grateful Dead, Country Joe & The Fish, The Animals, Pink Floyd, and of course The Beatles. For me, at least, the drug culture had not yet reached Beirut, and, even if it had, I was already seriously anti-drug from my judo training. My upstairs American neighbor, Jack, used to say I was so 'straight arrow.' So, I would not have thought of myself as the likely person to become known for wild parties. But with my big apartment, my setup was definitely not the usual for a college student. And with school off and on, we students were bored; there were not a lot of choices, so Saturday-night parties became the thing to do. I liked to think mine were the best.

In 1968, I wrote a letter to my mother, which said:

> I'm giving a big party this weekend sponsored by the Vonnegut-inspired 'Society for Immediate Nuclear War.' In conjunction with 'The Church of God the Utterly Indifferent.' Dress is from Mod to hideously gaudy. I am going to set up the movie projector and have a movie running silently backwards on one of the walls. One of the bedrooms will be a bomb shelter, one of the bathrooms the local Church of God the Utterly Indifferent, the other bathroom will be the tomb of the lobotomized android from hell. This with weird lighting and occasional spurts of electronic music will create a near-psychedelic experience in my very own home!

This party reputation apparently got around, and eventually it reached the boys in the Wichita Vortex Sutra band that my brother Stewart had played with at Christmas in 1967. They had been hired for a gig at the American University, and they came to ask me to help them make it special. I think they were thinking of it being how we imagined the psychedelic happenings in San Francisco were that we were all reading about.

The gig at the university was held in the art department and turned out to be a wild success. To give the psychedelic atmosphere, I set up my black lights and brought bottles of fluorescent paint for the band and their girlfriends, who had decided to dance with the group as part of the show. I made the mistake of leaving the bottles of fluorescent paint on a table near the band, and when students found them, they ended up on all their faces, clothes—no more paint, and a complete mess in the room. The students basically wrecked the place. Wichita Vortex Sutra was banned from the university after that.

It was my first experience of working a rock concert, and I quickly learned how much I didn't know. But the Wichita boys loved it, and they wanted me to be part of all their gigs in the future.

A few weeks later, I was approached by a rather shady-looking promoter who said he was bringing a British pop group to Lebanon in the summer, to do a month-long engagement at one of the mountain hotels. Summer in Beirut was hot, and anyone who could afford it moved up to the cool of the mountains. Beirut emptied out each summer, and the mountain night life was hopping. He had heard of my 'shows' and wanted to buy my lights off of me and hire my 'dancing girls.' As I didn't have anything planned for the summer, I said no, but he could hire me instead, and I would bring my lights. As for the dancing girls, I contacted the girlfriends, and they were also up for it.

The hotel was one of the nice ones in Shimlan, about an hour's drive up the mountain from Beirut. The group was Rupert's People, who had a semi-hit that got to #30 in the British singles charts. They were in the mold of The Hollies—long hair but well-manicured, with nice Carnaby Street clothes. They were certainly not like the scruffy progressive-rockers that were beginning to take off in London at that time. I can't remember all the details, but the band were happy that there was someone there

31

MILES A. COPELAND III

who could communicate with them. Anyway, we soon became friends, and I found myself called in to help them every time a problem came up—which happened a lot.

The promoter was actually a jerk who didn't much care about what I or the band thought unless he had to. One day, without telling me, he placed an advertisement in the English-language *Daily Star* newspaper, advertising 'RUPERT'S PEOPLE and Miles Copeland's Dancing Girls.' I prayed no one I knew would see the ad.

Mostly, I solved problems by threatening that if he didn't pay their fee or cover the hotel bill, they would not perform that night. It was always something, until one day they joked that I should be a rock-band manager. It was a flippant remark—in one ear, out the other.

In May, after graduating from university, I flew to London to re-join my family. I was there only a few days before Rupert's People showed up and hit me with the crazy idea that I should be their manager. At first, I thought they were joking. I knew nothing about the UK music business, or indeed the music business anywhere. They explained that my help in Beirut had convinced them that I had the necessary chutzpah, and they could help when I needed it. I started seriously thinking about it. Then I got a letter from the US Draft Board. I was to report for duty in Richmond, Virginia, to be inducted into the US Army.

It was 1969, the height of the Vietnam War, and all the young Americans I knew were plotting ways to get out of it. 'Say you pee in your bed at night,' 'Say you are gay'—there were all sorts of scams to get out being bandied about. Funny, though, I never heard of 'bone spurs.'

My brother Ian was already there. I was resigned to having the experience too. I hoped it would be in Germany, or anywhere else but Vietnam. The only thing I had done was go to a doctor in Lebanon and ask him to look at my feet and tell me if my high arches were enough to keep me out of the army. I was told no, they were not bad enough, but he gave me a letter anyway that said I had high arches and put an official seal on it with a Lebanese stamp. I said my goodbyes and flew to Washington, DC, to catch the bus to Richmond, where I was to report to boot camp and probably spend the next two years of my life in the army.

Arriving at the induction center, I realized quickly that it was a cattle call, and I was just a number. After stripping down to our underpants, all two thousand of us were put in a large hall where a tough-looking sergeant asked if any of us had a reason not to be in the army. Three of us raised our hands. The sergeant went to the other two and dismissed their complaint, sending them along with all the others. He then came to me and said, 'What's your problem?' I said I did not want to get out of the army, I just didn't want to get a job where I had to march. I had high arches and it hurt to walk long distances. He asked if I had proof. I handed him the letter from my Lebanese doctor. He was impressed with the letter—it looked official, with a nice Lebanese stamp on it picturing a Phoenician ship. He told me he was a stamp collector, then he said, 'OK, let me see you walk.' I obliged, and then he stopped me and went to get what I imagined was a doctor. Then the two of them asked me to walk again, insisting that I 'walk like you always walk.' Well I had never thought about it before, and now concentrating on my walk must have made me appear as a virtual cripple. They made me walk a second time. And a third time. 'OK, you're outta here.'

I couldn't believe it. I was the only one of two thousand inductees who reported for duty in Richmond that day to be rejected—and I wasn't even trying! I walked out of the induction center and headed to the bus station, afraid to look back. I was waiting for 'Just kidding, get your ass back in here.' It never came. I called home to give the news, and later I got a cable from Rupert's People that said, 'God bless your feet.'

CHAPTER 5

COLLEGE
EVENTS

· · · · · · · ·

Back in London in July 1969, I took up residence in my parents' house at 21 Marlborough Place in St John's Wood. It was a big house with ground-floor kitchen, living room, and dining room; my parents' bedroom and my bedroom on the first floor; and two more bedrooms on the top floor. My brother Stewart had converted one of the basement rooms into a drum studio, with soundproofing that dampened the sound to the neighbors but didn't do much for the house itself. Also in the basement was a small room I made into an office.

The St John's Wood area was an upmarket part of north-west London, only two blocks from EMI studios on Abbey Road and the famous 'Beatles' zebra crossing. Our Abbey Road street sign got stolen so often that the borough finally just painted the name on the brick wall.

At age twenty-five, living at home was not yet awkward, but I knew that with no more college, and no two years in the army ahead of me, it would not be long before I had to embark on a career. I had already lost interest in the Middle East, so when Rupert's People came to see me a week or so after I got back from the USA, to again talk me into managing them, I said yes. It was not official in any way; no contracts were exchanged, it was just, *OK, let's do it.*

Now that I had no fear of being inducted into the US Army, one of the first things I did was to get with the program in what was being called Swinging London. That meant a trip to Carnaby Street and Kings Road to buy my first bellbottom trousers and a hip suit, which I did for a cool £16 (around $38 at the time, or $350 in today's money). And I started to let my hair grow.

In the evenings, the Rupert's boys began to show me around, so I could find out what I had gotten myself into. The first club I went to was a place called the Country Club, not far from the St John's Wood house. It was where I met what was to become my first real management client. I say first real client because Rupert's People were not really a committed group at that point. They had no transport, no equipment, and they all had day jobs. They must have thought I was going to finance them— like I was the archetypal 'rich American' many British people assumed Americans were.

There were only a few people in the club, and it was definitely not a happening place that night. But I thought Tanglewood, the three-piece group who were performing, were really good. After their set, the drummer came to the bar, sweaty and looking dejected. I said I really liked what I saw. A conversation started up, and soon he told me that it was their last show: the guitarist was leaving to go back home to Torquay in south-west England, where the band originated from. A recording-studio friend had encouraged them to come to London with promises to help, but it never lived up to anything. It was basically a tale of woe. It ended up with me suggesting that I might be able to help, and to call me. That was Steve Upton, drummer and de facto leader of the group.

A day or so later, Steve and bass player Martin Turner, who was the older brother of the guitarist who had quit, came over to the house in St John's Wood. One thing I liked about them was that they were committed: they had their own van and equipment, and unlike Rupert's People they had no intention of taking day jobs. I can't remember all the details, but I agreed to take them on, and we agreed we would use the studio Stewart built as the rehearsal room, to audition to find a replacement guitarist. They then helped me work out an advertisement for a lead guitarist to put in the classified section of the *Melody Maker*. The *Melody Maker* at the time was the biggest weekly music magazine; it was aimed mainly at music fans, but if you were a musician looking for work, this would be the place to look.

> Wanted, lead guitarist—must be positive thinking, creative and adaptable for strongly backed group with great future.

For the first auditions, some people showed up with no guitar; few owned any equipment, and some were completely useless. So, we started asking questions on the phone calls to filter out the losers. First question was, 'Do you own a guitar?' If the answer was no, that was an automatic reject.

Eventually it got down to two players: Ted Turner, a young, good-looking kid from Birmingham, age eighteen, who was an avid fan of Peter Green from Fleetwood Mac; and Andy Powell, from Hemel Hempstead. We couldn't make up our minds, but then Martin suggested we take both of them and make them *both* lead guitarists. Harmony guitars could be a good gimmick. That's what we did. By the end of August, we had a new band.

Rehearsals started at the end of August in the basement studio at Marlborough Place. I would stick my head in every now and then to register approval or make a comment. Even my father came down a couple of times with his trumpet to play along. He could still get decent notes out of that old trumpet (which is by the way now in the CIA museum in Langley, Virginia).

When it came time to find a name for the band, we all put names into a hat. Two of the names I put in were Wishbone and Ash. Martin took out all the names and rejected them, one after another, until he was finally left with Ash and Wishbone. He said let's put them together, and voilà: Wishbone Ash was the name.

Now the biggest problem was looming. For a guy that knew virtually nothing about the music business, it was all very well having a group, but how the hell do you put them on the market? I could not go to my father to ask for money to make a record, and I had never booked a show and did not even know anyone who did. I was still learning about the business, reading music magazines to try to educate myself on what was what. When I came across an advertisement on the back pages of the *Melody Maker* for a 'Booker's Bible,' which had the names and contacts of all the clubs and promoters in England, on sale for only £25, it looked like that could be my salvation.

I called the phone number and Rick Simms answered, sounding exactly like an East End street hustler, but he was a fast talker, and finally he said he would bring me the book and spend a week with me using it, so I could see how good it was. It sounded too good to be true, but I was desperate. I knew Wishbone Ash would soon be asking me when their first gig was.

Rick had no car, so he asked me to pick him up at his mother's house. I figured if I knew where he lived, that would ensure he was not just hustling me. It was only two miles north from me, so I agreed. When I met him, he looked just like he sounded: a classic crook, short, half bald—he even had cauliflower ears. When he talked, he reminded me of the shyster street venders in Beirut: 'You, my friend—I give you special price.' I knew what the Wishbone boys would say when they saw him. All I could say was, if he's a crook, he's a stupid one. I know where he lives. I paid him the £25.

I set up the phone for Rick in my small basement office and he started calling. Within half an hour he'd booked a show, and by the end of the day three more. All the while I was listening to his pitch and getting an idea of how to book a band. The next day he booked three more, then asked if I would advance him a commission on the dates. I was picking him up and taking him home each day, so, as crooked as he looked, I was becoming more comfortable and indeed relieved that there were actually gigs on the books, so I agreed to pay him the advance.

The first gig for Rupert's People came a few weeks later, by which time I was out a total of £150. At that time, the average weekly wage was £17, so £150 was real money. I rented a van for the band, and they borrowed the Wishbone Ash amps and speakers and set off to the gig. It was at a school and it worked fine, which was a huge relief as there were another eight shows coming up—a few for Rupert's People, and a few more for Wishbone Ash. Things were looking good, and this management thing was turning out easier than I thought.

The next gig was another for Rupert's, and they set off as before. Several hours later, I got a call: they couldn't find the gig. The address they had was a residence, with no club in sight. I called Rick and he said I'd got the address wrong: it was not N8, it was N18. I waited for the group to call me back and gave them the correct address. An hour later, the same thing. This time I drove to Rick's and told him there was no gig at the new address. He apologized and said he must have gotten the address wrong. He was shucking and jiving, and I got that sinking feeling that he *was* the crook we all suspected.

When I got back home, I went down to my office and started calling all the venues Rick had booked. The first one told me they no longer booked live bands: it was a disco now. The next one said they'd never heard of Wishbone Ash; another one said they wouldn't book a band from Rick if he was the last agent on Earth; one after another, every gig was phony. I felt like a complete fool.

Worse, I was going to have to face the Wishbone and Rupert's boys, and I would get the *I told you so*—a confirmation that I was out of my depth already. Out of sheer desperation and embarrassment, I picked up the booking book and started calling. Most of the numbers turned out to be correct—the ones that were not I crossed out. When I got a promoter on the phone, I used the pitch I had heard Rick use, and, lo and behold, after a few calls I'd actually booked a show. I booked three more before Wishbone Ash showed up for their rehearsal.

When they finally arrived, I gave them the good news/bad news line and got the expected *I told you so*, but they were happy about the shows I had booked, so it looked like I would live to fight another day. I might have been a fool, but I was not a complete fool.

It is hard to overstate the 'flying by the seat of our pants' nature of things for all of us at this time. While I was trying to get Wishbone Ash off the ground with bookings, they came over every day to write songs and rehearse. The Marlborough Place basement became their hangout, and their friends became my friends, and my brother Stewart's, and Ian's, too, when he came back from Vietnam. When Wishbone were not around, us three brothers would use their equipment in the studio to mess around ourselves. I even jokingly came up with a band name: Marty Mortician & The Coffinettes. Ian could play a few notes on bass, Stewart was a soloist most of the time on the drums, and I was a shit singer so, as far as I was concerned—not serious and just a bit of fun. Ian was also just dabbling, but Stewart was serious. He was going to be a musician. Recordings do exist somewhere, though I hope no one ever hears them.

Once I had gotten over the fear of cold calling, booking gigs was not so hard. The first show I booked was November 10, 1969, at Dunstable Civic Hall, with The Ainsley Dunbar Retaliation. A nice hall supporting a good group, only an hour's drive from London. Some clubs were close enough to me that I went in person. Klooks Kleek was in West Hampstead, a mere ten-minute drive from Marlborough Place, and it had quite a reputation for having great bands. Fleetwood Mac and Led Zeppelin had played there. But it was tiny, holding less than 150 people. One forgets how 'Mickey Mouse' some really famous clubs were back in those days.

Looking back, I realize that one advantage was my American accent. Those club owners were used to getting an English agent on the phone to them, some with obvious regional accents, and they knew how to smell a rat from their fellow Brits. But an American accent was rare, and they could have figured I might be somebody important, so they gave me the benefit of the doubt.

The most ballsy move I made was at Bedford College in Regent's Park, not far from the house in St John's Wood. I couldn't get anyone on the phone, so I went to the college to see about booking the group to open for the Colosseum concert coming up on February 20, 1970. Finding there was no support, I told the person who seemed to be in charge that Wishbone Ash would be opening the show. No one had said no, so I told the group to show up, set up their gear, and open the show like it was all cool and arranged, which they did. The Colosseum people thought the college had arranged it, the college people thought the Colosseum people had arranged it, and Wishbone Ash performed their set with no problems. It was just like all those times at the Syrian border or Beirut airport, looking like I officially belonged there, so no one had thought to question me. The worst that could happen in England was a no—there was no risk of a machine gun being pointed at me.

I was coming to believe that England was going to be an easy place to get ahead in. What convinced me most was the prevalent idea that 'If it hasn't been done then there must be a good reason for it.' I heard this view expressed more than once. When I heard another piece of advice, 'Always stand in the longest line at the grocery store,' that was it. Having come from Beirut, where standing in line was considered stupid and the accepted logic was to shove yourself to the front of the line, I had to ask, 'Why on earth would you do that?' The answer convinced me that England was the place to be: 'Because they obviously know something.'

That advice came from Doreen Boyd, the mother of Lindsey Boyd, the girlfriend of Allan Fordy, who was the 'social secretary' at University College London. Doreen had been the fan-club secretary for The Rolling Stones, and soon I hired her to do the same for Wishbone Ash—and, even later, she took on running the Police fan club. But that story started with my biggest problem: how do I get venues on the college and university circuit to book Wishbone Ash if no one had ever heard of them? I knew advertising in *Melody Maker* could promote the band, but the advertising rates there were huge, and I didn't have the money. Besides, there were no more than two hundred or so people I needed to get to who actually booked shows—*not* the two hundred thousand punters who bought *Melody Maker* each week. Spending at a price to reach two hundred thousand people when I only wanted two hundred was obviously stupid. Or I could send mailers, but it was well known that most mailers—even if they do make it to the intended person—go right in the wastepaper basket. What I needed was a credible and affordable way to reach that two-hundred-person target audience.

I had learned that all of the college concerts were run by a student at the 'student union' called a 'social secretary.' Some had concerts each weekend, some only one a month, but it was by far the best circuit in the country, with nice venues and the best pay. Most of the social secs were amateurs who went through a local agent who helped them find the artists and negotiate the deals but kept their contacts a closely guarded secret. The social secretary would call the local agent, who would call the agent who represented the artist, and the two agents would split the ten percent commission. In early 1970, I launched a little magazine that changed all that.

I figured if I could create a magazine written by social secretaries *for* social secretaries that helped them with the concerts, and mail it to them each month for *free*, they would not throw it into the wastepaper basket ... *and* I could make sure nice articles about Wishbone Ash were in it, to create demand for the band. For credibility's sake, however, I needed to find a front person who would be the face of the magazine and keep me out of it.

Even an idiot would know that nice stories written by the Wishbone Ash manager about his artist would not be believable.

The person I found was Allan Fordy. As the social secretary of University College London, he would be respected by other social secretaries around the country. He regularly booked concerts, and he knew the drill. I met up with him and Lindsey Boyd, and together we hatched a plan. He took his role seriously, and he liked the idea of helping his fellow social secretaries, so he said yes. And, with that, *College Event* was born.

I pretty much wrote the first issue, but I made some serious misspellings, so in the second issue I included an apology (under a pseudonym, of course) saying the secretary who was responsible for the misspellings had been fired. Lindsay brought in her mother to do the typing, so by the second issue it was a four-person operation. From then on, once a month we would assemble at Doreen's house, she would type, and we would compile the issue. Doreen died in 2019, and, when I look back on it, I realize how quietly important she was, for *College Event*, then Wishbone Ash, and finally The Police.

At the start, the magazine was simply a set of mimeographed typed pages stapled together. What became revolutionary about it was that, after a few issues, it listed all the artists on the circuit that were touring, their approximate price, and the coup de gras: their agent's contact phone number. Within weeks, the social secs dispensed going through their agent middlemen and called the artist's agent direct. That little magazine actually revolutionized the concert business in Britain, and all because I wanted the colleges to know who the hell Wishbone Ash were.

CHAPTER 6

WHERE WILL YOU
BE YESTERDAY?

• • • • • • • •

As an American in London, I escaped easy categorization, but there were some disadvantages, too. There were many times I had people on the street say, 'Don't you Americans ever say please?' Like we were all rude. Actually, in America, you would ask the time first, then say thank you afterwards. In England, you had to say please first, then ask the time. No wonder I was often accused of being rude. To the average Englishman I probably was.

The guys in Wishbone Ash would recount various stories of me as a brash American doing things that were not done, offending people, but they begrudgingly admitted it moved things forward. I probably did have some crazy and pushy ideas, but perhaps in a staid country like England they worked. Where the general assumption was that the glass was half empty, I operated under the assumption that it was half full. In England in 1970, a bit of positivity could go a long way. The truth is that it never occurred to me that we could fail, so I never thought about it. It was blind ignorance, pure and simple.

That first year as manager of my first band must have seemed pretty strange to both me and the band members. We were all new to it, and we were feeling our way as we went. As the band's guitarist, Andy Powell, later said, 'Miles had a plan, and his plan was to be a success in the music business. He didn't know exactly how he was going to do it, but he was going to cut through it like a knife. While we were in the rehearsal room, he was plotting and formulating. It didn't matter how wacky the ideas were, he just threw them against the wall, inevitably some would stick.'

Anyway, in that early part of 1970, I booked another twenty concerts for the band, and then made a serious effort to get a professional agent on the job. I saw a small ad for a John Sherry Agency in the back pages of *Melody Maker* and, not knowing anything about the company, I gave them a call. Ed Bicknell answered the phone. It turned out he had seen *my* tiny weekly ad in the back pages of *Melody Maker* too, and he was intrigued. It was two witches stirring a cauldron with the name Wishbone Ash and a phone number. Ed took on the group and turned out to be a booking machine, filling up the date sheet very quickly. Meanwhile, the John Sherry Agency turned out to be two small offices in Dryden Chambers off of Oxford Street and no more than Ed, John, and a secretary who turned out to be John's wife, Nina. (Ed went on to manage Dire Straits.)

That first six months working with Wishbone Ash was really a culture shock for me. Steve and Martin had a one-room apartment called a bedsit about a mile from St John's Wood in Chalk Farm. When I first saw that apartment, I was shocked that on the left of the room was a single bed where Martin and his girlfriend slept and on the right of the room was the single bed that Steve and his girlfriend slept on. No division between the two. You can imagine what my first question was. Heat was purchased from a box at the entrance of the room, a shilling at a time. There was no telephone. I can't remember a kitchen or a bathroom. A far cry from the house in St John's Wood, and worlds apart from the way I grew up in the Middle East.

The actual gigs and the travel up and down the M1 motorway in that van were also a revelation. The M1 was the only multilane freeway in the country at that time. After a show up north, we would drive back to London and stop to eat at one of the several motorway cafes on the route. The infamous Blue Boar was about halfway between Manchester and London, a cafeteria-style setup where the only safe thing to get was eggs and beans. You *could* order a steak, but I would be surprised if they were not old shoes. England was famous throughout the 70s for bad food, but the Blue Boar took that to a whole new level: downwards. Alternatively, you could find a fish-and-chip place where you would be served fish wrapped in newspaper. The black ink would be on the fish. Occasionally, one could find an Indian restaurant open. Eating was not one of the pleasures one looked forward to in England.

One of the last gigs I booked was another show at Dunstable Civic, this time supporting Deep Purple. Ritchie Blackmore, Deep Purple's guitarist watched Wishbone's set, apparently liked the band; he called his producer friend, Derek Lawrence, to tell him about them. Derek had produced the first Purple albums, so he was reasonably well known among English record producers at the time. Derek eventually talked me into letting him get the band a record deal with MCA Records in Los Angeles and have him produce the first album. Derek got the deal. The advance was $20,000, and when I showed that check to my father, he finally realized I was going to make this work. From that point on, he never mentioned getting a 'real job.' I had one.

This was the first record deal I had ever made, and no doubt I was green. Derek was to get an advance of $1,000, so he said, in his usual *aren't I cool* manner, 'Make sure you pay me in *ones*.' I went to Chase Bank on Barclay Square to arrange it. They must have thought this a pretty strange request. They said they did not keep that many ones and to come back the next day.

When I gave Derek the bag of ones, he looked at me like, *What the hell is this?*

'You said ones,' I said.

'I meant one-hundreds!'

Derek produced the first three albums for the band, which all featured great album tracks but never managed a clear hit single. The Wishbone Ash strength was always the lead guitars; the vocals were only adequate. Worse, they rarely wrote more than ten songs for each album, which meant there was nothing to choose from, and they were dead against covering anyone else's songs. That would have been tantamount to selling out and credibility-destroying. I did make a few attempts to come up with lyrics for them, and, to my surprise, they did use 'Where Were You Tomorrow,' which they put on their second album, *Pilgrimage*. That was the first and last song credit of my career—they did not go for my follow-up, 'Where Will You Be Yesterday.'

With that first album, Wishbone Ash were named the 'Brightest Hope' in England, in the annual *Melody Maker* poll; by 1972, their third album, *Argus*, was being voted 'Best Album Of The Year.' There was respect, money was made for all of us, but we never experienced the superstar frenzy that I would have later with The Police.

As manager, all I could really do was control the live performances and try to develop the image—or, as everyone now calls it, the *brand*. Very early on, I realized the value of a clear image. This was not from any training but simple common sense. Like if you saw a picture of a guy with a cowboy hat on, you immediately thought, *country act*; a guy with an acoustic guitar, *folk act*. For Wishbone Ash it had to be the two lead guitars to give the band their defining visual look. Andy's flying-V guitar also added to it, and, when I saw it, I made sure we bought it. We never did manage to get the perfect two-guitar photo, so we had to settle for the Andy Powell/Martin Turner photo we used. That led me to come up with the two-guitar silhouette logo, which we used on advertising, T-shirts, and ever-increasing merchandise offerings.

The MCA deal did have one advantage in that, as a US-based company, the label quickly got behind getting the band to America to tour. If I had culture shock in London at the beginning of my management experience, I also had culture shock arriving in Los Angeles on the first Wishbone Ash tour of the USA.

It was February 22, 1971, and it was the first time the band had been to the USA—and their first flight on an airplane as well. As a proud American, I wanted them to experience my home country, so we arrived first in Washington, DC, so I could show them around the capital the next day. I remember Andy Powell jumping on the bed in that first Holiday Inn hotel—he was thrilled that the beds were big and there was a TV set in the room. 'Man, this is living!' It was more like kids in a candy store, huge cars, wide roads; they had their first McDonalds hamburger. They were also drinking beer in the rental car that I was driving around in, which got us stopped by the police. You can't drive in the USA with open alcohol in the car, which I either didn't know or had forgotten about, but in any case, I had to plead with the cops that this was a British Pop Group on their first day in the USA and promise never to do that again. Thankfully, we were let off.

The MCA Records deal included 'tour support,' which meant financing for the first tour of America, as it was expected to make a loss. MCA was based in Los Angeles, as was the booking agency that organized the tour, so it made sense to get to LA as soon as possible, to meet the record execs and personnel we would be working with. When we arrived at the airport, we were met by a big black Cadillac limousine, which certainly gave the impression that MCA was taking care of us. On a trip to the Sunset Marquis hotel, just off the Sunset Strip in West Hollywood, which was apparently where bands often stayed, the limo driver offered us all huge joints, like it was the normal thing to do. I was shocked. This was against the law, and the fact that this happened so nonchalantly freaked me out.

After checking the band into the hotel, I took a taxi to the MCA building at Universal City, to tell our head of A&R (artist & repertoire) what had happened. At his office, I closed the door behind me to tell him privately about the shocking thing that had happened with the limo driver. He must have thought I had two heads, but he covered it well—he said he would look into it and make sure it didn't happen again. I can only imagine what he must have said to people after I left the office.

The first West Coast dates were at the famed Whisky A Go-Go on Sunset Boulevard. I was surprised that it was not bigger—an impression I had from buying the Johnny Rivers album *Live At The Whisky A Go-Go* back in 1964. After the last Whisky show, guitarist Ted Turner disappeared, and we all thought that the 'Jesus freaks' had gotten him, like they had one of Fleetwood Mac a few months earlier. People began to say, 'It's happened again.' We never really knew where Ted went, and we were probably afraid to ask. It was a scare, and it showed just how innocent Ted really was. He had no problem taking joints when offered, unlike the other band members, though normally he was pretty responsible. Thankfully, Ted eventually turned up, and the tour carried on with no more problems.

America is a big country, and it could seem a daunting task to break the country by touring alone. On their second US tour, Wishbone Ash supported The Who at four large shows, including one in St Louis in front of thirty-five thousand people on August 16, 1971. In the dressing room before the group went onstage, Steve Upton voiced the opinion that constant touring was never going to break the band in America. I disagreed, and just at that moment Roger Daltrey and Pete Townshend came into the dressing room to say hi to their fellow Brits and show mates. Daltrey had heard Steve's comment and said, 'Touring is exactly *how* you break America.' He then recounted how The Who had played every shithole in the country over and over until they finally worked their way up to playing the huge 'shed' venues. Townshend agreed. Coming from The Who, that was a great confirmation that what I and the band were doing was the right thing. I've always liked those guys ever since.

Those Who dates were also a fun window into the wild antics of a successful rock group. Roger Daltrey told me that he always made sure he was booked to be in the bedroom furthest away from Keith Moon and Pete Townshend. That night I saw why. Keith wired up his room's TV set with a long extension cord and threw it out of his window into the swimming pool. He wanted to see if it would still work in the pool.

After the first few tours with Wishbone Ash in the USA, my center of gravity shifted to New York. None of the acts I was then managing were going to attract a super-agent, so I had to set my sights on finding someone who might see me as his ticket to success. Making the rounds of the New York agencies, I came across a young agent called Richard Halem, who was keen and needed acts to represent, so taking me on gave him acts that made him more employable. He was good enough to get the concert dates I needed, but not good enough to acquire a superstar act that would take his attention away from booking my acts. So, for now, it worked.

CHAPTER 7

THE LOST CITY
OF MOO

. . . .

Back in England by 1971, I was regularly working out of the John Sherry offices at Dryden Chambers, so we set up a partnership, calling it the Sherry/Copeland Artists agency. Soon after, my brother Ian returned from Germany, where he had served his last months in the US Army. Ian was always a character and a bit of a rebel, but the US Army did indeed sort him out, so, when he asked me about a job, I figured he might make a good concert booking agent. But just because he was my brother, I couldn't make my partner pay a fat salary, so here is the desk and the phone, and *you have to prove yourself.*

Ian started that first week on a salary of £5 per week. He took to it like a fish to water, and within a few weeks his salary began climbing. I would stick my head in the booking room every now and then to hear how he was doing. His main line was, 'I have a great act for you and am offering it to you for FREE! Well, almost free.' Then he would quote a fee, saying it was so low for such a great act that it might as well *be* free. When female social secs began coming to the office to see Ian, I knew I would not have to worry any more about nepotism. After Ed Bicknell left in July of 1972, Ian became chief booker, and one of the top booking agents in England.

Meanwhile, I began to add other management clients, starting with Renaissance in 1971. They were already represented by the agency, but they needed help. Their problem was that line-up changes had resulted in not one of the original band members remaining in the group. In other words, Renaissance were not really Renaissance. But the music was good, and Ed Bicknell asked me to get involved, so I did. We talked about changing the band's name, but a totally new name meant starting from absolute scratch. Keeping the name Renaissance meant at least some recognition. Then a funding opportunity came up that looked like it might be the solution.

It was to be my first record company venture. Wishbone's producer, Derek Lawrence, convinced John Sherry and me to join him and a well-known UK music publisher, Ben Nisbet, to form a record label. The idea was that Derek would produce, I would sort out touring in America, John would handle touring in Europe and the UK, and Ben would oversee the relationship with EMI/Capitol Records, who would fund the venture as Sovereign Records. It sounded pretty good to me, especially the funding part. My first move was to get the label to fund the recording of the first Renaissance album.

Annie Haslam was the lead singer, and funnily enough John Tout, the keyboard player, was from Rupert's People. The only thing missing was a great guitar player. In December of '71 we held auditions, and we found the perfect player in Mick Parsons, who happened to live in Devon, right on the way to Annie's parents place a bit further south. I was invited to Annie's for Christmas, so we took Mick and dropped him off at his mother's house and said we'd see him in a few days when we headed back to London for the first rehearsals. When we came back and knocked at the door, his mother answered in tears. Our guitarist had gone out to celebrate with his friends and died in a car accident. It was a shock. We drove back to London in silence.

Rob Hendry, our second choice of guitarist, was a completely different kind of player. The resulting album was *Prologue*, released in 1972. It was not a huge success, but the album got some action in the USA and put the band once again on the map in the UK. The next album, *Ashes Are Burning*—with a title track featuring Andy Powell of Wishbone that became the band's anthem—was their first album on the US *Billboard* charts. That success opened the door to Sire Records in the USA—home of the next band I took on for management.

The situation in England for The Climax Blues Band was much the same as for Renaissance. They had been on the circuit for seven years and had no upward momentum. Also, like Renaissance, they had an inbuilt problem with their name. They really weren't a blues band, and blues was not a hip label anyway. Again, changing the name was discussed, and again we decided to keep it.

With Wishbone Ash, I had built an ability to tour the USA, so that became the obvious place to try to establish both Renaissance and Climax. For both bands, the USA would be a new territory, and any success there would hopefully splash back to the UK. It was the same problem I had with The Police five years later. In effect, for all three, that is what happened.

Renaissance built a strong following with great concerts on the East Coast, especially New York. The image was upmarket and orchestral, culminating in sold-out shows at Carnegie Hall. For those I took out a full-page ad in the *Melody Maker*, with 'SOLD OUT' across the middle. The idea was that if you sold out Carnegie Hall, you must be great. Renaissance were in fact the first British band to sell out three consecutive dates at Carnegie Hall, so it *was* a big deal—at least we could make it seem like a big deal, which was the point.

For Climax it was much the same. For their sold-out concert in New York, at the Academy of Music in June of 1973, I also took out a full-page ad in the *Melody Maker*—again with 'SOLD OUT' across the middle. That was pretty good going, as I had only signed the band seven months earlier. For a guy who started out knowing absolutely nothing about the business, in my view I was proving to be a pretty good manager.

At the start, I had been trying to get Climax interested in me managing them for several months, but I never got anywhere on the telephone. When I noticed they had a concert at the Marquee Club, just down the road from my Dryden Chambers office, on December 11, 1972, I arranged to meet them there, to see if we could finalize a deal. I wasn't hopeful. Climax were from Stafford in the Midlands, and they had a kind of inbuilt suspicion that I could feel in each of the conversations I had with them. Perhaps it was because I was an American or just because I was from London—I never knew which.

I went to the Marquee for the meeting at the arranged time, and they didn't show up. I waited an hour and then, thinking I was stiffed, said *fuck it* and walked back to my office. On the next block I had to stop at the corner to let a speeding van pass by. The band in the van saw me and I saw them, so I walked back to the Marquee. Upon meeting them, they were not at all the standoffish band they had been on the phone. Seeing me 'waiting for them on the street corner' had struck a positive chord! I learned that they thought if I was so keen that I would wait for them on a street corner then I must really be serious about wanting to manage them. I didn't let on that I had given up, thought they were pricks, and was walking back to my office. We made the deal, and I became the manager.

Much like Wishbone Ash, Climax were a real rock band and therefore should be able to build a good following all across the world just by touring. Peter Haycock was a super guitar player and a kind of child prodigy, having started the band at age fifteen, so he was still pretty young. To overcome the word 'blues' in the name, the focus became CLIMAX. Then came the search for that killer photo to market the band. When guitar-maker John Veleno showed up at a Climax concert in New York with his shiny aluminum guitar, we asked Peter Haycock to try it out onstage. When a spot hit it and reflected like a mirror, Peter began to point the reflection at various members of the audience; I thought, *Aha, that's a good gimmick*. I leaned over to the Veleno guy and said, 'We'll buy it.'

I had seen Climax essentially as a great live band, and all the imagery should be to highlight that. Richard Gottehrer at Sire Records had a different aesthetic idea, and he went for non-rock images like a postage stamp for the *Stamp Album* and a radio for the band's *FM Live* album. I grew to respect Richard's musical ideas, but I didn't think much of his visual concepts. He was very insistent, though, and Sire was funding the albums. Consequently, when we recorded a live album by Climax at the Academy Of Music in New York, the USA got Richard's idea for a sleeve while in the UK I managed to change the Polydor Records sleeve to be a live photo of Peter Haycock onstage. Originally, I thought the photo had been taken by my then girlfriend, the photographer Jill Furmanovsky, but when I looked at the sleeve, I saw her in the photo, and I realized that in fact I had taken it. It became my one and only front-cover photo credit.

ↂ

In 1972, Glen Turner—Martin's brother from Tanglewood, who I had first seen in 1969—showed up in a new band called Cat Iron, with his younger brother Kim on drums, Tony Brinsley on bass, Mick Jacques on guitar, and a singer. I thought Cat Iron could be another band to take advantage of the funding from Sovereign Records, so I agreed to take them on. The first thing was to turn them into something more interesting, like a theatrically oriented rock band—give them all cool names and come up with strategies to get press coverage and some shocking stage antics. Along the same lines—although I didn't know it at the time—as Alice Cooper in the USA.

It was a fun idea that would allow me to try out stunts with someone else's money. The youngest member, Kim Turner, was into it, even when I suggested a press stunt whereby he would marry an eighty-year-old woman. I have no idea how the thought came to me except that, knowing the British press, they would have gone wild at the news that a teenage pop star was to marry such an elderly lady. Luckily for Kim, I never found an eighty-year-old willing to go along with my stunt. In the case of the singer, I quickly learned that you can take a horse to water, but you can't make him drink. In Cat Iron, the singer just did not have it in him to be a convincingly wild front man. I really needed someone like Stiv Bators from The Lords Of The New Church, the band I would put together years later.

Cat Iron did teach me some lessons, however, and did give me a talent of another sort. The band gave me Kim Turner, who joined me again in 1977 to help with the punk groups I was working with and would end up as my partner in managing The Police and Sting. Tony Brinsley, who in Cat Iron I dubbed 'Diamond Brinsley,' later became my tour manager for The Bangles and chief accountant of the company. Mick Jacques later joined my brother Stewart in Curved Air. Glen Turner went back home, and I have no idea what happened to the singer. All I have left of him is the poster: him in all black and the cat in pink.

There was one stunt with that band that provided a window to the future. We tried it out at a college in Chatham, where strangely enough the social secretary was Hugh Burnham, who later became the drummer in Gang Of Four. We worked out a stage prank where my brother Stewart, who I had made the band's tour manager, would dress up as a policeman and walk out on the stage just before the last song to stop the show, yelling about the noise and the appalling goings on. A strobe light would go on, and the singer would grab Stewart and pull down his pants, revealing a huge, two-foot-long penis (I think made out of an old sock stuffed with fabric). All as the strobe light was flashing and the band were blasting away in aggressive throbbing music.

'Kim came from behind the drums, shrieking, with a massive pair of shears,' Tony later recalled. 'He approached the policeman, who was struggling and complaining, and suddenly snapped the scissors on the phallus. The lights went out. The band then launched into a short final song and the show was finished. There was no applause; the place was just stunned, shocked, speechless!'

At the next show, the strobe didn't work—the singer panicked and lost the plot. Then someone in the audience yelled, 'You're a cunt,' and he went limp and stayed that way through the remainder of the show. It was now obvious he was never going be the front man the band needed. He had to either be a bit crazy or have the arrogance to pull it off, and he had neither. The band fizzled, and I'd learned a valuable lesson. However, Stewart did become a policeman—as drummer of The Police—and Kim Turner, drummer of Cat Iron, became their tour manager. A complete reversal of roles! Some years later, Tony Brinsley worked as tour manager for Gang Of Four, and when Hugh Burnham heard Tony had been in Cat Iron, he said he remembered that show in Chatham as the most outrageous thing he had ever seen.

꙳

In May of '74, a serious monkey wrench was thrown into the works. Wishbone Ash guitarist Ted Turner had found a girlfriend in Los Angeles who was sweet and reasonably pretty but as far as most of us were concerned lived in cloud-cuckoo-land. She moved in with Ted back in London and used to bring me paintings she had done of flying saucers she had seen the night before. She used to see a lot of them. After they visited me, I would shove the paintings in a drawer and pull them out again when I knew they were coming over. They were shit paintings. Finally, on May 2, 1974— my birthday—Ted called a band meeting and announced that he and his girlfriend were leaving to find the Lost City Of Moo, somewhere in Peru.

It was a shock. Ted resigned from the band and soon after left for Peru. As far as I know, they never found the Lost City Of Moo.

Ted's departure happened right after I was considering managing the English group Home, but before I made a decision the band dissolved. The lead singer had issues that I never did come to understand, but the other band members were great. Best of all, they had a super lead guitarist by the name of Laurie Wisefield—indeed, in every way a perfect replacement for Ted Turner. As luck would have it, it was almost perfect timing. A few months earlier, I had agreed to a partnership with Luke O'Riley, a DJ I had first known from a radio station in Philadelphia who was now living in London and working as a tour manager for my company. He had proven himself as the tour manager on The Climax Blues Band's first American tour, and now he had a pretty convincing pitch as to why we should take on Al Stewart. He had seen firsthand the audience response to the Al Stewart songs he had played on the WMMR station. Al had never been to America, and WMMR had proved there could be a receptive audience.

Being able to offer a British music artist a US tour must have been enticing, and Luke and I must have been convincing, as we quickly signed Al for management. One of the first things we did was talk him into building a band for his first US tour. Touring as a solo act might brand him as a 'folkie,' and he was more than that. *And* I had just the band he needed: the members of Home, including Laurie Wisefield. Al hired the band, and we soon had him off for his first US tour.

As the tour was ending, Wishbone Ash's other guitarist, Andy Powell, had agreed to fly to New York for a performance with Renaissance, who were recording a live album at the Academy Of Music. I asked Andy to meet Laurie and decide if he was right for Wishbone Ash. They hit it off and Laurie joined the band, and now Wishbone were back in business as a double-lead-guitar act. Disaster averted, monkey wrench withdrawn.

Meanwhile, my brother Ian was becoming the top agent at the Sherry/Copeland Agency, and, as the company expanded, we needed more space. Frankly, so did I, so I moved into my own office on Stanhope Street and adopted a new company name, British Talent Managers (BTM). I also opened an office in New York—or, more correctly, had it opened for me. I had been using a law firm in New York called Hoffer, Rich & Grubman, where the junior partner was a young hustler named Allen Grubman. We had become friends, and he was the main guy I dealt with; in fact, I rarely saw any of the others.

I met Allen one morning at the HR&G office in New York in May of '74 and he said, 'Let's go have breakfast.' We walked a block to the Sheraton Hotel coffee shop on Sixth Avenue, and Allen hit me with his idea: 'I gotta leave that place, I am doing all the work and I can't take it anymore. Will you come with me?' I could hardly stay with a firm where I knew no one, so, yes, I would go with him.

Allen was quick. 'As your lawyer, my first advice is you need a New York office—come with me.' We left the Sheraton and walked to 55th Street, where Allen showed me my new office. It was two rooms and a reception. He pointed to the left room and said, 'That's your room, to the right that's my room, and Paul Schindler was at the reception.' I would pay half of the rent and become his first client. That was the start of the Allen Grubman law office, which became the premier law firm in the music business. He remained my lawyer until 2001.

❧

With artists like Wishbone Ash, Renaissance, and The Climax Blues Band on the roster, it was not surprising that I was on the list of managers to call in the UK. One day, out of the blue, I got a call from Darryl Way. I had not known him nor did I have any idea of why he had called me. He had been the violin player in a successful British band, Curved Air; he was now playing with a new band called Wolf. The most I remembered about Curved Air was that they were the first to make an album picture disc, which got them a hit in the British pop charts.

Though not too excited at the prospect, I agreed to go see a show by the band somewhere in London. Darryl was an impressive player and an obvious star, but the band was not up to his standard, so I was going to pass. After the show, Darryl asked me what I thought, and I said, almost flippantly, 'You were great but not the band. If I were you, I'd fire them and start over.' I didn't think much more about it; I left and assumed that would be the last I would hear from Darryl. Musicians don't usually like to be told the blunt truth.

The next day I got another call from Darryl. 'OK, I fired the band, you are my manager, so what do I do now?' Though somewhat taken aback, I felt I had some sort of obligation to take him on. After all, he had taken my advice, and that was a good start to any relationship. I must have been flattered that a flippant bit of honesty would actually have been listened to. So, without any prior intention, I ended up as Darryl's manager.

The first task was to organize a new and better band. I brought in several players I knew, including Mick Jacques from Cat Iron on guitar and my brother Stewart on drums. I was never about nepotism, but I knew Stewart was ready, so why not give him a shot? I made sure that Darryl knew it would be up to him in the end. Without me pushing, Darryl himself decided to give the drummer's job to Stewart. He later told me he figured that if my brother was in the band, I would pay more attention than otherwise. For Stewart, it was a big break, and indeed the first professional band he was a member of.

As fate would have it, in 1974 a large VAT (Value Added Tax) bill was levied on Curved Air, and it seemed the only way to pay it off was to reassemble the original Curved Air to tour and hopefully make enough profit to pay off the tax bill. Back came Sonja Kristina as singer, Florian Pilkington-Miksa as drummer, and Francis Monkman on keyboards. The original bass player was not available, so we brought in an American musician, Philip Kohn, to complete the touring line-up. To add to the financial viability of the tour, I suggested a live album be recorded, which I could put out via the new BTM label deal I had just organized with RCA Records. This turned out to be quite convenient for me personally, and it did in fact help Curved Air pay the tax bill.

The Curved Air situation had put a hold on Darryl's new band, so Stewart took on the role of Curved Air's tour manager, which also conveniently kept him in the frame. The eighteen-date tour of the UK included Cardiff University and Bristol Polytechnic on December 4 and 5, 1974, respectively, where the album was recorded. It actually turned out to be a great live album, and it got amazing reviews in the press.

Luckily, the tour was successful enough to pay the tax bill, cover the tour costs, and make a small profit. That made Darryl and me think seriously about continuing as Curved Air and to forget the new band idea.

Kind of, if it ain't broke, don't fix it, and let's face it: Curved Air proved they could make money. I was definitely into the idea, and Darryl was listening to me, so we looked at pulling it together. The key players were Darryl on violin and singer Sonja Kristina, who quickly agreed to join in with the plan. Francis and Florian, however, opted out. That opened the door to Stewart taking over on the drums and Mick Jacques joining on guitar, and we already had Philip Kohn on bass. In effect, Curved Air absorbed the new Darryl Way band, and a new Curved Air was born. The advantage from the start was that Curved Air had a name and a market already established, so it was certainly easier to book concerts for them than a new band fronted by Darryl.

Meanwhile, Stewart was now in a professional touring band; he married the lead singer, Sonja, and was now a real 'muso' rock star. I will always remember the day when Stewart told me, 'I am one of *them* now!' He had crossed over from the business side, the management of musicians, to *being* a musician. Stewart recognized the difference. He could now be a prima donna, shoot himself in the foot, be his own worst enemy, and it was perfectly natural, for now he was a 'muso.' He could complain about the dressing room food. The shitty hotel. The limo is too small. Be unrealistic. Like it was his JOB to complain—that's what musos are *supposed* to do. It was like he was warning me that he had gone over to the 'dark side' and was no longer my brother—or, at least, not the brother he had been before. I thought it was funny at the time. But in every joke, there is a grain of truth.

Curved Air proved to be a good training ground for Stewart. He had seen the business side as a tour manager, and now he saw the artist side as a musician. The lessons of excesses in the business and their realities definitely were absorbed and would be put to good use in the future.

By 1974, the BTM management company was expanding. New offices in London and New York, and a new record label in partnership with RCA records, made me think expansively. The British group Caravan joined in that year, wanting me to deliver their first tour of the USA, which I did. And my brother Ian volunteered to be their tour manager for that tour, which turned out to be a valuable education for his future, too.

In late 1974, I had a surprise visit from Lawrence Impey, one of Stewart's school chums from his days at Millfield school in south-west England.

Lawrence, it seems, had decided he wanted to go into the music business as a manager. However, his father, a prominent lawyer in Bournemouth in the south of England, was concerned that his son didn't know the first thing about the business, so he should find a partner who did. The only person Lawrence could think of was me.

Lawrence was very enthusiastic. He told me he had discovered the 'next Beatles' and wanted to take me to Blackheath in South London to see his great discovery. I went with him and met five young lads, all around seventeen years old, in a band called Squeeze. Lawrence was right: they were great, so I agreed to join him and co-manage the group. I began to look for a record deal and set up gigs, leaving Lawrence to deal with their day-to-day affairs, although he quit when he realized that working for a year or more with no guaranteed income was not what he had in mind when he graduated from university.

The main members of Squeeze were Chris Difford, who wrote the lyrics; Glenn Tilbrook, who played lead guitar, wrote the melodies, and was the main singer; as well as Jools Holland on keyboards. Chris and Glenn were a sort of Lennon/McCartney writing team—actually more like Elton John and Bernie Taupin. As with The Beatles, the original drummer was apparently below par, so he was changed early on.

This happened when I got some interest from Island Records producer Muff Winwood, brother of Stevie Winwood. I was hoping Island might sign the group, but Muff wanted to check them out in the studio first. After a few hours, he pulled the plug on the session and said we needed a new drummer. He was blunt: the drummer was the foundation of a band, and if the drummer wasn't solid, you were building on sand. That put us on the road to looking for a replacement, and after many auditions we found Gilson Lavis. He was a great drummer but about two feet taller than the rest of the band, making it virtually impossible to get a photo that looked like the members belonged in the same group. Meanwhile, Muff lost interest, and I had to start looking for an alternative record deal.

Squeeze were quite different from all the other artists I represented in that they were a pop group that might actually be able to have a hit single. And they were very young, unmarried, and not yet jaded. They would prove an interesting transition, and challenge, for the future...

CHAPTER 8

STARTRUCKIN' 75

. . . .

The reality of my management time with Wishbone, Renaissance, and The Climax Blues Band was of trying to find a way around their basic weaknesses while maintaining the continuing effort to grow their fan bases. The surest way to build them, for me, was touring. Unfortunately, that could be a long process—as The Who had so eloquently told Wishbone Ash back in 1971. Any way I could shorten that process, the better. In the end, the StarTruckin' tour was the method I chose.

By the summer of '75, my British Talent Managers company had established itself in the main markets of North America and the UK but not so much elsewhere. I began to look towards continental Europe as the next potential growth area for the artists. This led me to develop a relationship with an enterprising agent in Holland by the name of Cyril Van Den Hemel, who had proved adept at booking countries in Europe that had, to that point, been difficult for me. He had booked a successful Wishbone Ash tour in late 1974 that included Germany, Denmark, Switzerland, Holland, Belgium, and France, which proved to me that he was a keeper for the future, so I got further into business with him. If he could do the same for my other bands, that would be good for both the management company and the new BTM label. Together, we started plotting, and we came up with the concept of a moving festival tour called StarTruckin' 75.

The StarTruckin' 75 tour was an attempt to find a way to faster establish all my management acts by piggybacking on the more famous acts we could

MILES A. COPELAND III

book as headliners, namely acts like Lou Reed and Mahavishnu Orchestra. It was perhaps the first moving festival tour of Europe (if not the world), and promoters quickly saw the concept as a winner. It linked several existing festivals with ones StarTruckin' created to join them together.

By making Wishbone Ash the headliner on the posters, the idea was to paint them and all my acts on the bill with the brush of being big and popular. Conceptually, it was a winner, and in fact it worked in the attempt to further the popularity of my management acts. Instead of playing to one or two thousand people per show and building from that, they were now playing to fifteen and twenty thousand people per show.

On paper, it looked great. The tour itself, however, was a growing series of mishaps. First, putting all your eggs in one basket turned out to be a bad idea. Like a machine with lots of parts, if one stops working, the whole machine stops—as happened all along the way.

The first hiccup was the transport. Two airplanes were chartered to transport the bands and crew and painted with the StarTruckin' 75 logo on them, which looked great. Showing up at the airport and seeing them, I thought, *Wow, we have our own planes!* When it was time to check the planes for takeoff, however, one was so overweight the pilot refused to fly. 'Get that shit off my plane!' he yelled. He had us take off most of the equipment before he would agree to fly.

I remember the cool and collected John McLaughlin—Mr. Vegetarian, clean-living Zen master of the Mahavishnu Orchestra—actually becoming so upset he started smoking again as he watched the plane being unloaded. I think I wrecked that guy's life. That should have been my first warning sign. Now there were trucking costs we didn't budget for.

The really big hurdle was with Lou Reed. He was to join the last part of the tour in time for the shows in Spain, where he was huge. But we hadn't heard anything about his arrival plans, and we were getting no response from his agency. I finally tracked him down at a hotel in New Zealand. When I was put through to his room, his partner, Rachel, answered and told me very politely that Lou could not come to the phone as he was in the bathroom. I said I would wait. 'It could be a long time, as Lou has been in there for a day already, and I have no idea when he's coming out.' That freaked me out, so I asked what the travel plans were. When Rachel told me they knew nothing about the shows and Lou had left the William Morris agency months before, I knew I was in trouble. It was looking like a serious disaster.

Thankfully, but at a cost, Cyril managed to replace Lou Reed with Ike & Tina Turner, who delivered a truly spectacular show. It was some consolation that all the shows were great and the audiences were happy, but for me it felt increasingly like knowing I was marching to my death and Cyril was paving the way.

By mid-tour at the Orange Festival in France, the impending financial debacle was becoming ever more apparent. So, I sat down with Steve Upton of Wishbone in his hotel and tried to pay him what I had at the time. It was a bag of money in various currencies—Danish krone, Norwegian krone, Finnish markka, Belgian francs, and German marks—which should have been close to what I owed the group. Steve didn't want to deal with all those currencies, though. 'Keep it,' he said. 'Pay us in English pounds at the end of the tour.' Half of me wanted him to take that money, the other half knew I had other bills to pay, so I put the money back in my suitcase. I don't think Steve had any idea how bad the situation was.

It went from bad to worse. The promoter in Orange cut the fee, and the absence of Lou Reed and the increased cost of Ike & Tina meant the tour sank into deeper trouble. Needless to say, those currencies I had tried to pay Wishbone Ash with were soon spent, and by the end of the tour there were no pounds to pay the group what I owed them.

In the end, what kept me from actual bankruptcy was going to all the debtors and promising that if they gave me a chance, I would pay them fifty percent of what I owed within two years, or they could bankrupt me now and likely get nothing. The realization that what goes up can easily go down was a lesson I needed to learn, and boy did I learn it.

There was another lesson. My partner in this fiasco, Cyril, unbeknownst to me, was often high on cocaine and hence living in a world devoid of reality—a reality I did not see until it was too late. I never took drugs, so I had no idea what the signs were. I terminated my relationship with Cyril, and ever since then I have watched out for any hint of drugs with anyone I worked with.

In spite of its problems, however, in many ways the StarTruckin' 75 tour was actually a kind of masterpiece. As far as I know, it was the first traveling music festival of its kind, long before Lollapalooza or WOMAD or Amnesty International. It was a big idea, but it was too big for me.

⌘

I flew to the States in September and found the situation there much the same as the one I had left in England. Rats leaving the sinking ship. Allen Grubman took over my vacated office, and my one staff member disappeared. Meanwhile, Wishbone Ash had relocated to the USA soon after the end of StarTruckin', so I went to see the band at Martin Turner's newly rented house in Connecticut. I had to tell the band the bad news that I could not pay them. I felt so bad about it that I resigned as manager and tore up the contract in front of them. Five years of fighting together, and now I was officially the ex-manager of my main client, Wishbone Ash.

At the same time, my agent friend who'd been quick to write me off left me with no more US agency relationship. My only meaningful calling card in the USA was The Climax Blues Band, who would soon be looking for their next US tour to support the new album, *Gold Plated*, that they were working on back in England. A chance meeting with fellow manager Shep Gordon saw two agents recommended to me. One was Johnny Podell in New York and the other the Paragon Agency down in Georgia, neither of whom I knew.

I set up a meeting with Johnny and was almost immediately put off by his open use of cocaine. I had learned my lesson from Cyril, and I had no intention of working with a drug-taking agent. Truth be known, I was always anti-drug, but the StarTruckin' fiasco had made me *rabidly* anti-drug. I was out of there. Next I called the Paragon Agency. Alex Hodges was the boss, and after I explained I was looking for an agent for Climax he invited me to Macon to meet his team.

Paragon was unlike any other agency: nice antebellum house, garden, and Southern hospitality. The atmosphere reminded me of my days at college at Birmingham Southern in Alabama: serious, but without the hectic tension of New York or the hipper-than-thou posing of Los Angeles. At the end of the meeting, Alex asked me if I knew any agents that might be interested in coming to work at Paragon. I said I could only think of one, but it would be a drag for me, as he was my best agent in England. But I always thought he would do better in the USA. It was my brother, Ian. So, I gave him Ian's contact information, and Alex promised to call him. When I left the office, I called Ian and told him to expect the call. Alex did call, Ian went to Macon, and he got the job. I am sure being able to bring The Climax Blues Band to Paragon helped, but Alex seemed more interested in a good agent, rather than just what that agent could bring. I am also sure Ian charmed them no end, and that's why he got the job. In any case, Paragon booked the next Climax US tour.

No sooner had I returned to the UK when the bailiffs came into my fancy Stanhope Street offices and cleaned them out. Furniture, desks, typewriters, copy machines—all they left were piles of promotional posters, stickers, and badges, which I presume they felt were of no value. I packed up all those posters and promotional materials, hoping I could sell them at the upcoming concerts that were still on the schedule, and took them to my parents' house in St John's Wood. I was now once again living with them at 21 Marlborough Place.

With no office, I called my old partner, John Sherry, and asked if I could move back in with him in Dryden Chambers off Oxford Street. Luckily, he had space, and he did me the courtesy of not saying, 'I told you so.' It was a far cry from those nice Stanhope offices, with my own secretary and staff. I was down but I was not out.

For some reason, The Climax Blues Band continued as a management client. I did promise them that if they stuck with me, I would give them my full attention and deliver them a hit record. They recorded *Gold Plated*, turning in the usual really good album, but upon hearing it I knew I would not be able to give what I'd promised, so I insisted they go back in the studio to record a hit. I suggested some covers, but lucky for them they wrote 'Couldn't Get It Right' on their own; we recorded it, and it became the single we needed, a hit in both the UK and the USA. After so many years as a lower-mid-level touring band, Climax performed for the very first time on the UK's *Top Of The Pops* TV show on November 4, 1976, and they eventually got to #10 in the British charts in late November. It did even better in the USA, reaching #3 in the charts. In spite of the shit I was in, I delivered what I said I would.

By the end of 1976, I was left with only two official clients: Squeeze and The Climax Blues Band. I helped Curved Air when I could, but Stewart was getting other ideas, and the group did not seem to be long for this world.

The only good news of the 1976 period was that all those posters and promotional materials I had taken came in handy. As I had no income, I arranged with my ex-management bands to let me sell the posters at their shows. At some shows I made a few hundred pounds, in some cases more than I would have made in commissions. In a world of shit, it was uplifting. I had cash in my pocket again, and I could eat. From that point on, I have had a healthy regard for merchandise.

My co-management deal with Al Stewart essentially fizzled out without any formal separation. My supposed partner just carried on by himself with Al, who was touring the USA at the time. I presume Luke decided he didn't need me anymore, and, like many others, just wrote me off. All I knew was one day he called me on the phone, probably after a few drinks—actually a lot of drinks—screaming that he never wanted me to mention Al Stewart again or he would sue me. As he ranted, I thought of my mother's oft-quoted expression, 'I knew that rat when he was a mouse.'

Curved Air carried on with concerts in Europe and England for the rest of 1975 and throughout 1976, but the band slowly ground to a halt, eventually performing their last date on December 11, 1976. They did manage to give me a bunch of good support slots for Squeeze, though, and they let me sell posters at their shows.

Thankfully, the next US tour for The Climax Blues Band was booked by Paragon, and it went well, but by early 1977 things were not looking good between me and the band. My credibility had been severely punctured by the StarTruckin' fiasco, and the wives were bitching that their husbands were away too much of the time. They all imagined they should have more money. There were also some embarrassing incidents at my Dryden Chambers office when Colin Cooper, Climax's long-haired sax player, showed up when a bunch of punks were visiting, and they made fun of him. To a British punk, Colin was the epitome of an 'old fart,' and they told him so to his face.

At the end of 1976, I was back in New York for the Climax dates, and fortuitously I took the time to meet up with an old friend who I had worked with, off and on, doing publicity for some of my artists. Jane Friedman may have appeared frail in stature, but she was quick and strong with opinion and not afraid to tell it like she saw it. I always found her to be a useful window to see what was going on. Jane had become immersed in the underground scene in New York and seemed genuinely excited about it creatively. She was working with Patti Smith at the time, and her boyfriend was John Cale of The Velvet Underground. Jane was seeing the future, and she encouraged me to check out people like Cherry Vanilla, Wayne County, Blondie, and others, plus the clubs that these new artists were performing in—CBGB's, Max's Kansas City, and the like. I took the time to do what she suggested, and whatever had excited her also seemed to do something to me as well. I met Cherry and Wayne, a seed was planted, contacts were made.

In February 1977, The Climax Blues Band fired me. So much for appreciation! That termination put the final nail into my 'progressive rock' past and forced me into a new era. My only holdover was Squeeze—although of course I was once again in a seedy Dryden Chambers office.

CHAPTER 9

THE OLD AND
THE NEW

. . . .

My comeuppance after the disaster of Star Truckin' 75 landed me back in my old offices at Dryden Chambers off Oxford Street, London, with my first British partner, John Sherry. Sting once told me, 'Be nice to the people on your way up because you might need them on your way down.' John turned out to be one of the few people who were there when I was down.

While I was down and pretty much broke, it just so happened that a whole new generation of music was bubbling up among England's disenchanted youth. Some might like to say it was a cultural, economic, or political shift, but to me it was no more than a new generation sticking their heads up, bored with the past and wanting their own identity and music. They didn't want to look like the past or to like the music of the past. In fact, they aggressively and vocally opposed it, which is why the term 'punk' was so applicable to them. To this new generation, the Led Zeppelin era became the era of old farts.

Part of the aggressiveness against the past was simply because 'the past' had rejected them and refused them entry. It was like, 'If you won't let me in, then fuck you.' I could relate to that. And, as I no longer represented any of those groups, that sentiment suited me fine.

Meanwhile in the mainstream record business, the executives saw punk simply as a musical fad that would soon go away. They heard music badly played and forgot that every ten years or so, a new generation comes along wanting its own thing. These executives were stuck in the rules of the previous ten years, forgetting that even The Beatles were rejected by every record company because *they* broke the rules of their time, too.

So, in a very real way, the punks and I were in the same boat. Like them, I had no money, and I'd been counted out by the mainstream music business. How this worked for me was simple: the punks wouldn't care that I had no money, so long as I was prepared to pay attention to them and take them seriously, and able to deliver entry into the music business— either through gigs or record deals. Having no other option, it was natural that I would gravitate to them, and that is what I did.

The most notorious new group, the one that got all sorts of press coverage and seriously rocked the boat, was the Sex Pistols. They were the gods of this new generation, and they made a big deal in the press that the mainstream refused them entry. To me, it seemed that the same doors that were closed for me were also closed for them.

It was sheer luck that on the floor above Dryden Chambers, Malcolm McLaren, the manager of the Sex Pistols, had a small office. As the Pistols were becoming more notorious and newsworthy, I could not help but become intrigued. I kept reading that no one would book them, so I took it upon myself to come to the rescue. I started calling clubs to see if I could get them some dates. It was easier than I had thought, so I went up to meet Malcolm to offer the group the dates, fully expecting to get a warm welcome. He was nice enough but dismissive too, and he kept giving excuses as to why he couldn't do any of the dates. I kept moving the dates and going back to see if this time he could do them. After the third time, he started yelling at me: 'Don't you get it? I get more media attention saying no one will touch the group than I would get if I actually played dates. You are fucking me up! Get the fuck out of here!'

As I left his office, I threw out one parting shot. 'How about Europe? I have an offer to do Amsterdam.'

To my surprise, his whole demeanor changed. 'Europe we can do,' he said. So, I became the first person to book the Sex Pistols for a European tour.

Malcolm couldn't go with them, so I took the group myself, realizing that being in the Sex Pistols camp would give me credibility with the other new bands that seemed to be popping up everywhere. Besides, I was pretty curious to see what all the fuss was about.

On January 4, 1977, the band and I flew from London Heathrow Airport to Amsterdam. The *Evening News* reported that the band were hung over and had 'vomited and spat' their way to the flight, which was categorically denied by the EMI representatives the paper said accompanied the group to Amsterdam. I was with them: they were not hung over, and there was no vomiting or spitting along the way. I also don't remember any EMI representatives traveling with us. Perhaps the paper was quoting me and assuming I was with EMI. As far as I was concerned, it was the British press just making it up to sell more papers—which was exactly what I assumed Malcolm wanted.

In Amsterdam with the Pistols boys, it was apparent that *they* thought they were a group, and they were very happy to be actually playing a gig. I don't think they realized that Malcolm had no interest in them doing gigs unless it worked for his media strategy. We stayed at Hotel Wiechmann, a little place that was frequented by all the British groups because it was cheap and in the center of town. The owner, Mrs. Body, was a sort of rock'n'roll mom—she made the groups feel welcome at their Dutch home away from home.

I'd had Squeeze stay there a year before, and before that The Climax Blues Band and even Wishbone Ash, so I knew Mrs. Body and her hotel well. On the morning of the Pistols' show, however, all hell broke loose. The hotel phone was ringing off the hook. Mrs. Body was freaking out that every newspaper one had ever heard of was calling and speaking to *her*. She called me for help, and when I got to her office, she handed me the phone.

'No comment.'

'No, the band are not available.'

'No, it's untrue; they did not wreck the plane or spit on the stewardess.'

This was front-page stuff, and they all wanted quotes from the band, or Mrs. Body, or me. I am sure if I had said Johnny Rotten had spit at the passport controller, it would have been on the front pages all over England.

The furor was over EMI's announcement that the Sex Pistols were being dropped and their contract terminated. This stemmed from the incident on Thames Television's *Today* show where several members of the band had used words like 'fuckers' and 'shit' during an interview. Whether Malcolm knew this was going to happen and that the band being out of the country would make them hard to get to, I don't know, but it sure was a feeding frenzy, and it was impressive to be a part of it.

The Sex Pistols shows at the club itself went well enough, and, contrary to some press reports, they were *not* cancelled. Johnny Rotten was a character, as one would expect. There was a kind of twinkle in his eyes, and I couldn't help but think he saw the humor in all of this. The bass player, Glen Matlock, was the best musician, which is why Malcolm got rid of him and put the crazy Sid Vicious in his place. Most of all, my impression was they wanted to be a band but were being pushed by the press, and indeed Malcolm, to be more newsworthy by being outrageous. By being so encouraged, they became, in effect, a plaything for the media—and for Malcolm himself. To be honest, as much as Malcolm is credited as being a manager, in the traditional sense he was not a manager. He was great at getting publicity, but he was never about working for the band or delivering what they wanted. He was working for himself.

The most amusing part of the UK press response to the punks was when the Sex Pistols and The Clash banned reporters from their early gigs. At the door, reporters were literally told to 'fuck off.' This was such a shock that it made them want to get in even more. Whether this was a strategy to get more press or to keep the press from finding out that the bands were crap musically, I don't know, but I do know that the press went crazy, and the coverage continued for much longer than one would have expected. Funny thing, though: when later groups tried the same thing, the press just said, 'Ho hum, we won't be writing about you then,' and left. The press smelled a rat—this was a calculated maneuver to get coverage, whereas the Pistols and Clash just didn't give a shit.

As any media person knows, the press wants shock stories—they sell more papers than sweetness and light. And it usually doesn't take too much prodding to get bands to exaggerate. Give them some smoke and they will report a fire. In the end, that is what a lot of the 'punk' furor in the British national press was all about.

Fashion was also a big part of the punk scene. Safety pins, ripped shirts, wild colored hair, mohawks, spiky hair—anything to rub the establishment the wrong way. In fact, fashion played a bigger part in the punk scene than people may realize. Clothing stores like Vivienne Westwood's Sex on the Kings Road were gathering places for the early punks who wanted to look different. Secondhand clothing shops specializing in the weird and unusual played a part. The punks ran away from the scruffy, long-haired, blue-jean informal look and now wanted to stand out in a crowd. At one of the early Clash gigs I attended, I was struck by three things: members of the press trying to get in for free and being turned away; how bad the band were as musicians, but also how no one seemed to care; and how cool they looked in white shirts with paint splattered over them, like some modern art painting. I left laughing to myself, thinking, *This really is shit, but it's also really great.*

As punk was making bigger and bigger news, the people on the periphery, like myself, also began to get coverage. At one point, there was a feature on me in a major national paper as the architect of the phrase 'new wave,' as a 'cover up' for the horrible punk rock sound. The article was complete nonsense, but I liked it as it made out that I was more important to the scene than I really was. Like my father used to say, 'Any press is good press—just spell the name right.'

The *Sunday People* newspaper was convinced of punk's evil and gave a great flavor of what the press was pushing in late 1976 and early 1977. 'This is the truth about Punk Rock,' the paper announced. 'For many weeks a *Sunday People* team of investigators has probed this bizarre business. Their verdict on this cult is simply this. It is sick. It is dangerous. It is sinister.' The paper claimed to be convinced that the 'system' was threatened by punk, and that punks were in 'rebellion against everybody and everything.' The journalists found a highly educated punk who spoke of the need for 'another Hitler and the abolition of the monarchy and Parliament.' The following week, the paper described punk as a 'freaky music craze masterminded by Svengalis such as Miles Copeland.'

After several years of being counted out, it was nice to see one's name in print as a Svengali of a new movement that was gaining such huge attention. For me, it was the beginning of a new era—I was beginning to rise like a phoenix from the ashes.

ᕙᕗ

From what I could see, the mainstream music scene in London in 1977 was one of confusion. With all the national press coverage punk was getting, one would think the establishment would be getting excited and have recording contracts at the ready, pens drawn. But no, the doors were closed. Consequently, the bands were forced to go it alone. Small independent record labels sprung up, along with a spirit of irreverence for the traditional music business, most of which resulted from being denied access. Stiff Records was one of the first to gain attention, with such groups as The Damned and Elvis Costello.

The main club at the time was the Roxy. It was tiny and really a dump, but that made it easy to sell out, so it was all the easier to give the impression of something happening. It launched in January 1977, and it quickly became *the* happening place for punk in London. I spent a lot of time at the Roxy that year, and I made sure all the bands I worked with performed there.

One of these bands was The Police. My growing interest in the punks had also inspired Stewart, and he soon launched his idea for a stripped-down, punk-vibe group of his own—suitably named The Police. Having met Sting after a Curved Air show in Newcastle, he talked him into joining the new band, and then roped in his friend Henry Padovani as well, largely because he looked the part.

Stewart's next step, unbeknownst to me at the time, was to record the band's first single, 'Fallout' / 'Nothing Achieving,' at Pathway Studios, which he got a friend to pay for. My first involvement came when he wanted to get the single pressed up and distributed. That's when we came up with Illegal Records—the first of my indie labels.

I quickly went about learning how to release a recording from start to finish. I knew about the recording studio and the mastering process, but I had never actually gone to a factory that pressed the records, or the printer that made the sleeves, or the label maker that made the labels to go on the records. It turns out it was not that difficult: record the music, take the tapes to the master room to get mastered, take the masters to get the metal plates made, take the metal plates to the factory for pressing along with the labels I had organized with the label printer, and then finally go to the sleeve printer to get the sleeves printed in time to get them to the pressing plant to put the records in them.

Often, I was late with the printed sleeves, so I had to bag the records myself. Then, with the product in hand, I would borrow my parents' car and drive around to the record stores that would buy the records, get the money, and think, *Wow, I really am in the record business from A to Z.* It was also a great education as to why all those many pages existed in record contracts dealing with 'free goods,' 'returns,' 'damaged goods,' 'packaging costs,' and various discounts. Now I was personally experiencing what all those things meant.

Wanting to catch the momentum of the punk scene at a time where any 'punk' single could be sold, I created Illegal Records, first for the Police single but also later for releases by John Cale, Wayne County & The Electric Chairs, The Cramps, The Lords Of The New Church, and more. It was so basic that the words 'Illegal Records' on the record label were drawn by me with a black felt-tip pen. I always thought it was stupid to have label names that meant nothing. Surely the label name could also be cool, and a hip part of the marketing for the record?

As far as punk was concerned, though, The Police didn't fit age-wise, and Squeeze didn't fit it lyric-wise. And they could actually play their instruments, too, so they didn't fit musicianship-wise either. Andy Summers, The Police's new guitarist, had after all been in Soft Machine—the most progressive, self-indulgent, scruffy long-haired rock band ever, with thirty-minute songs, long solos, and no recognition of their audience. Sting had come from a jazz band, Last Exit, and Stewart had been in Curved Air. You can't get much more old-school than that.

Though I had signed Squeeze when I was strong in the progressive-rock scene, now that I was no longer part of it, I could see the writing on the wall, and I came to the view that they should be part of the new music scene that was developing around us. Cut their hair and they had a better chance going for the new, especially because they were young. But it was also obvious that they wouldn't relate to the aggressive side of the punk scene—spitting, pogoing, spiky hair, and anti-establishment politics were not part of the Squeeze mentality.

Squeeze were in the age group of the punks, but musically they seemed to belong more to The Beatles' generation. They were anything but political, to the point that Billy Idol's bass player once chastised me, 'How can you manage a group like that? They sing LOVE SONGS!' To the Generation X guys, it was all about your 'stance.' By contrast, Stewart, in his efforts to make The Police a punk group, wrote political songs like 'Nothing Achieving' and 'Fallout,' was concerned about the image, and had an aggressive performance style.

Squeeze were none of that, and nor would it have made sense for me to push them into it. I liked their music, and I saw no reason to change it—my job was to make it fit in with what was starting to happen. Mostly, what I could do was affect the image. But giving Squeeze an image was no small task. Glenn had a resistance to anything contrived—and no sense of fashion anyway. It's like he lived in a world of pure music, and he could have just as easily worn pajamas onstage as blue jeans. Jools always had an image. Gilson, who was twice as big as the rest of the group, was also not an image person, so I can't say I ever got a photo that fully represented the group. Once, in Arizona, I tried—I took them to the desert for a photo session, hoping to get photos that would make it into the papers, like I had done with The Police. All through that photo session, I could not help but think that Glenn did not really want to be there. Jools took it in his stride and saw the fun in it, but Glenn must have seen it as something phony. Well, it was contrived and phony—like all advertising inherently is.

I remember the day I decided the band needed some new clothes to wear onstage. I gave Glenn and Chris £500 and sent them off to kit themselves out. Glenn came back with what looked to me like women's clothes, a kaftan, and both of them bought funny shoes—totally useless onstage, and definitely not image-making nor image-defining. I probably should have hired a clothing designer for the group to help create a cohesive image, but then again, Jools would most likely have gone one way and Glenn another, and the rest somewhere in between.

I tried various ways to get Squeeze included in the new movement without *pretending* they were punks, including booking them onto one of the first shows at the Roxy, hoping I could get them some attention in the press and, eventually, a record deal. When Island lost interest, I went to RCA and got another rejection.

Undeterred, I created Deptford Fun City Records for the release of their first single, 'Packet Of Three,' and later for Jools Holland's 'Boogie Woogie 78.' In reality, Squeeze were from just south of the Deptford area, in more upmarket Blackheath, but it was close enough. Deptford to London was what the Bowery was to New York City—definitely *not* a fun place. So, calling Deptford a 'fun city' was a joke to give the band a rough edge that might add to their 'street credibility.' At least that was the idea.

To sell records from all these different labels, I created an umbrella distribution company called Faulty Products (with an inverted *F* in the logo). Again, a bit of irreverence in a name. In the beginning, it was just me; later on, I hired a salesman to help me, but it was never more than a few people.

࿇

From a pure marketing perspective, with Squeeze and then with The Police, it was important to do everything we could to be identified with the future, not the past, in spite of the fact that neither fit what was going on. Luckily, although the record-store buyers were reading about punk, and had people coming into the store asking what recordings were available, they were not really *au fait* with what was hip or not in the actual punk scene. In that context, I could sell Police and Squeeze singles almost as easily as Generation X or other 'real' punk bands, as long as they 'looked right.' Perception was nine tenths of reality. If the record sleeve looked punk enough, and the recording was unpolished enough, that worked.

The first real punk label was created soon after a guy named Mark P. moved into my office at Dryden Chambers and we created a partnership we called Step-Forward Records. I never liked the name, but Mark wanted to make the point that the label was to be a launching platform for this new generation of musical artists. It was to be a stepping stone for an artist, not a long-term commitment.

Mark P. was actually a very interesting character. His name was really Mark Perry but, not wanting the dole office (British social security) to find out what he was up to, he used the name Mark P. At age twenty, he had created a fanzine for the punk movement called *Sniffin' Glue* that was really just a bunch of Xeroxed pages stapled together. It was not well written, it was laced with swearwords, it made liberal use of the felt-tip pen to highlight a point, but it was brutally honest, and soon it became *the* fanzine that mattered. *Sniffin' Glue* was as important to the punk world as *Rolling Stone* was to the mainstream, and getting on the front page was a big deal.

One day, Mark came into my office to interview Chelsea, one of the bands I was beginning to work with, and soon others began showing up for interviews there as well. Before I knew it, Mark had essentially moved in; my office became his office. He had no other convenient place to go, and not only was Dryden Chambers centrally located but it was tatty enough to fit the image. I don't think *Sniffin' Glue* would have fit well into a gleaming modern office building.

Meanwhile, for me, it was not a bad idea to be at the media center of what was going on in the punk world, so I made space for Mark and went along with it. With the Sex Pistols' office upstairs, in many respects the entire punk world now began flowing through my office. So, realizing the benefits, I helped Mark expand *Sniffin' Glue* by suggesting he print more copies and then distributing them as I was driving around selling my records. Mark's sidekick, Harry Murlowski, requisitioned the camera that I had left on my desk and immediately maneuvered his way into becoming the official photographer for the magazine. I never saw that camera again. It was brand new, but months later, when I suggested to Harry that he buy it, he offered me a pittance, declaring, 'But it's used!'

It was not long before *Sniffin' Glue* got to a circulation of twenty thousand copies, making it by far the biggest and most important fanzine of the era. Meanwhile, Step-Forward Records signed Chelsea, The Cortinas, and Models (with Marco Pirroni, later of Adam Ant fame, on guitar). Then came The Fall and Sham 69. Our semi-hits were Chelsea's 'Right To Work' and 'Fascist Dictator' by The Cortinas, which BBC Radio's famed DJ John Peel played on his show. Hearing those songs on the radio proved we were on to something—this was real.

Chelsea were fronted by Gene October, who had a great look but was the classic English 'wide boy.' Almost every time I saw him, his first words to me were, 'Lend me a fiver.' Even if he had money he would ask. I also never knew if he'd signed his real name, Jonathan, to the contract, as when I asked his name, he was so sheepish that it took a few minutes to get it out of him. 'Gene, you have to sign the contract with your real name, not your stage name.' His lyrics were very much punk, though, and with his face he could definitely pull off 'angry.' Gene could look angry even when happy. When 'Right To Work' was played by John Peel on the BBC, it soon became a punk anthem. Of course, his wide-boy demeanor meant he went through musician after musician, starting with Billy Idol and the Generation X guys. One would work with Gene for a while, then move on. He was also not the type of artist that a major label was going to sign, so consequently Step-Forward and IRS Records in America got enough songs from Chelsea to release two full albums. We never even bothered to have a long-term contract with Gene: we just went album by album, song by song.

The Cortinas were the second act signed to Step-Forward, and they were a different story. They were five young lads from Bristol who were basically nice people from reasonable families. I even had them stay at the house in St John's Wood in March 1977 while they were in London to record their first two singles for Step-Forward. Mark and I had first seen them perform at the Roxy, and we were impressed: they were pretty good musicians for their youth, but I can't say they were particularly angry or politically motivated. Songs like 'Fascist Dictator' had a suitable punk feel, though, and made them players on the scene, so we could see that this was a band that could go places. The drummer's father acted as their manager at first, before realizing it was too much for him and turning the band over to Kim Turner and me.

Kim had recently showed up in London looking for a job. He was a musician—formerly the drummer in Cat Iron—and he knew his way around a sound board. Young and enthusiastic, he had no problem working with all the punk bands, so he was a useful savior I called upon to pull the various bands together, most of whom had no clue about what it takes to set up for a music performance. He and Harry Murlowski became my two jacks of all trades that I threw at each problem, event, or opportunity that came up that I could not handle or attend to myself.

Step-Forward was always meant as a springboard for artists to move to bigger labels, so when CBS wanted to sign The Cortinas, we made the deal. The resulting album, *True Romances*, moved the band away from their original punkish esthetic, either because the producer was old-school or because the CBS people who were watching over it were—whatever the case, it didn't have the hard edge that their fans expected. I could blame Kim for this—Kim was there day-to-day from the start, so he should have seen what was happening—but most of all I blame myself for not spending more time in the studio to correct what became an album that was appealing to no one. As one critic said, '*True Romances* sounds more befitting of a bunch of middle-aged pub-rockers than five teenage punk rockers.' It was a shame, though, because I really liked that band. Besides the music, they had an endearing way of introducing the band members to the audience. Jeremy Valentine, the lead singer, would announce, 'On drums we have . . . Johnny! On guitar we have . . . Johnny! On bass we have . . . Johnny! On rhythm guitar we have . . . Johnny! And my name is . . .' he'd begin, and the entire audience would shout, 'Johnny!'

The most serious and long-lasting signing to Step-Forward Records was The Fall, from Manchester. Mark E. Smith was the leader and mainstay of the band, and he had a definite point of view, both politically and socially. The Fall maintained a loyal if cult following for many years with music that has been called tense and abrasive, but it was Smith's caustic lyrics that usually caused the most attention. Critic Simon Reynolds of the *Melody Maker* would describe them as 'a kind of Northern English magic realism that mixed industrial grime with the unearthly and uncanny, voiced through a unique, one-note delivery somewhere between amphetamine-spiked rant and alcohol-addled yarn.'

The Fall turned out to be the most important Step-Forward signing, partly because they lasted longer with the label than any other band, but mainly because they had something enduring to say and were influential within and beyond the punk movement. Long after Step-Forward was no more and Mark P. had moved on to Alternative TV and dropped *Sniffin' Glue*, The Fall remained relevant.

Sham 69 would be the last signing to the Step-Forward Label. With Jimmy Percy as lead singer, they were more unruly than our other signings, so it was probably just as well that they were last. After they came into the Dryden Chambers offices to sign the contract, the Indian chap who ran a travel agency on the ground floor came up to ask, ever so politely, 'Please can you ask your guests to not piss in my window?' Yes, that was Sham 69. The next time they came to the office, I asked Jimmy to refrain from his repeating the same stunt, and he agreed. When they left, a few minutes later, the Indian chap was back in my office: 'Please, they are still pissing in my window!' The third time they came in was for a *Sniffin' Glue* interview, and it happened again. From then on, Sham 69 meetings were not held at Dryden Chambers.

Just as Step-Forward Records was making a name for itself and *Sniffin' Glue* was becoming super-successful, things changed. Mark P. decided to form a band of his own, calling it Alternative TV. In true punk fashion, he had written some songs and decided to sing them as front man onstage and no longer be a commentator from the sidelines. The crazy times were becoming even more crazy.

Kim began working with Mark, who turned out to have lots of musical ideas, and together they managed to pull together a reasonable group to play them. Kim virtually became the bandleader when Mark booked a gig at the 100 Club on Oxford Street and decided to record it as an album. Harry Murlowski became the manager/roadie/general do-whatever-it-takes guy. The resulting album was *The Image Has Cracked*, which Mark decided should be released on the Deptford Fun City label, because Deptford is where he lived. That told me that there probably would be no more signings to Step-Forward.

When the album was released, in May of '78, it was an instant success. I had to keep re-ordering copies from the pressing plant to keep up with demand. Sometimes there was a delay, as factories were not always available. Sometimes the records were warped and had to be sent back. Even so, it didn't take long to sell over twenty-five thousand copies. To do that with virtually no advertising in a market where a hundred thousand sales was a gold album was a really big deal.

Unfortunately, Mark had forgotten all about his fanzine, which I thought was a big mistake, but he had come to the view that his reasons for starting *Sniffin' Glue* were no longer relevant. The music business was waking up, with bands like The Clash and The Cortinas signed to CBS— and Mark was now an artist himself.

The success of the first Alternative TV album meant we were all excited when Mark announced he was ready to record a second. We assumed he could do no wrong, so when he told me he didn't want me interfering in the process, I agreed to stay out of the studio until the album was finished. Harry would check up on him from time to time, but I was never given any idea of what was happening. I figured, *How bad could it be?* If anyone had his finger on the pulse of the punk scene, it was Mark P., so it was easy to give him rope. Meanwhile, I made sure I had the pressing plant lined up to give me twenty-five thousand albums, and the printer the sleeves, so we were ready for the expected hit.

Finally, Mark gave me the tapes, and it was off to the mastering room of Trident Studios on Wardour Street, London, with the studio's top mastering engineer. The tape started with some noises—furniture being moved around, clearing of the throat, a few burps, paper shuffling, a fart or two—so we moved it forward. This happened a few times, then the engineer said the tape was over. I thought there must be a mistake, so I gave him the second tape, which I thought was the album's B-side. It was the same. Just a series of noises in no discernable order. These couldn't be the tapes of the album!

I called Mark to come down to the studio asap to sort it out. The pressing plants were waiting. To my shock, he said, 'Yes, that's the album.' There was virtually nothing on it but a collection of sounds with no reason for being there. I called Harry immediately and told him to go to the factory to cancel the pressing order. Harry could not believe that it was as bad as I said, and he insisted we keep the order in place, as we had tons of orders from the stores to fulfill. I managed to cut the order in half, but that was still a lot of vinyl. I was stuck, and too committed to totally back out.

The album title was *Vibing Up The Senile Man*. There was not much on it to vibe up anyone, certainly not a senile man! However, hoping that I must be missing something, I started to deliver the albums to all the stores and distributors that had ordered them. The next day I got irate phone calls from those same stores and distributors: 'Come and take this shit back.' You can't fool all the people all the time, but we fooled no one any of the time on this one. It was an unmitigated disaster. Today, it must stand as the very worst album ever recorded and released by anyone at any time. This was not a 'fuck you' album like Lou Reed had once made to get out of a record contract: it was supposed to be a serious album by a serious artist. But it was total shit—and I released it.

☙

It's hard to describe the craziness of those early 1977 punk days. As new groups popped up, most of them came to my office to get a record deal. For one group I hired Pathway studios, where the first Police single, 'Fallout,' was recorded. The fee was eight pounds an hour, paid in advance, so one could cut a single A- and B-side for around £80 in less than an afternoon. The day before the booking, I got a phone call from one of the musicians, 'Sorry, me band's broke up.' I was stuck with a studio paid for and no group to record.

That night, I went down to the Roxy club, figuring there was bound to be some punk group playing there, and found Menace. I had never heard of them but they sounded fine, and they looked punk enough, so, when they finished their performance, I went into the small dressing room to offer them a deal to record two of their songs. They were surprised, but, like I said, it was a crazy time, and they agreed without much discussion. They asked when, and I said, 'Tomorrow morning at ten o'clock.' That day in May 1977 we cut 'Insane Society' and 'Screwed Up,' put it on Illegal records, and I was out selling it to record stores two weeks later. It sold just under ten thousand copies.

For a while it seemed any single would sell as long as it sounded and looked right for the punk market. Menace worked, but a few singles later I recorded The Pigs and Gardez Darkx, pressed up several thousand copies, and got stuck with them. The stores started to listen to the records before they bought them, and they now wanted to know if the group had a following. The bubble had burst.

CHAPTER 10

JACK OF ALL TRADES

. . . .

My father used to tell me that there was a difference between being broke and being poor. It was an attitude. I was broke, but I was not poor, and I knew the business. I was soon being approached by many punk acts who wanted to work with me, even some from the USA. For some I became the booking agent, for others the record company, and for others the manager. In some cases I was all three.

In early 1977 I organized the Television/Blondie tour of the UK. Television came from my friend Jane Friedman in New York. Blondie from producer Richard Gottehrer, who I knew from Sire Records in New York. I contracted the one promoter who still gave me the time of day, John Curd at Straight Music, to promote the tour. John might have been rough around the edges, but he knew how to promote, and he would prove a valuable ally for the future. He was not one of the fair-weather friends, and I never forgot it. (John did The Police's *Ghost In The Machine Tour* in 1981-82, and he was always my first call when I needed a promoter.)

At this point, Blondie were unknown in the UK, but Debbie Harry was certainly photogenic, and the tour got a lot of press, so it worked for the band. However, their manager and I did not get on—he was a real jerk, self-opinionated and totally arrogant. It turned out the band had problems with him, too, and not long after that they fired him, resulting in a nasty legal battle. As for Television, they never followed up on the success of that tour, but I kept working with their manager, Jane Friedman, long after.

One of the most interesting of the New York acts I worked with was Cherry Vanilla. She had been a publicist for David Bowie and had apparently built up a credible reputation of her own, calling herself the First Lady of Punk. I had met her on a trip to the States in 1976 and encouraged her to come to England, where I thought her reputation could work in her favor. In February 1977, she came over with her guitarist boyfriend and musical director, Louis Lepore, to try her luck in the UK as a musical act. But she had no band. She did have two things that worked for me, however. First, she was a great self-promoter, afraid of nothing, willing to flaunt her sexuality, so I could easily book gigs for her, and the press would soon be on board. Second, her having no band provided the ideal way to put The Police in the picture.

If Stewart and Sting could be her backing band in return for The Police being given the opening slot on her tour, it would be a win-win for both Cherry and The Police—and indeed for me, as I was having trouble booking shows for The Police. Especially ones that would pay them. Cherry agreed, and Sting and Stewart joined Louis in the Cherry Vanilla band. (The Police's guitarist at that time, Henry Padovani, sat it out.) I booked a good tour of thirty concerts, and The Police, with Henry on guitar, opened them with a half-hour set each night.

On that same trip to New York back in 1976, I also met Wayne County. Wayne was a gay man whose boyfriend was his lead guitarist. In the small underground New York scene, he was known for his outrageous performances, the most notorious of which involved him sitting on a toilet onstage and defecating in it. No one knew for sure if he actually did it, but the rumor was that yes, he really did. He was also known for wearing a dress made of prophylactics onstage.

The main thing was, like Cherry Vanilla, Wayne was a fixture of the New York underground scene, and he knew how to get press, so I figured he would also do well in the new London scene. He was definitely anti-establishment, and he understood the value of shock. He moved to London shortly after Cherry, and I started booking shows for him as Wayne County & The Electric Chairs. To give added support, I soon had him in the studio recording an EP, *The Electric Chairs*, which we released on Illegal Records in September '77.

Wayne was not to everyone's taste. At the Reading Festival, which had an audience of more traditional rock'n'roll types, he was pelted with so much mud that he and the band left the stage soaked and covered in brown.

One day, my brother Stewart came back from a show in Holland at the Paradiso that The Police had done with Wayne, Cherry, and Johnny Thunders. 'You won't believe this,' he told me. 'It was fly-posted all over Amsterdam.' He then showed me a poster. It listed the four acts, then the bottom half of the poster said, 'Plus Miles Copeland in drag.' It was funny, but at least it was not all over London. What had happened was, I had to cancel and move the show several times, and on the third printing the poster maker must have gotten pissed off, so he decided to display his displeasure with that poster.

Meanwhile, things were not going well with Wayne County and his guitar player. The problem was that Wayne had decided that he was in fact a girl and was going to have a sex change. His boyfriend did not want a girlfriend, so this was an insoluble problem. If Wayne went through with his sex change, he would lose the boyfriend. A year or so later, in New York, I felt a tap on the shoulder and I heard, in a sweet voice, 'Hi Miles, it's me, Jayne.' Wayne County has been Jayne County ever since. Needless to say, the boyfriend moved on.

One might have imagined from all his outlandish stage antics back in the 70s that Wayne County was some sort of tough, wild guy. In fact, Wayne was always a sweetheart; a real 'wouldn't hurt a fly' type of person. I dealt with some real wackos during this period, but I would have to say Wayne was not one of them.

John Cale was another interesting artist I met in New York. He had gained status from his membership of The Velvet Underground, which was a band that the punks looked up to. Like the punks, The Velvet Underground had developed anti-establishment credentials, so John had become a hip producer for this new era of punk bands. He was also fascinated by the CIA and all things skullduggery, so he took every opportunity to push me into conversations about the inner workings of government behind the scenes, and of course conspiracy theories. He imagined I knew all sorts of secret stuff from my father's connections with the CIA—a view I did not always discourage. Needless to say, when I later agreed to distribute a label for John Cale and Jane Friedman, it was called Spy Records.

In the UK, I had John produce the first Squeeze single, 'Packet Of Three,' for Deptford Fun City, and soon after that came his own single, 'Animal Justice,' for Illegal Records. The front cover photo showed John in a blindfold, tied to a pole, about to be shot. Funny thing: it was pretty much the same as the cover of The Police's single 'Can't Stand Losing You,' released a year later—with Stewart on a melting block of ice, a rope around his neck—which the BBC banned. I guess about-to-die imagery was good branding at that time. Sweetness and light were definitely not part of the punk scene.

*

Throughout 1977, when I was more of an agent than manager in London, I used to get calls every day from Billy Idol or his bass player in Generation X, along with countless other punk bands, asking me to get them gigs. Generation X looked upon themselves as the most important punk band after the Sex Pistols and The Clash, so booking shows for them naturally got other bands to follow them to my door.

The good thing about Generation X was that they actually *wanted* to do gigs. As I had learned from Malcolm McLaren, the Sex Pistols were a non-starter, and, try as I might, I could not get the manager of The Clash to commit to anything. Bernie Rhodes was the manager in question, and the rumor was that his main focus was getting the band to read Mao's *Little Red Book*. Unlike Malcolm, he didn't seem to care much about media attention—he was more about political revolution and attacking the status quo. I didn't see any effort to get gigs for The Clash. To be frank, what little I knew of Bernie I did not like, and I came to think The Clash were a lot smarter and savvier than he was. In fact, I didn't even consider him to be a real manager. The vibe I got from both him and Malcolm was that the artist was working for the manger, rather than the other way around.

While all this was happening, I was still making the rounds, trying to get a major label interested in Squeeze. I had released 'Packet Of Three' in

April of '77, but they deserved and indeed needed a real recording studio to make an album, and I didn't have the money. I needed to sign them to an established label that had some money.

Most labels were shy of anything that looked punk, but I figured A&M might be different, since they'd had the balls to sign the Sex Pistols in March, even though it did not take much to make them drop the band a week later. I figured A&M wanted in but didn't want to deal with Malcolm McLaren types any more than they wanted to deal with bands who would be outrageous for the sake of it.

A&M knew me from a management relationship I had with one of their artists, Joan Armatrading, and it was pretty evident just looking at me that, though I was into the punk scene, I was not out to shock—I was out to do business. And Squeeze could fit the bill of looking and sounding new, but they were not crazy for the sake of it, and they were making music that the A&M folks could understand. I must have figured right because, in August, A&M signed Squeeze—the first punk-era band the company signed and kept for more than a week.

Meanwhile, I had managed to build a circuit of clubs that would book the punk bands, but often I would get a call on the day of the gig from a band saying they could not find a van and had to cancel. Most of the bands were hopelessly unorganized. Then, one by one, bands like Generation X and others got managers who promised them all sorts of things, and I got the inevitable call: 'Sorry, but we have to cancel all the gigs you booked— we are going in a new direction,' or some other lame excuse. This usually meant the band disappeared, but as they were so thirsty for action, they were primed to fall prey to anyone selling good news about their future. Even my brother Stewart and The Police!

One day, Stewart came to see me at Marlborough Place with some great news. He had just signed to a great manager who could do all sorts of things for The Police: an Iranian guy with lots of money who had a recording studio and was going to book a major tour for the band and break them wide open, apparently. All this was going to happen when Stewart and Sting returned from Germany after a month working as backing musicians for a German act called Eberhard Schoener. There was not much I could say: I still had no money, and I could not promise anything to compete with this great offer. I wished him luck, but I also had the feeling of unfair rejection.

People like to say that I paid little attention to The Police in the early days, but in actual fact I booked more gigs for them than for all of the other bands I was working with put together, right up to the Police tour of the USA. In all, I booked seventy-six shows for The Police during this period, including the thirty with Cherry Vanilla, seven with Wayne County, and three with Spirit. Squeeze came in second with thirty-six UK shows and a week in Holland (not including all the shows Ian booked for them in the USA).

The truth is, Stewart was impatient. He wanted The Police to be big *yesterday*. I could have booked twice as many gigs and he would still have looked for greener pastures. After all, he was a muso.

☙

In the month that followed, Kim Turner came across a studio just outside London in Leatherhead called Surrey Sound, run by a doctor who had built a recording studio behind his office and was hoping to get into the business as a recording engineer. Doctor by day, would-be recording engineer by night, Nigel Gray offered one month of recording for £1,500, all in. That was a price close to affordable to me, so we checked it out.

For now, it seemed, Stewart and The Police were out of the frame . . . until a month later, when Stewart returned to London and came knocking at the door of Marlborough Place, freaked out and beside himself with anxiety. 'That fucking manager was full of shit, he did nothing, not one show booked, no tour—what the hell am I going to tell Sting? This is the end. He's going to go back to Newcastle.'

I have to admit that while on one hand I was sorry for Stewart, I also felt a sense of vindication—he might finally have to admit that the work I did was not so bad after all. But I doubt Stewart thought about that. His focus was keeping Sting. So, I said, 'OK, how about this: why don't we record a Police album? I can give you one month to do it at a studio in Leatherhead, and you can start as soon as you are ready.'

Stewart's eyes lit up. 'Great, I can give Sting the bad news and then the good news.' He was convinced that Sting would be excited about finally doing an album, and that would be enough to counter the bad news. He was right. The Police started recording their first album at Surrey Sound, and I became their official manager from that point on.

This story has been recounted in a number of books, mostly by people who got it wrong. The truth is, it was my idea to record the album to help my brother out. How bad could it be? I would release it on Illegal Records, and at the price it would cost me I should be able to earn the money back through the distribution system I had built up. Of course, I didn't have the money either, but it wasn't that big a number, and I figured I could find it somehow.

I made the deal with Nigel Gray, and The Police started recording their first album. The sessions went OK until towards the end, when I had a chance to hear all the songs. The Police were selling themselves as a punk band, so that is what I expected in the studio. Something was missing for me, and I said so, to the point of depressing the group. Then I asked if there was anything else to listen to, and Nigel said, 'Yes, one more.' But the band quickly added, 'Don't play it—he will hate it. It's a ballad.'

I insisted I hear it—after all, I was there, I had made the hour-or-so drive to Leatherhead, and, besides, I was paying for it. Eventually, Nigel put it on, probably to stop the back and forth between me and the band, and out came 'Roxanne.' While I was looking at the downcast faces of Sting, Stewart, and Andy as they listened to that song, I was internally having a eureka moment.

At the end, I looked at them and said, 'Gentlemen you have created a classic—it's bigger than I can do on my own, so I am going to take it to A&M Records and get you a real deal to release the album.' To a man they looked at me, incredulous: 'You like that?' Needless to say, Sting had a few more songs like that lurking in the back of his mind, like 'Can't Stand Losing You.'

It was the turning point in all of our lives. 'Roxanne' changed the game. What the band had not realized was that I wasn't looking for something specific, just something that worked. That didn't mean I wouldn't be open to a left-field inspiration that was unexpected and special. 'Roxanne' was just that. This was perhaps the perfect example of my father's perceptive description of me as having 'flexibility.'

'Roxanne' was not a punk song any more than The Police were a punk band. The Police could have the energy of punk and the anti-establishment ethic of punk but, musically, Andy, Stewart, and Sting would have a hard time actually *being* punk. Andy had no respect for any punk band musically, and Sting simply hated punk. It was only Stewart that wanted The Police to be punk, but it was more about being of the future, lean and mean, in control of their own destiny, breaking the rules that Stewart got off on, not the lousy musicianship. In short, 'Roxanne' was a lot more honest to what The Police had become than 'Fallout' had been.

Getting a deal with A&M Records would be no small feat, however. A highly regarded label signing an act with nothing on paper to recommend it would seem to be a long shot, if not simply way out of reach. No fanbase. No tour in the works. No great press. Actually, no press at all, save a few lines in *Melody Maker* by the journalist Caroline Coon (a super Clash fan who later claimed to be a Police fan) that said, 'The Police, yawn.' The only thing that The Police had going for them in such a meeting was the music itself.

I knew from experience that every record executive who signed acts listened with two thoughts working at the same time: *What is this going to cost me, and do I like the music?* There would always be the inevitable cautionary tales popping into their thoughts, too: *Is there a single, can this be a hit, what will my boss say, what if it's a failure, will this cost me my job, do I want to take the risk?*

I had a growing relationship with A&M since Squeeze signed there, so they knew I was serious and a straight shooter. Still, getting a record deal was rarely easy, no matter how good the music was. Knowing this, I started the conversation by telling them, 'I have a great record for you, and you can have it for FREE. No advance, no risk on your part, it's yours—just pay me your highest royalty when it sells.'

That might sound crazy but, knowing there was nothing to suggest the band was worth signing *except* the music, I knew it was the only positive to rely on. They only had to hear the music and never need let risk or financial questions interfere with their thought process. I wager that it was the first time they had ever based a decision on whether or not to sign an act *solely* on the music. In short, it was an easy yes—a nothing-to-lose proposition. I got the deal, and The Police were to be released on one of the world's most prestigious record labels. Now they really had a chance to be in the big game.

This proved to be a very valuable lesson for the future. If you make it easy for the answer to be 'yes,' you are likely to get yes for an answer. If you make 'no' easy, you are likely to get no. I am sure that if I had asked for an advance, The Police would never have gotten the deal with A&M.

I soon came to realize that there was one other benefit to our A&M deal. Not asking for an advance and virtually eliminating risk for the company had the effect of making them willing to go along with any crazy idea we came up with, from a US tour with no help from the American company, to the album sleeve and the album title. The attitude was, *What the hell; if that's what they want to do, no problem.* It was a nice freedom to have.

With the first album title and the screen-printed album sleeve portrait of the band, there was no issue. Driving home from A&M in a taxi, I was thinking we should combine the image of commandos with outlaws, so the name *Outlandos* came to mind. That sounded too harsh, so I thought of adding *Love*, but that sounded too wimpy, so I thought it would be better in French. I ended up with *Outlandos D'Amour*: outlaw commandos of love. It had a nice ring to it, and when the band approved, that became the title.

For the second album, the band again looked to me to come up with a title. I thought of combining 'reggae' with 'blond' and came up with *Regatta De Blanc*. By the time of the third album, the band were less willing to go along with my title ideas. I was thinking of three blond guys conquering the world: *Tri Mondo Blond Domina*. We went around in circles, eventually compromising on *Zenyatta Mondatta*. And then, for the next album, Sting came up with the title.

℘

Meanwhile, while I was working to sort out the UK, my brother Ian was doing the same in America. In April of 1977, Ian had left London and moved to Macon, Georgia, to take up his new job at the Paragon Agency as Special Assistant to the President for Foreign Acts and the West

Coast. As usual, Ian fit right in almost immediately. He even married the niece of Phil Walden, owner of the agency. The Climax Blues Band tour had gone well, but that was up the traditional street of the agency, and when Climax fired me, they fired Paragon, too. That left Ian with some embarrassment.

Without Climax, the only acts I could deliver were all new wave or, worse, punk. Between the two of us, Ian and I realized that if I was to be any help delivering acts to Paragon, he had to open doors to the kind of acts I now represented. A band had to be found that could unlock those doors.

The obvious choice was Squeeze. They had a US record company prepared to give tour support, and they were not too punk-like to immediately offend the American record establishment. Even so, Ian made it clear that it would not be easy getting everyone at the agency excited about the punk scene, even if it could be called 'new wave.' Even in faraway Macon, the vibe was not good.

Ian was game to take on the challenge, but on one condition: he needed the band to perform in Macon, Georgia, so that the Paragon people could see for themselves that this 'punk' thing did not mean angry bands that could not play. I agreed, even after he told me the only venue he could find in the town was a discotheque. It was a case of 'beggars can't be choosy.'

Squeeze's first album was released in America in March of '78, under the name 'UK Squeeze,' there already being another band called Squeeze in the States. It had some good pop songs on it, like 'Bang Bang' and 'Take Me I'm Yours.' It was not the angry sound of punk, but at the same time it was a long way from the long-haired rock acts that were promoted by Paragon's owner, Capricorn Records, and the bulk of the major labels of the time.

Meanwhile, both of us looked at a Squeeze tour as a way to find support for the future: Ian with clubs, venues, and promoters who would book future tours, and me with radio, press, and record stores who might get involved to promote the releases I hoped to work. I had hired an assistant, John Lay, to help me with Squeeze in England, and we both went with the band to America. I went as manager, driver, tour manager, and new-wave scene investigator—and I also ended up helping John as a roadie.

The fun part of taking Squeeze to America was to once again experience the country through the eyes of people seeing it for the first time. It was almost like that first Wishbone Ash tour of 1971. All of Squeeze except the drummer, Gilson Lavis, were still in their teens, so it was a thrilling time for them, but even for me, who had by now seen it all, it was still refreshing. We all traveled in a rented van and truck, with John Lay and me taking turns driving them. It was the first time I had used a CB radio, and I had great fun talking to the truckers and others while we were driving. My handle was 'Georgia Hotdog.'

There was a kind of camaraderie on the road, especially with the truckers. One night, late, as we were driving towards Macon, I got stopped for speeding by a highway patrol car. I had been talking on our CB radio to a trucker on the way, and he must have been behind me, and I will always remember him saying, as he passed by, 'That you, Hotdog?' Yep, it was me. I also remember going through one town and getting stopped by another police car and made to follow it to the local courthouse. The town was apparently a notorious speed trap, and it made all its money from unsuspecting drivers like me. The speed limit was twenty-five miles an hour, with signs conveniently hidden by bushes. I had no option but to pay the fine or stay in town several days to await trial.

For me, the tour was as much a fact-finding mission as it was a string of concerts for Squeeze. That mission was often as simple as seeing a young kid in punkish-looking clothes and asking where he bought his records, what radio stations he listened to, what clubs he went to. Whenever I could, I would go to the local radio station to try to get the DJs to play the Squeeze record. I would pry information out of club owners, bartenders, or indeed anyone in the audience that looked like they might be helpful. My brother Ian was doing the same but on the phone at the Paragon Agency, trying to find any club or venue that would book bands that were remotely associated with the new wave or punk.

It was not an easy tour. I was back to cheap hotels and roughing it in a van, and in many ways it was even worse than that first Wishbone Ash tour. Unlike Wishbone, Squeeze were not looking to support big acts: in the music scene we were claiming to be part of, there were none. Every Squeeze date was a headlining date, which meant a lot of shithole clubs and small audiences. Chris Difford in his book tells of one show where the audience consisted of a man and a dog, and then the dog left. And it sometimes meant shithole hotels as well.

That first tour consisted of forty shows in fifty-seven days from May 23 to July 19, 1978, making it the first real tour of British new wave in the USA, paving the way for The Police and so many other bands to follow. It enabled both Ian and me to make valuable contacts, to open people's eyes and change minds, so in many ways it was one of the most important tours ever for a British band in the USA. Without that tour, Ian would have had a much harder time delivering a Police tour three months later. It showed the world that the doors existed for this new generation of music, and there were bands that could open them. A lot of bands owe Squeeze a debt they don't even know about.

CHAPTER 11

KLARK KENT AND
MELVIN MILKTOAST

· · · · · · · ·

With The Police now signed to A&M Records ahead of the release of their first single, 'Roxanne,' in April of 1978, there was the beginnings of interest in the band—a tiny bit of smoke but not yet any fire. 'Roxanne' was in fact banned by the BBC, as it was 'about a prostitute.' The band's second single was 'Can't Stand Losing You,' and even that was banned because the sleeve showed a photo of Stewart hanging himself, and the BBC 'didn't want to encourage suicide.' It seemed the forces were lined up to prevent The Police from getting on the radio.

The first actual chart action for the band was a left-field idea of Stewart's called Klark Kent, which came between the first two Police single releases. Klark Kent became one of the funniest and strangest parts of the Police story. Stewart had written a song called 'Don't Care' for the band's first album, but Sting couldn't relate to it, so Stewart recorded it himself, with Nigel Gray producing, at Surrey Sound. It was Stewart completely solo, singing and playing all the parts.

At this early point in The Police, the last thing any of us wanted was for it to appear that the band members were already going solo, so Stewart dreamed up the idea of taking on an alter ego, 'Clark Kent,' and disguising himself with a mask as part of the image. We invented a label called Kryptone Records and released the single via my independent distribution setup in early June 1978. At that time, colored vinyl singles were popular, so we decided that as an added bonus, to help the record sell, it would be manufactured in green vinyl, à la kryptonite.

As 'Don't Care' started getting radio play and seemed like it might actually be a hit, I went to A&M to see if they would go for it. They jumped on it, re-releasing it in mid-July. Their only stipulation was that we change the name from 'Clark' to 'Klark' to avoid problems with DC Comics.

The mask idea was straight out of the sense of humor we Copeland siblings had developed, which probably came from our father. The concept was that to really be free, you had to be free from all the inhibitions you would have if anyone knew who you were. Therefore, only by disguising oneself with a mask could you truly be free to express yourself. It was a concept that actually made some sense—at least to us . . .

To promote the single, we decided to do a stunt for the press at London's famed Speaker's Corner at Marble Arch, at the corner of Hyde Park. Kim Turner and I and a few others donned masks and watched Stewart mount his soapbox and wax eloquently about this philosophy. Anyone getting up on Speaker's Corner tended to draw a crowd, especially the more outrageous ones, and Stewart in his mask definitely qualified. There were the normal hecklers we had hoped for, and I recorded it all on my portable tape recorder. Mostly what I recorded, however, was the sound of myself, fighting off laughter.

To everyone's surprise, 'Don't Care' went to #48 in the UK singles chart, and 'Klark Kent' was invited to perform on *Top Of The Pops* on August 31. Entering the singles charts and being invited to perform on the country's biggest music TV show was a pretty big deal for all of us, especially Stewart. He quickly assembled a group to perform that included Police-mates Sting and Andy Summers, plus Kim Turner, Florian Pilkington-Miksa from his Curved Air days on drums, and Stewart on vocals.

To keep our identities secret, we all showed up at *Top Of The Pops* wearing masks, me included. At the first run-through, the producer—a real arrogant prick—came to me saying Klark Kent could not wear the mask as it would scare the young viewers, and insisted he take it off. I protested, and the producer said, 'I want to speak to Miles Copeland!'

I answered, 'Mr. Copeland is not available, and I was given authority to act on his behalf.'

'What's your name?'

'Melvin Milktoast,' I answered. This really pissed him off, as I was obviously fucking with him. I quickly had to say, 'Millhoss, Melvin Millhoss.'

'Well, Millhoss, that mask has to come off.'

Then an A&M rep showed up and tried to sort out the situation, all the while looking at me, thinking, *What the hell is going on here?* We all went to the dressing room, and Stewart decided he could paint his face green and still get away with it. The others could keep their masks on, as did I. That's how it was performed.

If I could go back to do it all over again, I would have pulled a Malcolm McLaren, refused to take off the mask, and walked out of the show. That would have gotten a lot more press than the TV appearance got us, and it would have been a better story in the long run. But, then again, *Top Of The Pops* was a big deal, and I don't know if Stewart would have gone along with it. In any case, it was the first appearance by The Police on British TV.

Nothing happened for Klark Kent in the USA until two years later, when I had my own record company, IRS Records, to release the single. The liner notes followed the Klark Kent storyline, with the usual irreverent IRS approach to releasing records. It was pressed as a ten-inch vinyl album packaged in a twelve-inch sleeve bearing a sticker that stated, 'You have just purchased an IRS product. Keep in mind, however, that this is no ordinary record. It has been specially sealed under clinical laboratory conditions guarded by twelve armed security officers. Upon contact with light, this eight-song album will shrink to ten inches and turn green. Exercise extreme caution.'

Klark Kent put out several more singles, and we later used the instrumental track 'Theme From Kinetic Ritual' to open our MTV show, *IRS Records Presents The Cutting Edge*. A couple of other songs found their way onto charity albums as well. Needless to say, the Klark Kent story was too much for my father to resist. In his inimitable style, he wrote the Klark Kent biography:

> 'Klark Kent' first came into my life as he was sitting next to me on the Concorde flight from Washington, DC, to London. Speaking in what he claimed to be his native Sanskrit, he explained that he had

been in Washington testifying before a congressional committee on church politics. His expertise in this subject had been attained while studying in a Moslem seminary in India. He underlined his religiosity (he claimed to be a 'Sufi,' a kind of Islamic mystic that is rarely seen on the Indian subcontinent) by saying his noonday prayers in the aisle of the jet air-plane, jostling the stewardesses as they were trying to serve lunch, and annoying the passengers with his shouts of, 'Which way is Mecca? Which way is Mecca? Which way is Mecca?' while shifting his body to accommodate to the turns in the direction of the aircraft. Later, he confessed, in substandard broken English, that he was 'a mere computer programmer,' currently out of work but living on the sum of one million four hundred thousand dollars which he had won from IBM in a successful suit against the company for stealing his 'invention.' He was most secretive about the invention ('Do you want me to sue you?' he asked coyly when I questioned him about it), but he adumbrated the notion that it had to do with capturing radio signals from distant galaxies, systematizing them through computer analysis, and reducing them to simple melodies which he played on the various instruments on which he is proficient.

The biography went on from there with even more outlandish panache.

Klark Kent was a fun aside, but for now, the essential problem of resistance to The Police in the UK persisted. Something bolder had to happen, so I thought, why not do what I did for Renaissance and The Climax Blues Band and go for action in the USA?

ఆ

Three months after the first Squeeze shows in the USA ended, I thought booking a US tour for The Police would be relatively easy, as they were a trio, so the fee could be half of what Squeeze's had been. Stewart's concept of lean and mean minimalism meant that the band could virtually break even at $300 a night, and it did not hurt that Laker Airways was offering £90 tickets from London to New York. With only three in the band and Kim Turner as soundman/roadie—plus the punk ethic of minimal equipment and production—I thought it should be cheap.

When I called Ian to organize the tour, however, he made it clear that it wasn't going to be easy. With no domestic record release and no record company support, he was unlikely to get much help from anyone else at Paragon. He would have to book it almost entirely on his own.

'I know,' I said, 'but can you do it?'

Stewart was *his* brother, too. Plus, Ian had written lyrics for one of The Police's songs, 'Nothing Achieving,' and he was already a believer. So, he was game to try.

With Ian's gift of the gab and what he'd learned from the Squeeze tour, he managed to book twenty-three shows in twenty-five days. I can't say they were all classy clubs: in reality, some were dives, and some rarely booked live bands, but it was a US tour. Who was to know, back in England, that The Police played in some serious shitholes? In fact, it should have been impossible, as no unknown British band had ever toured the USA before without a record release or the financial support of a label. On top of that, with Ian managing to squeeze an average fee of $500 per show out of the promoters, the tour actually made a profit!

This was another really important lesson: the more affordable something is, the more likely there will be takers. If The Police had not been such a small outfit with minimal requirements, Ian would not have been able to book the tour, and I would not have been able to afford to get them to the States. Affordability got us into the game.

Even so, even after the relative success of the Squeeze tour a few months earlier, arriving in New York with The Police in October 1978, I was surprised at the complete lack of interest from the A&M Records New York office. I expected negative reactions, but not from the record company that I had just been working with a few months before.

It was October 19 when I went to the office to give them tickets to the Police show at CBGB's the next day—*free* tickets. I was ushered in to see the office manager and told not so politely that I had no business being there, and I should take my group and 'go home.' Apparently, it was unheard of that a manager would offer free tickets and not ask for tour support. I still remember Gail Davis's parting words as I left her office: 'We are *not* giving you any money. Go home.' She even followed me to the door to make sure I left the premises.

The CBGB club had started as a country, bluegrass, and blues venue (hence the name), but by 1977 it had become the iconic home of New York's underground music scene. It was small and in a seedy part of the Bowery, but for the new scene it was *the* hip place. That there were rats scurrying around the back door where bands loaded in did not matter. The Ramones had played there, The Dead Boys, Richard Hell, Patti Smith; even The Damned from the UK. And, of course, Squeeze on their first tour. If you were in the punk scene, you played CBGB's.

The Police flew in on the evening of the 20th: they were running late and caught a checker cab straight to the club. Jetlag aside, this was the band's first gig in the USA, and pretty soon the adrenalin kicked in. I was not surprised that no one from A&M came, except the unpaid college intern; there was an air of anticipation in the venue, but still few there knew anything about the band. With Sting in his English army tracksuit and adrenalin pumping through all three of them, The Police played a blistering set, and for the encore they played the same songs again as they didn't have any more songs. The anticipation in the audience quickly turned to excitement, and Jane Friedman, who was in the audience with me, said, 'This is going to be huge.'

I traveled with the group to the Rat Club in Boston—a venue whose name suited it—and then back to New York before meeting up with the band again in Philadelphia and DC. They did well in the big cities; in the smaller cities, where most of the venues were dives, it was hit and miss. After all, The Police were an unknown band.

There was one show in northern New York State that had all of four people in the audience. Many a band would have opted to cancel, but The Police decided to give them the best show they had ever seen. Those four people had actually bought tickets, and one had to respect that. One of the four turned out to be Oedipus, the young, up-and-coming DJ at MIT's college radio station in Boston. He was so impressed with the band—he loved the song 'Roxanne,' which the band had given him, and went back to play it incessantly on his radio show. That goes to show, you never know who might be watching, so no matter how big or small an audience, it pays to do your best *all* the time.

Oedipus was a critical catalyst in the story of The Police. This episode points to a truth in marketing: if you can get one super-fan, you can get two, then four, and so on. From acorns large oak trees grow. His airplay led to the single being added by other stations, and eventually to it becoming the #1 import in the USA in January 1979 and showing up on *Billboard* radio charts. Those radio charts are what all the mainstream record executives scoured every week. And soon they'd all be paying attention.

છ

Upon our return to the UK, The Police performed at a small club behind a pub in West London called the Nashville Rooms, and it became obvious that something had happened while they were away. Interest in the band must have grown in our absence, and we could see that the Nashville Rooms crowd was largely there to see The Police. They got more than they expected. Playing that run of shows—often two shows a night—in the USA had turned The Police into a tight performing machine, and they had a new air of confidence onstage. The outcast vibe of a few months earlier had vanished.

I don't know if it was the US tour alone that made the Brits wake up to The Police, but it was apparent that 'Roxanne'—though it was never hit on the UK charts—had percolated while we were away into becoming an underground hit. The second single, 'Can't Stand Losing You,' had also scratched the surface. The band's music, with its sprinkling of reggae, was getting noticed by musicians in other bands, some of whom were at the Nashville Rooms gig. Up to that point, reggae had been a relatively fringe interest, but the punks brought it into the mainstream, playing the records at shows, partly as a way to not play old-fart music. The reggae ethic actually fit well with the punks. It was relatively underground, cheaply recorded, often with political or social messages in the lyrics, and not considered mainstream. In any case, The Police were now on the UK music map *because* of the music. This was all the more interesting given that the country's biggest broadcaster had banned both of their singles.

Not long after the Nashville Rooms gig, we scored the opening slot on the Alberto Y Lost Trios Paranoias tour of the UK. They were an interesting band with a large element of comedy in their show, and they managed to appeal to a broad spectrum, including even some of the punks. The main thing was that they were *not* associated with the progressive rockers—or, as the punks preferred to call them, the old farts. The Albertos had booked The Police to help sell tickets, but they didn't expect to be completely overshadowed by their opening act, which is what happened. I have to hand it to them—they kept their humor about it, and they even began to mimic The Police in their set as part of their act. It was a good tour; The Police could now feel some wind in their sails, and they ended the year on a high.

CHAPTER 12

THEN EVERYTHING CHANGED

· · · · · · · ·

On Monday, January 15, 1979, I got a phone call from Jerry Moss, the M of A&M Records. He had just seen the January 13 issue of *Billboard* magazine, which showed 'Roxanne' by The Police was a top 'add-on' on East Coast radio. From the *Billboard* chart, he saw that it was an import on A&M Records, and he asked, 'Does that mean it is A&M in the US, too?'

I said, 'Yes, it does.'

'Well, we'd better do something about it,' he said.

'Yes, you'd better.'

He agreed to rush-release the record and get A&M behind it. 'And the sooner you can get the band back here, the better.'

My next phone call was to Ian at Paragon. It looked like that first Police tour, as fly-by-the-seat-of-our-pants as it was, had paid off. I then made a quick trip to Los Angeles, to meet the A&M people and set up the release of the *Outlandos D'Amour* album.

The first issue was the album sleeve. The art department insisted the sleeve be black, with just the name of the band and the title on it. They were afraid of the image of the three band members with short blond hair that was on the sleeve in the UK. They were actually frightened by the back sleeve, with photos that screamed 'punk' to them. I insisted on the front sleeve but finally relented on the back sleeve, which ended up with just printed information. Meanwhile, Ian got on with booking a new tour, which began on March 1, 1979, with three nights at the Whisky A Go-Go in Los Angeles and ended April 9 at the Walnut Theatre in Philadelphia. With that, The Police were launched on what was to become a dizzying ride to the top of the music business.

There was one big problem, however. A&M Records did not have any real idea what they were dealing with. They had not yet fully bought into this new-wave thing; they had their way of doing things and we had our way. To Ian and me, it was simple; if the object was to enter the house and the front door was locked, the obvious thing would be to find an open window—a side or back door. On January 5, *Billboard* magazine had an article implying that 'punk was dead,' in effect saying the front door was locked. Ian and I simply looked for another entrance, which to some people might have made it look like we were rebels.

But we were not rebels. More than anything, fueled by the energy of the small but growing audiences we could see on the street, it was simple impatience. I was happy to take advantage of record-company support when it happened, but, when it didn't, one resorted to operating independently. Whereas I saw support on the street, the record company was looking at the charts. They did not see what I was seeing. Apparently, this did not sit well with the powers that be.

It was not long before I so upset the radio promotion department that I got an irate phone call from the president of A&M, Gil Friesen, telling me I was about to ruin my band and turn off the company. He insisted I fly immediately to Los Angeles so he could 'educate me' on how to properly work a record company. His secretary set up a ticket, and I duly reported to his office on the A&M lot in Hollywood.

Gil was a smart guy, and he sincerely believed I was doing harm to The Police by not following the company norms. After twenty minutes of telling me off for going around the promotion men, and especially for calling radio stations myself, his main point was that by doing so I was embarrassing the promotion men and turning them off the band. *They* were supposed to be the ones who called radio and set up the press, not the manager of the band. In short, I was making them look bad.

I listened respectfully, then I gave my response. We believed in what we were doing, and, out of respect, we did not expect his promo men to do all the work for us. If they didn't have time for us, I understood. We were perfectly happy to push the ball along ourselves, until such time as it was worth their while to help us. But we were not content to sit by and do nothing. Most of all, if we weren't prepared to be fighting in the trenches, how could we ask anyone else to be there with us?

I then recounted an incident when two A&M radio men showed up at a gig and told me enthusiastically how much they had enjoyed seeing the group. The Police had not played yet, so, a bit perplexed, I asked if they were at the show the night before.

'No—we just saw them, they were great!'

They had not realized they had just seen the opening act. Four guys, black hair, all American. I asked them if they had ever seen the cover of The Police's album: three guys, blond hair, English? From the deer-caught-in-headlights look, it was obvious these guys had no idea who The Police were or what they looked like, and they had probably never heard the music either. That was a pretty graphic illustration of what we were up against.

With that, Gil said 'stop,' got on the phone, and asked every department head in the company to report to his office immediately. In a few minutes, the room filled up, and Gil turned to me and said, 'OK, Miles, now tell them what you just told me.'

A bit surprised, I did my best to recount what I had told Gil. It was the turning point for us in the label. The story of the two hapless radio guys mistaking the support act for The Police could not have made the case better for me. I owe those guys.

Though the mainstream record companies didn't know it yet, 1979 was to become a major transition period for the music industry in the world's biggest market. At the beginning of the year, there was little understanding that there was a new generation with a desire for their own music and for doing things their own way. The objection of the A&M art department in Los Angeles to the *Outlandos* album sleeve was a good example of the prevailing attitudes. Horrors—a band with short dyed blond hair looking like punks might shock people out of their comfort zone! Had they forgotten about The Beatles with long hair? The Stones wanting to get busted for drugs? Alice Cooper biting the heads off of chickens? Elvis Presley gyrating onstage? When did rock music become so tame and afraid?

Those three blond, short-haired guys sold 340,000 albums in the USA with a hit single that got to #12 in the charts. They were on their way. By the end of that year, there was no question a change was happening—not just for The Police, but for the industry as a whole.

From my perspective, the year 1979 could be neatly divided into two periods and two continents. At the beginning of the year in America, it was all about The Police, and in England it was all about Squeeze. The call from Jerry Moss on January 15 set in motion the beginnings of The Police's march to success in America. In the UK, Squeeze's second album, *Cool For Cats*, released that same month, delivered four hit singles, two of which reached #2 in the UK charts and made them my most successful management client. Meanwhile, my brother Ian was well set up at his job as an agent at Paragon in Macon, Georgia, and things were looking good for all of us.

By the end of the year, Paragon would be no more, and The Police would be well on their way to becoming a supergroup, overtaking Squeeze as my most successful management client. The last half of the year saw the formation of my IRS Records and Ian's FBI concert-booking agency. In the UK, the business had outgrown the Dryden Chamber offices, and we now had our own premises in Ladbrook Grove, north-west London. It was a year of upheaval, big risks, big changes, mistakes and successes. For me, it cast the die for the next decade and beyond.

It must have been a confusing time for Squeeze. By the time their 'Cool For Cats' single reached #2 in the UK charts, they were off to the USA as the support act for their labelmates The Tubes. A&M Records had pressured Ian to have Squeeze support The Tubes in Britain and North America. The pitch was that, as a headliner, Squeeze would play to a few hundred people each show, whereas with The Tubes the numbers would be in the thousands. A&M saw it as a great opportunity for the band. Of course, none of us knew then that a few months later, Squeeze would be happening big on the UK charts. On the positive side, The Tubes were not associated with the 'old fart' world, and their anthem 'White Punks On Dope' had the right kind of anti-establishment feel about it. On paper, it made sense. On the negative side, The Tubes were downright outrageous, and they would inevitably garner most if not all of the press attention. To compete, a support group would need a killer show and a killer instinct, but that was not Squeeze.

Ian and I had our reservations at the outset, believing that the type of bands we were working with were better off headlining. The problem was that A&M was very insistent, and it was a bit early in the game to bite off the hand that feeds. So, begrudgingly, we agreed to look on the bright side. It was not long, though, before we both came to the conclusion that we had made a mistake. That tour will not go down as one of my smarter management decisions.

Back in Europe in May, Squeeze did their first major tour, taking in Scandinavia, Germany, and Holland. Meanwhile, the *Cool For Cats* album continued to do well, spawning the biggest UK hit singles of the band's career. Perhaps the exposure of the Tubes dates in the UK had helped? I can't say. For the US market, I don't think it did much. By July, it was back to touring the States as a headliner, and back to the smaller venues. It was not until the end of the year that Squeeze would return to performing as a headliner in Britain in the large venues that they deserved. Of course, by that time, The Police had exploded on the scene.

Nineteen seventy-nine must also have been confusing for The Police. At first, breaking reasonably big in the USA at the beginning of the year was completely overshadowed by the complete bedlam that was occurring in the UK and much of the rest of the world by the end of the year. The *Outlandos* album got to #25 in the US album charts, but the second album, *Regatta De Blanc*, did less well. This was after the band did three tours of North America, totaling ninety-five shows. In the UK, where they had done only twenty-two shows, *Regatta De Blanc* entered the charts at #1, making The Police without question the biggest band in the country. That couldn't have been clearer on the night of December 18, when they performed two shows in London on the same night: the first show at Hammersmith Odeon and the second one across the street at the Hammersmith Palais.

The Hammersmith gambit was one of those stunts that I dreamed up that the band were happy to go along with. The Hammersmith Odeon was the proper upmarket venue, with nice seating for a happening band, but the Hammersmith Palais, with no seating, was more 'street' and funky, in keeping with the band's image. To further highlight that image, I rented an army half-track tank as a cool idea to drive them across the street between the two venues. Little did I know that it would also prove to be the *only* way we could have gotten across. After the first show, as we climbed into the half-track and entered the intersection, we saw it was totally blocked with thousands of fans—and the real police desperately trying to clear the streets to let traffic through. It was anarchy!

That is not to say that the US tours did not have memorable dates as well. There was May 8 at Madame Wong's on the second US tour. Madame Wong's was originally just a Chinese restaurant in Chinatown in Downtown Los Angeles, but by the late 70s it had become a hip punk/ alternative club for bands like The Motels and even The Ramones. What attracted me was simply the name: 'The Police Raid Madame Wong's' had a nice ring to it. Then, to hype the 'three blond Police' image, we announced that entrance was free if you were a blond: natural, dyed, or a wig would do. A few days after the gig, I got a call from the owner of a wig store on Santa Monica Boulevard, thanking me for the stunt. Apparently, he had sold more wigs for that show than he had sold for the entire year.

The name The Police obviously had promotional value, too, so radio stations and promoters often came up with some play on the word to attract business. In Washington, DC, the record company created a 'The Police will pay your parking tickets' promotion. Stewart often said, when asked how he arrived at the name, 'Cars all over the world are promoting my band.'

For a band with a name like theirs, an obvious stunt would be a Police concert in a prison. On their third US tour, I organized a performance at the federal men's prison at Terminal Island, Los Angeles. The five-hundred-capacity hall was as packed as one could imagine. What I didn't imagine was the overpowering smell of marijuana in the place. That gig was as close as I ever got to being high. It was not just a crass publicity stunt, either: we donated musical equipment to the prison's arts program, to help prisoners develop skills that might help them in the future.

Meanwhile, in Continental Europe, the major event was the annual

Pink Pop festival in Holland on June 4. Reputed to be the oldest pop festival in the world, it was sold out to over fifty-two thousand people, though the real police claimed it was over seventy thousand. The Police went on late in the afternoon, before everyone was tired and drunk out of their minds, and delivered one of their strongest performances ever. The result was that one show broke them wide open in Europe. The *Regatta De Blanc* album went straight to #1 in the Dutch charts when it was released there a few months later, just as it did in England.

There was a sense of giddiness about all this success. A month later, The Police toured Scandinavia and played a bunch of dates in Germany. Kim Turner was with them as tour manager and called me from Stockholm to go over the latest information on the upcoming German shows. He needed to give a list to the band, so I told him the first date was in Berlin on June 20.

'How do you spell that?' Kim asked. He had left school at age fourteen to join Cat Iron, and he was not good at reading and writing, so I said 'B-E-R-L-I-N.'

'OK, where are we next?'

Hamburg on June 21.

'How do you spell that?'

'H-A-M-B-U-R-G.'

I got the idea Kim didn't know any of these cities, so the next one I said was Auschwitz: 'A-U-S-C-H-W-I-T-Z.'

'What's after that?'

I couldn't resist, so I said, 'Mein-Kampfs-burg. M-E-I-N-K-A-M-P-F-S-B-U-R-G.' Then 'B-E-L-S-E-N.' I hung up the phone, and about twenty minutes later Kim called again.

'OK, very funny. The band want to know the real dates.'

✧

As noted above, there were two major events of 1979 that were personal to me and my brother Ian but that also impacted all the acts we represented now and were to represent in the future. The first was the creation of IRS Records in Los Angeles, and the second was the creation of Frontier Booking International in New York City.

One would think that anyone would have had to be blind not to notice the 1979 vacuum in the US music industry—just as there had been in England in 1977 and 1978—with little outlet for all the new bands that were bubbling up all across America. Perhaps the music executives thought the 'underground' would *stay* underground. I, apparently, was one of the ones who saw things differently. To me, the underground was one day going to be very much above ground. It seemed obvious. The question was how to make that happen. One approach would be to do what I did with Squeeze and The Police—to sign them to an existing major US record company and battle the preconceived ideas. Another would be to try to 'go it alone' in some way, as I had done in the UK with Faulty Products.

To go it alone in America, my first step was to hire a salesman I had met at Bleecker Bob's record store in New York City. That record store was the perfect window into what was going to happen in the future. It specialized in the American underground bands and imports from the UK, and the salesmen there were real music fans who knew their stuff. I was glad to see the Police 'Fallout' single on sale, as well as Squeeze and the other records I had released in the UK.

I met salesman Bob Laul at Bleecker Bob's right before the first Police show at CBGB's. He had previously worked for the independent distributor that handled A&M Records, before it moved to RCA distribution; that meant he was already familiar with selling Squeeze, so he seemed the perfect guy to start with. He joined me as my first US employee in April of 1979. Meanwhile, my friend Jane Friedman had offered me a desk in her office with a telephone while we worked out ideas for a John Cale label. We had already worked together on the Television tour of the UK, so her office became my focal point any time I was in New York.

Bob moved into that office and took over the desk Jane had provided. His first brief was to sell the records I brought in from the UK. Not only me: I loaded up the bands when they traveled to the USA and even got Bob to go to London to load up on all the records I had released there. At the time, I couldn't pay a regular salary, so I told him to pay himself from the sales he made. Those sales helped me get a pretty good idea of the demand for records from the artists I was working with in England, as well as some of the artists that my brother Ian was picking up in the USA.

That made me confident that there was a market, even if to a big company it might seem like a relatively small one.

Meanwhile, the US success of Squeeze and The Police had other artists back in England, like Gene October, pressuring me to put out their albums in America. 'What about me?' If Gene October wasn't asking for a fiver, it was, 'When are you releasing my album?' I had recently signed the Birmingham group Fashion, too, and part of the deal was a US release. The Fall, Alternative TV, and others might do business in America. What I really needed was a distribution system in the USA that could do more than the Bob Laul one-man operation in New York.

The success of The Police and Squeeze—plus my apparently being looked upon by A&M since the Gil Friesen lecture as someone with a vision for the future—made me think I might be able to talk Jerry Moss into letting me launch a record label in America with A&M. It wouldn't be an easy sell, so the obvious approach had to be the same strategy we'd used to get The Police signed in the first place. Namely, make the answer an easy *yes* by offering a nothing-to-lose argument.

Meeting with Jerry, I explained that I had more artists in England with albums that I thought would sell in the USA, as well as acts I had come across during the Police and Squeeze tours who already had product. The artists could be promoted through the contacts I had built, and with the touring my brother Ian could provide. Some of the artists were already selling via my imports. All I needed was the distribution and help from his company, only as and when *his* people at A&M felt it was warranted.

The deal was, I would sign the acts on my own, with no advance or investment required from A&M. All Jerry would have to do was release the albums. He could have his promotion people work the records, or not. It was up to him. Essentially, the pitch was that there was virtually no risk on his part. It was an easy yes, so he said OK. Then he asked to hear the records I was proposing to release.

'Ah,' I said, 'that's the only catch. I won't take your money, but you don't ask to hear the music.' I knew if he heard the albums, that would be the end of that. I then added, 'And you have to release every album I give you.' *What the hell*, he must have figured—he agreed.

We had some discussion about a name for the label. He thought a name should be something along the lines of Chrysalis, but I had already decided to continue in the footsteps of choosing institutions that had conflicting connotations. The name should have an element of 'jolt' about it. My father's history with founding the CIA, and my brother's band The Police, had already set the stage. I liked double entendre. So, I hit on calling the label the International Record Syndicate—and IRS Records was born.

Trying to launch a record label with no money might sound crazy. Normally that would be true, but at that time I could count on two things. First, I knew from my visits to the growing number of specialist record stores like Bleecker Bob's that there would at least be *some* sales, no matter what band I released. As long as the music fit into the new scene, musically and image-wise, and was at least (in my opinion) good, there should be sales enough to cover whatever small investment I would need to make.

Secondly, there was virtually no competition in the North American market at that time, so there would be no bidding wars between record labels competing to sign the artists. That would encourage artists to ask for small advances, if any—ones that I could afford. Given that this music scene was not about spending large amounts of money, the artists would presumably not need big advances anyway. In other words, to be in the game, I would not need much money, nor would the artists. Small independent labels in the UK would be all too happy to have releases in the US market, even if they got no advance up front, while US artists at that time had few places to go.

I knew this window of opportunity would eventually close when US labels woke up to what was going on. Any success I had was bound to foster competition. With any luck, I would have time to build a cool roster before that happened.

A major selling point that made A&M an attractive partner was their intern program of twenty-eight young college reps around the country. I had met many of them on the Police and Squeeze tours, and I looked upon them as supporters of what I was doing—and they were *free*. Unfortunately, that turned out to be a very short-lived plus. Within a few weeks of agreeing the IRS deal, the entire college department was terminated for financial reasons. A&M was experiencing financial problems due to its switchover from independent distributors to RCA's national distribution network. As they were losing the A&M business anyway, some of these distributors took the opportunity to challenge bills and, in some cases, refuse to pay.

Upset as I was about losing a free asset, I decided to hire some of the reps myself. A&M was based in Los Angeles, and the local college rep there was Jay Boberg. He had helped me on the Squeeze and Police tours, so there was already a relationship. Plus, having someone on the A&M lot to watch over the IRS label and give me a window into what A&M was doing or not doing for The Police and Squeeze could be handy. I decided to offer Jay a job. Problem was, I didn't have much money, and I was not about to start paying out the usual record-company salaries. So, I had to offer more than money.

My offer to Jay was a five percent share of the company each year he stayed with me up to five years—and to make him vice president of the label. To be the vice president of a record label at that young age, and have the chance to own twenty-five percent of the company, had to be enticing. That must have cushioned my offer of a salary of $100 per week. Thankfully, he went for it. I am sure his parents and friends must have thought he was crazy. But, in reality, if he had asked for a real salary, I would not have been able to hire him. Because he was affordable, I could hire him. Because he was young, unattached, and probably had few living costs, he could afford to join what we both hoped would become a successful business. Turned out it worked for both of us.

Jay also had one other advantage. Whereas I tended to be brash— or, as Kathy Valentine of The Go-Go's describes me in her book, a man of 'unshakable conviction, interesting, handsome, opinionated, and charismatic, but a little like a combustible droid'—Jay was much calmer, nonthreatening, and, as Kathy put it, 'a little nerdy.' It made for a good yin-yang at the Los Angeles office.

Jay brought in his friend Carlos Grasso to create the art for the album sleeves, and it was Carl who created the 'IRS Man' image. For an office, A&M gave us an unused storage room on the lot that had just enough room for three desks. On the East Coast, I hired the local A&M college rep, Kathy Bacigalupo, who worked out of A&M's New York office. She had been A&M's 'East Coast special projects representative' before the termination of the college intern department. With Bob Laul also in New York, IRS started with four employees plus me.

IRS Records now had a team that could keep things going while I was off working with my management acts. More importantly, A&M allowed the IRS staff to be part of the weekly briefings where strategy was set for all the acts they were working. That gave me the inside scoop on what was happening with IRS Records, but also to what was going on with The Police and Squeeze. My CIA father would have appreciated the situation.

The first act to be released on IRS was the Buzzcocks, from Manchester, England, who typically no US record company was interested in. It was not long before we had sold over twenty-five thousand copies of their *Singles Going Steady* album, which to our minds at the time was a success. We had not followed the standard record-company practice of shipping out tons of records only to get most back in returns. Our sales were therefore genuine, as the A&M salespeople had done just as I had suggested to Jerry Moss they do: only manufacture and distribute the quantities they had actual orders for.

This philosophy of shipping out records you know you can sell ran completely counter to the normal practice of record companies at that time. It used to be a joke that some albums 'shipped gold and came back platinum.' For IRS, what was shipped is what was sold.

Also released in 1979 were the records by acts aligned with my UK Faulty Products operation, like Fashion (*Product Perfect*), and The Fall (*Live At The Witch Trials*), and from the US the strange but soon to be legendary Cramps (*Songs The Lord Taught Us*). Ian encouraged me to sign American artists he had started booking, like Wazmo Nariz and Skafish, both based in Chicago.

Fashion were by no means an important part of my story or that of IRS or Faulty Products, but they are one of those acts that have lingered in my mind as a failure that should have been successful. It could have been my fault or the band's fault or their management's fault—or most likely a combination of all three. In any case, I feel compelled to write about them, even if only briefly.

They were a three-piece band from Birmingham, England, that had all the elements to convince me that they were going to happen. In fact, when Derek Green, the managing director of A&M Records in London, saw them supporting The Police, he said, 'Miles, looks like you've got another one.' They also looked great: the lead singer/guitarist in the center was about six foot five, his bandmates on either side of him a foot shorter.

We released *Product Perfect* in July 1979 in England and in September in the USA. Then I put Fashion on all the gigs I could throw at them, including an entire Police tour of America. As far as I was concerned, they were given a real shot. Then, right after returning to England from the Police tour, their front man, Luke Sky, quit. He left a short note: 'Gone to America,' which turned out to be untrue. Fearing one of his bandmates would track him down in New York with a knife, he actually went to Bordeaux, France. (Talking to Luke since, it turns out he had become paranoid at the time and was convinced the band were out to get him, when in fact they were not.)

All I was left with was a memory and a great album. Many reviewers have called the *Product Perfect* album a 'little-known masterpiece,' which it was. For me, it was yet another example of a great band with a future that somehow went awry.

Meanwhile, Wazmo was in the mold of a Devo, with a strong 'nerd appeal.' Image-wise, he was straight and normal, but he wore two ties, so he came across like he had a screw loose somewhere. Skafish was just plain weird but a brilliant musician. He could do amazing things on a piano while standing on his head. He had a huge nose, which accentuated his hermaphrodite image. Much as I'd experience with The Cramps later on, walking into a restaurant with Jim Skafish had the entire room staring at us. His best song, 'Disgracing The Family Name,' pretty much sums him up.

As the year ended, the nascent IRS Records was considered interesting—like it was cute or something—but as yet no one thought much could happen with it except the five of us in the company. If it hadn't been for The Police and Squeeze looking like they might be big, I think most of the A&M staff might have said it was a waste of time. Outside of A&M, that was certainly the case.

Even some local LA bands wondered about IRS, especially the ones that knew of my supposed connection to the CIA via my father. I was considering signing local band X, and I invited the band's guitarist, Billy Zoom, to meet me on the A&M lot. He listened for a few minutes to my pitch, then interrupted me with, 'X will never sign with IRS because we know you are backed by the CIA to study youth trends.' He got up and walked out of the office. As he left, I said, 'If that's true, get them to send me a check!'

Meanwhile, even before the first album was released, our IRS office received our first letter. In it was a check from Circus Disco for $16,000, made out to IRS. It was to pay their taxes. I was very tempted to cash it.

℘

The most dramatic event of the year for Ian and me was the closure of the Paragon Agency, leaving my brother without a job—and creating a huge problem for IRS Records.

It was in July of 1979 that disaster struck. Ian called me to explain that the Capricorn Records label, which had been losing money and owned the Paragon Agency, had cleaned out the Paragon bank account. Capricorn was going broke, and now Paragon was broke. It was over, and Ian was out of a job.

I was already in New York for Squeeze's shows at the Bottom Line club, so Ian flew up to see about getting a job at one of the New York agencies. From what I understood, the discussions he was getting were more about what artists could he bring with him, rather than Ian as a great agent. The Police were not yet a big act, nor were Squeeze, and some of the other bands Ian had acquired, like Ultravox, were interesting but also not yet the kinds of big names that would warrant hiring someone, let alone paying a decent salary.

Ian came to see me at my office with Jane Friedman to tell me about the possible job offers, and Jane in her usual fashion said, 'Let me tell you what I think.' She was not one to mince words, and she made it apparent she had little time for the traditional booking agents. Her pitch was simple: Ian should go on his own. None of the established agencies knew what he knew about the new bands, so why sell out to people you don't need? We had already decided that the strategy of being headliners worked, so what could a big agency offer anyway?

It was the same conclusion I had already come to with regard to the record business. This was a unique time where we knew what was going on, but the rest of the business had so far missed it. Do it now or the time will pass and you will never get another opportunity. That was pretty convincing. Then Jane pointed at my desk and said, 'All you need is a desk and a phone, and you can use my office to start.'

Squeeze were just finishing their US tour, but The Police were supposed to be back in the States at the end of September. I had committed Fashion to be the support band. I was already working on renting the Hotel Diplomat in New York for three nights at the start of that tour, so I was keen for Ian to be back in business as soon as possible. For me, the idea of an agency free to focus on the kind of bands I was now working with was more than attractive. Jane was convincing, and I was for it, but Ian had to decide for himself. It was a big step—it's not easy to start your own company with little income guarantee. In spite of the risk, the convincing argument was, 'This is the time, and there will never be another.' That pushed Ian over the edge, and he went for it.

In keeping with the Police and IRS image, and indeed our father and the CIA, Ian came up with FBI as a name, but wasn't sure what it would stand for. I suggested Frontier Booking International. According to Ian's book, the agency officially started on August 1, 1979, and the first bookings were made right out of Jane Friedman's office.

Ian's major issue quickly became money. He didn't have any and neither did I. At the same time, none of the bands were yet earning fees that would make an agency pay for itself. Ten percent of $2,000 is just $200, which doesn't pay for much, especially in New York. Ian went to my lawyer, Allen Grubman, who agreed to help and waived his fee until Ian could afford him, so at least the legal side could be dealt with. All I could do was suggest Ian call Jerry Moss, to see if Jerry would give him a loan. He did, and Jerry did, and FBI was off and running. By the end of the year, Ian was looking for his own offices, and FBI had become a reality, soon growing to become *the* US agency representing the new wave.

CHAPTER 13

SQUEEZE
A LONG STORY
. . . .

A manager friend of mine once told me, when you first start a relationship with a new unknown artist, you are a hero—you can walk on water, a sort of god. When the artist finally succeeds, *they* walk on water, and you become the janitor. I am afraid to say that this is often the case. The fate of the manager is all too often to be left out of the credits, or shit upon, or both. So, whenever one hears horror stories about record deals, artists being screwed, managers ripping off artists, there are usually two sides to the story. From my fifty years in the business, I can safely say there are shits everywhere you look, both among artists and managers, as well as good people. And most stories shift radically one way or another depending who you talk to. In the final analysis, the truth is always in the eye of the beholder.

It has to be true, however, that with the explosion of The Police, the starting of IRS Records in America, and all the other things I was doing, it must have looked like I had less time for Squeeze than I had during '78–79. I did have a good tour manager/assistant with them the whole time in John Lay, but Squeeze would not have been easy for anyone. Did I do my job? I think so, but perception is often nine tenths of reality, so it should be no surprise that by October 1980 I was no longer the manager of Squeeze.

The truth is that Squeeze were in many ways the most difficult management client I ever had to deal with. There was so much talent in one place, but it was like a jigsaw puzzle—you saw that it was going to be a beautiful picture, but some of the pieces just wouldn't fit. Like a painter with a complete set of colors, but some are oil paints and some are water paints. The simple fact is that Squeeze from the very start were really two bands. Chris and Glenn were one and Jools the other. Starting with the musical interests, both were very different—Glenn and Chris liked traditional Beatles-style pop; Jools liked Ray Charles and Bessie Smith, boogie-woogie and New Orleans jazz. Their personalities were also poles apart. Jools was instantly likable, funny, and looked on the bright side of life; Chris and Glenn were guarded. I can't say I ever really knew Glenn. Jools would be up for anything, keen to try new things and generally game for adventure. But with Glenn and Chris, I could never be sure how they would react.

Even the name 'Squeeze' turned out to be a problem. In the USA another band had the name, and so too in Australia, so the band's name became 'UK Squeeze.' It was also not a name that leant itself to cool marketing ideas, nor did it say anything strong. It did not have the vibe of names like The Police, The Clash, The Sex Pistols, The Cramps. It was just a name of a band.

In spite of all that, we did have some great times, and some funny ones as well. As always, there were plenty of learning experiences for both band and manager. And, of course, I am proud to say I managed Squeeze and played a big part in their careers.

On an early US tour, we played a club in New Jersey that had the biggest bouncers we had ever seen. Apparently, they were a team of bodybuilders who had worked with the club owner, who had also been a bouncer. At the end of the show, as the band's roadie, Mike Hedge, was loading out the equipment, one of the exit doors was closed; instead of getting the key, he kicked the door in, and as it opened it hit the owner. Upon seeing that, a herd of bouncers descended upon the roadie, who burst into the dressing room calling for help. The Squeeze guys were in their underpants, midway through changing out of their stage clothes, so all of us looked on in shock. Mike ran into the bathroom and locked the door, only to have it ripped open by the infuriated bouncers. They pulled him out into the center of the room and started pounding him to the ground. I ran towards the melee of bodies just as a barrel of water went over, taking me and several bouncers down with it. The biggest of them pulled the hapless roadie out and said, 'Run!' And run he did, into the parking lot and beyond. We later found Mike hiding under the bed in his hotel room. It was a close call—he was a bit bruised—and a lesson learned.

As I got to my feet, the bouncers came at me, yelling, 'When we are finished, we are going to own you!' The manager's son kept yelling, 'You are going to be working for me!' I shucked and jived, telling them I was shocked at what our roadie had done and promising he would never work in the industry again—anything I could think to calm the situation down.

Finally, the biggest bouncer, the one that had pulled the roadie to freedom, calmed them all down and had them leave the room. That impressed the hell out of me, so I made sure I got his name and phone number. When I saw Sting a few weeks later, I told him, 'I think I have found you the perfect bodyguard for the next tour.' Big Larry got the job and would work regularly for Sting for the next few years. I will never forget August 28, 1980, in Fréjus, France: The Police were performing, and we were filming the show for *Urgh! A Music War*. One jerk in the audience was heckling Sting. Sting looked at Larry on the side of the stage and nodded in the direction of the heckler, without saying a word. Larry made his way through the audience, picked the heckler up, and quietly removed him from the venue.

Urgh!, by the way, was a concept that movie producer Michael White created to capture the spirit of the punk and new wave movement. Michael, who had made the cult hit *Rocky Horror Picture Show*, plus *Monty Python And The Holy Grail*, was always interested in leftfield projects, and as I had become known as being at the center of the 'scene,' he asked me to help him put it together.

Squeeze toured the USA again in the first half of 1980, but they never seemed to crack the charts. They got lots of airplay, especially on the East Coast, but it did not result in the kind of visible chart positions that record companies respond to. The weird thing was, with all that airplay spread out, they were actually more successful than their chart positions indicated.

By May 1980, however, it was apparent to me that a rift was brewing between me and the band—largely, it seems, due to the exploding success of The Police. Squeeze had been my first signing to A&M Records, they'd had the first hit records on the British charts, and they were the first 'new wave' band Ian and I had taken to tour the USA. Until The Police came along, Squeeze were my #1 success—the top band I managed. Then The Police became #1, and they were also on A&M Records, so it is easy to imagine how jealousy could develop.

Around this time, I was personally getting a lot of attention in the press as the manager of 'the world's biggest band.' That apparently pissed off Jake Riviera, the manager of Elvis Costello, who, with Stiff Records, had previously been a press hot shot. I am told he resented the attention paid to me. One newspaper wrote, 'As manager of The Police, Miles Copeland III is just BIG . . . he could turn out to be the most significant entrepreneur of the new wave in Britain, and especially in America. He's outlasted McLaren, outshone Rhodes, and outreached Rivieria.'

Elvis Costello genuinely liked Squeeze, and would become good friends with Chris and Glenn, so Jake decided to go after the band and become their manager. Jake's pitch to the band was this: 'Miles is off with his brother and The Police and has stopped paying attention to you.' It all came to a head at a meeting the band called in the spring of 1980. At the meeting, Glenn or Chris—I can't remember which of them it was—said I was to be fired. Jools was apparently as shocked as I was: he stood up and said he knew nothing about this—and if Miles goes, so will he. That put the cat among the pigeons, and the conversation about firing me stopped cold.

I left the meeting still the manager of Squeeze, with a sad feeling about Chris and Glenn but huge admiration for Jools. When we spoke later, Jools was apologetic, but he warned me, 'Whatever you do, those guys are going to find fault—even if you give them a huge bag of money, they are going to see something wrong with it.' Whether we said it or not, we both knew that the writing was on the wall.

Perhaps naively, my view was always that the better I was doing overall, the greater would be my ability to generate opportunities for Squeeze, but not all artists appreciate that. I put Squeeze on the bill at the huge Milton Keynes Bowl gig that The Police were headlining on July 26, 1980, and I paid them a big fee for participating. I gave them the 6:15 slot, one band (UB40) away from the headliner, having learned my lesson with The

Tubes. I even went into their dressing room at that gig and handed each of them a big check, thinking it would prove that I was delivering for them, and that The Police's success would help not hurt them.

A few days later, I got a phone call from Jools. 'Remember what I said about giving them a bag of money?' Chris and Glenn were pissed off that I had given them the money in front of their girlfriends. Jools went on to say that he couldn't stand the atmosphere in the band anymore, and would I manage him if he left Squeeze?

'Are you sure that's what you want to do?' I asked. Squeeze were right at the point of becoming very successful, and they were making real money, so in that respect it was not the smart thing to do. But Jools had made up his mind.

'Of course I will,' I said.

Jools officially left Squeeze in October of 1980.

The funny thing was, now that Jools was out, Chris and Glenn were free to ask Jake Riviera to become their manager. I agreed a settlement, and then the band got the contract from Jake. It was so onerous, and Jake was so unwilling to make any accommodation, that the relationship quickly dissolved. The band then turned to David Enthoven, who had once managed King Crimson. He proved to be an able manager, and he was smart enough to stick with my brother Ian and FBI in the USA, until Squeeze broke up in December 1982.

Meanwhile, I remained interested in Squeeze, and I was glad to see them sell out Madison Square Garden to twenty thousand people in June 1982. The band never did have big hits on the US charts, but they proved over and over that they were a lot bigger than any charts would indicate.

CHAPTER 14

FAULTY PRODUCTS USA

. . . .

The launch of IRS Records in America solved some problems but not all of them. We quickly realized that A&M was too big a company to clutter up with too many releases and get the same attention as we would with careful releases spread out over time. After several years of releasing records in the UK, I had more product than A&M could legitimately handle. Also, it was evident that some of the UK artists would not have fared well in the A&M system, distributed by RCA. *And* those artists were still bitching about not getting their albums released. I needed another option.

With Bob Laul I had seen the value of independently dealing with the small record stores that really understood and sold this new music, so I began thinking I needed the same thing on the West Coast. The perfect guy to run it was a salesman at a record store I had met on the first Squeeze tour. I first met John Guarnieri at Mushroom Records in New Orleans much the same way I had met Bob Laul in New York—while checking out which local record stores might be interested in what we were doing, and looking for support wherever we could find it. John was also a DJ at the Tulane University radio station, and he made it pretty apparent he was keen on the music we were releasing and would relish the opportunity to work with me to help make it happen. John joined the company on February 2, 1980. He loaded up his Volkswagen minibus in New Orleans and drove to Los Angeles.

When John got to the IRS office on the A&M lot, he was greeted with, 'Who are you?' He explained I had just hired him to sell all the UK Faulty Products releases on the West Coast, and Jay Boberg pointed to a desk in the corner. That was the official start of Faulty Products USA. Soon, John picked up independent domestic American releases. Being a pure 'indie,' Faulty became more of an underground outlet than IRS could be, much like Faulty in the UK. To begin with, we released American acts like Missing Persons and The Humans. Later in the year we brought the Dead Kennedys to the company. However, that was not supposed to be.

The Dead Kennedys were a perfect band from my point of view: they were already controversial, they had a following and press savvy lead singer, and they fit the IRS Records ethic, but the band inadvertently also brought the first stumbling block with A&M. Jerry Moss called me into his office and asked me to not release the group on IRS. It had nothing to do with the music. It was the name: Dead Kennedys. Jerry and Herb Alpert had been close personal friends of the Kennedy family, and having a band with that name distributed via A&M would be personally embarrassing to both of them. It was a heartfelt request, so I had no choice but to agree or risk hurting the relationship I and the small IRS team were building and nurturing with Jerry's company.

Unfortunately, I had already promised Jello Biafra, the leader of the Dead Kennedys, that I would release his album, and that he'd benefit from the distribution the A&M deal provided, so it was an embarrassing stumbling block. I only had one option: to use the alternative distribution network of Faulty Products. For the Dead Kennedys, the solution was not ideal. I failed to deliver what I'd promised to Jello, and he had every right to be pissed off about it.

Faulty ended up as a footnote to the IRS story because after a few years, partly due to the success of The Go-Go's and signing The Bangles to Columbia, it become less necessary. There was also some jealous tension between Faulty and IRS. By far the biggest problem, however, was that it became a financial drain on me personally. Independent distribution was a tough game, as even A&M discovered. Getting paid was a never-ending fight. If you had no good-selling record at the time, you might not get paid until you had one.

Faulty got stiffed a number of times, which left me with a dilemma: do I pay the staff and the rent, or do I pay the royalties and the labels? It was not a pleasant place to be, and certainly not good for my reputation. In the end, I had no option but to pull the plug on the company.

By mid-1980, I had a second problem with A&M. During the first half of the year, we'd released The Cramps' *Songs The Lord Taught Us*, Skafish, John Cale's *Sabotage* album, and EPs from Oingo Boingo and Wall Of Voodoo. From the IRS Records standpoint, the label was doing fine. Each of the albums had covered the expenses and even delivered a small profit. That had to be pretty unique in the music business. I was surprised, therefore, when Jerry Moss invited me to his office to terminate the deal. From his point of view, eight albums had been released, but none had been a 'hit'—at least a hit in his way of thinking. To Jerry, IRS Records was not working.

I had been given a preview of what Jerry might be thinking about the music we were releasing when I tried to get him to loan me money to sign The B-52's. Jane Friedman had made sure I saw the band when they played at CBGB's, and I did, even before The Police played there. Not only did I like the music, I liked them, especially Fred, who after each song would ask the audience, 'Any questions?' I was ready to sign a single deal for the band's 'Rock Lobster,' but then I went on the road with Squeeze, and by the time I approached them again they had a manager and a price tag that was beyond my means. So, I went to Jerry Moss, asking for his help, and of course, as I needed his money, he had the right to hear what I wanted to buy. 'Sounds like a college band,' he said—he was not interested. Jerry 'got' The Police, probably because there was a sophistication to them, but he must not have related to most of the IRS music.

Anyway, I was taken aback when he said he wanted to terminate our deal. I asked him how much he'd lost, and he said, 'Nothing'—but he hadn't made anything to speak of, either. I then asked him how many acts he had broken on their first album. The standard of the time was the third album.

'Rarely,' he said, 'but IRS has released eight albums.'

'Yes,' I said, 'but it was the first album from each act, and *all* of them made money on that first album. How many times can you say you made money on the first release of an act? How many times can you say you made money in the first year of any deal you made—even if only a little?'

The answer was never.

'OK,' he said. 'I'll give you another year.'

I think Jerry Moss must have seen in IRS Records the same small beginnings that he himself had seen with Herb Alpert in the early days of A&M. In March of 1980, he told *Record World*, 'Miles is betting on himself, and I'll always bet on a guy who is betting on himself.' Meanwhile, after Jerry's respite, IRS released second albums from The Buzzcocks and The Cramps, plus The Damned, Sector 27, and The Stranglers. The label was on its way to becoming the hippest label in America—at least for what was now being called the 'new wave.'

Though we didn't know it at the time, our biggest acquisition was a staff member: another ex-A&M college rep by the name of Michael Plen, who in June 1980 became the first IRS Records head of radio promotion. In many ways, that single addition changed the game for us. It meant we were no longer totally dependent on A&M to get the most important of all promotional means behind our record releases: namely radio play. With Michael on board, we could at least generate some smoke on our own—*and* have an easier time convincing the large A&M radio team that there was, in fact, a fire.

Michael had started at A&M much as Jay had in the college intern team, then he was officially hired by the company as a local rep for Buffalo and later Kansas City. While he was there, Squeeze played a show at the World of Fun amusement park. It was a free open-air show with a five-thousand capacity, and it was full when the band started their set. Michael had invited along the program director of the local station, to prove to him that Squeeze would appeal to the Kansas City audience. About three songs in, people began to walk away; one song later, only about two hundred people remained. It was like a bomb scare.

The program director was not impressed. He turned to Michael and me. 'Well, I told you Squeeze wouldn't fly in KC,' he said. 'I'm dropping the record and I'm outta here.'

As Michel told me, 'All that were left were the two hundred devout Squeeze fans and me and you. You turned to me and said, *How are we gonna get this music, like Squeeze, broken in this country?* I said, Move me back to NY and I'll be your first head of promotion and travel all over the country spreading the word, like I'd already done at A&M for The Police and Squeeze.'

I called the A&M executives who looked after the promotion in LA and in New York, and me and Jay Boberg badgered them into letting Michael work for IRS out of the New York office. Michael moved to New York and officially became IRS's first head of radio promotion. Kathy Bacigalupo resigned, and soon after that she married Kim Turner.

☙

In its first few years, the IRS roster grew to include some of the most intriguing bands around.

Danny Elfman, the leader of Oingo Boingo, came to see me in 1980 to look at signing his band, figuring IRS might be different enough to give him a record deal. He had been trying to get a deal with all the major record companies in Los Angeles, but to no avail. The general consensus was that they were 'too quirky.' To me, they were in the mode of Devo or Skafish, so not punk, but not of the old school either. They were very good musicians, and there were a lot of them. They were by no means a lean and mean three-piece like The Police—in fact, they were more like three or four Police bands put together.

However, Oingo Boingo were impressive live, constantly performing and building their audience anywhere they could drive to in California. They played every dive I had heard of—and ones I had not—gradually climbing the ladder to sell-out status at Anaheim Stadium. They were good, they were different, and they were committed, so just the kind of act that would fit IRS Records. The only problem was that Danny wanted more than he thought IRS could give, and he kept pushing to have A&M Records take over.

For a while, Oingo Boingo were the most popular new-wave band from Southern California. 'Weird Science' and 'Dead Man's Party' were ubiquitous anthems for high-school students and became the ultimate party-pop. KROQ Radio in LA played them constantly, so it was always a mystery why other labels were not lining up to sign them. But they were definitely quirky, and the name Oingo Boingo—or, as people joked, 'Oin-gii Boin-gii'—might have put people off. People, especially in the music business, *do* judge a book by its cover.

The unfortunate thing was that early in our relationship, Danny came to me asking to borrow $50,000 to buy a house and offered to sign a publishing deal in return. He had not yet built any profile in the soundtracks that would later make him famous, so it was a risk, but, then again, the band was great, so I agreed. What I did not do was rush to draw up the publishing contract. He needed the money right away, though, so I gave it to him.

Many months later, by the time I had drawn up the contract and asked him to come see me, he said, 'I'm giving back your $50,000, plus $5,000,' thereby reneging on doing the publishing deal. At least he gave me the money back with a bit of 'interest,' but I was not a bank, and I did not give loans. I *was* in the business of signing publishing deals. So, basically, one could say I got stiffed.

The situation reminded me of the old saying, 'Neither a borrower nor a lender be.' It comes from Shakespeare's *Hamlet*, and it means do not lend or borrow money from a friend, because, if you do so, you will lose both your friend and your money. In this case, I lost both an artist and the deal I thought we had. The sad part was that I always felt Danny was embarrassed about it; he paid the $5,000 extra to be honorable, but he still knew it was not right, and he seems to have avoided me ever since. Needless to say, he went on to become one of the most successful soundtrack composers in the business, so I can claim to have been one of the few to recognize his talent and help him get started at the beginning.

✑

In 1981, I decided to create the perfect band for IRS Records—our own punk supergroup with a 'London meets New York' flavor. The singer would be Stiv Bators from New York's famed Dead Boys, and on lead guitar would be Brian James from The Damned in the UK. Add Dave Tregunna from Sham 69 on bass and Nick Turner from The Barracudas on drums, and what a band that would be!

Stiv was suitably nuts, so he would be the perfect demonic front man, and Brian James wrote hit songs like the Damned anthems 'Neat, Neat, Neat' and 'New Rose.' Brian and Stiv already knew each other, and they got on, so there was already some real chemistry even before I got involved. The music that resulted was slicker than that of the pure punk groups; *New Noise Magazine* would later describe it as a 'seedy concoction of spidery guitars, sleazy bass lines, jungle drums and gothic keyboards.' It was Iggy Pop meets Guns N' Roses, with a monkey wrench thrown in for good measure.

I wanted to call the band Lords Of Discipline, but they didn't go for it, so we ended up with The Lords Of The New Church. It was Stiv who pushed for it, mostly because of his Catholic upbringing, which he was convinced was the reason he was such a rebel. He was thinking the Lords could be the Four Horsemen of the Apocalypse. That probably made more sense with songs like 'Open Your Eyes' and 'Method To My Madness.' I wasn't sure what the message was, but Stiv had one, even if it was mostly obscure. The main thing was, it fit the image of The Lords Of The New Church, or, as we came to call them, 'the Lords.'

Stiv did have some strange views, and he was prone to some pretty wacky conspiracy theories. During a concert in Gateshead in 1982, supporting The Police and U2, he went on about his theory about the British navy sinking the Argentine battleship the *Belgrano* during the Falklands War, announcing onstage that it had actually been blown up by a neutron beam operated by a CIA satellite.

There were comparisons to The Doors, partly I think because of the unpredictability of their stage performances. Nevertheless, with players like Brian James involved, this was a band bound to make great music. They were great live, but at the same time seemed to court confusion and disaster. When I set up for them to appear on *The Tube*, which was their first big TV break in England, Stiv announced onstage that it was 'anti-heroin week' and advised everyone to take cocaine instead. That put my head in my hands, and, of course, the band were forever banned from the show. Not only that, they were banned from Channel 4 entirely.

Then there was the video for the song that was on its way to being a big hit for the group, 'Dance With Me,' from the album *Is Nothing Sacred?* Directed by Derek Jarman, it featured a little girl dancing around, which, when combined with the lyrics, apparently led MTV to believe the song promoted child pornography. MTV pulled it from rotation, and the controversy killed off the song. One step forward, two steps back—often the story of IRS Records. Yet the song had legs; today, the video has had more than one million views on YouTube.

Stiv Bators was already a legend thanks to his live performances with The Dead Boys. To me, he seemed to be out to destroy his body. He would hang himself onstage, jump and land on his knees, dance naked—one never knew quite what he would do. At *The Tube*, Stiv knew Paula Yates, the presenter, was coming into the dressing room with the film crew, so he stripped naked. His only concession to TV morality was to tape his penis with duct tape so that it was hidden between his legs.

My knees hurt just watching Stiv Bators perform. One day, I sat with him to discuss his more outlandish antics, as I was worried that he would actually kill himself even if by accident. He told me not to worry. 'This scrawny piece-of-shit body I am in is a tool for me to use, and when I have wrecked it, I will get another.' Stiv believed in reincarnation, and he was going to come back as one of the 'beautiful people.' That apparently gave him license to do all the crazy stuff he did. After he jumped and landed on his knees at one concert, he did the next show in a wheelchair. At another show, he even pulled a wheelchair-bound audience member onto stage, requisitioned the wheelchair himself, and lay his hands on the poor guy who, lo and behold, walked off the stage.

Of course, Brian James was the other key player, providing the base for the songs. I had recorded Brian on his own for an EP and a single, both featuring my brother Stewart on drums, *Ain't That A Shame* and 'Why Why Why,' and I always rated him both as a songwriter and guitarist. ('Why Why Why' b/w 'Where Did I Find A Girl Like You' was issued as an Illegal Records seven-inch on green vinyl; *Ain't That A Shame* was issued by both Illegal and IRS in 1979. The title track also featured on *IRS Greatest Hits* Vol. 2 & 3 and on *Never Mind The Sex Pistols, Here's The Bollocks*.)

Dave Tregunna and Nick Turner were pretty crazy, too, and it seemed that everybody was feeding off of each other. I sent Chris Lamson, Jay Boberg's friend and one of my newest tour managers, out with the band, joking it would 'make a man of him.' By the second day he was phoning me from somewhere on the East Coast, saying the band had just beaten him up.

I was both manager and record company for the Lords, so to me they were not as crazy as others might have thought, and it afforded me the opportunity to occasionally talk them into recording something even if they weren't keen. When I heard Madonna do 'Like A Virgin,' I developed a real disdain for the song, so I decided that the Lords covering it in a really trashy style would not only be funny but would also show the song as a real piece of shit. I told Stiv to trash it full throttle, to 'vomit all over it,' so to speak—which he did. It got to #1 on the UK Independent singles chart and stayed there for weeks. In return, the band made me do a cameo appearance as a kind of green Southern Devil in the 'Method To My Madness' video. My lines were, 'Well, boy, you better shut your mouth, can't afford the bail, now don't go telling secrets, this record's gotta SELL!'

I will admit I was hoping that Madonna would hear the Lords version and be really pissed off—until, years later, I heard she had chosen William Orbit to produce her *Ray of Light* album, and I thought, *Smart girl*.

The Lords saw themselves as the 'dark side' of The Police. In an interview with Jane Simons for *Sounds* in 1984, they said,

> Miles thinks we're crazy. People ask him about us, and he goes, 'The Lords are outta their fucking minds!' You see he had a band like The Police, which is very laconic, very logical, and they make a lot of money. Then he's got a band like us, who are the complete opposite. We are walking fuckups. Like, we don't care about making it, we just care about having a good time. We're the dark side of Miles. He loves telling people stories, 'Did you hear what the Lords did now?' like burning down a hotel in Finland, or me getting arrested for pulling a knife on someone, or what we did to the road manager. Or street surfing on top of a car. Miles loves all that stuff!

I never did understand how Stiv was so quiet and mouse-like when I spoke to him on his own. Onstage, he was an unrestrained psychopath. Later, when I filmed the TV show *My Britain* (see chapter 22), one of the sequences showed me scolding Stiv for not having the band rehearsing and writing songs, and what was the drummer doing on vacation in Europe? Stiv is seen to answer sheepishly, 'That's not true,' and I retort, 'He's in the fucking South of France!'

As with many of the IRS bands there was a 'due date' that seemed to kill them off before their time—but then when you look them up on YouTube, you realize that someone is watching. The Lords' biggest four or five songs have around four million views. For me, their best of, *Killer Lords*, is one of the best albums IRS ever released. They may have been fuckups, but they were *my* fuckups.

It is no wonder that Iggy Pop paid tribute to Stiv after he died in Paris on June 4, 1990. For me, if Stiv was right that he was to be reincarnated into a 'beautiful one,' we should now be looking for a thirty-year-old politician of anarchy, or perhaps a charlatan evangelist preaching, 'The Lord works in mysterious ways.'

℘

And then there was Stan Ridgway and Wall Of Voodoo. When Stan first came to see me at the IRS office in Los Angeles back in 1980, it was the fastest decision I ever made to sign a band in my entire career. Probably less than one minute into the first song he played: the Wall Of Voodoo version of the famed Johnny Cash song 'Ring Of Fire.' It was done in the inimitable Wall Of Voodoo style: spaghetti western guitar à la Ennio Morricone, with techno synthesizers, drums, and keyboards, and a kind of sarcastic talk/singing voice. Before it even got to the middle eight, I had to know if we could make a deal, so I stopped the tape and said, 'What's it going to take for us to sign you?'

Stan looked surprised and said, 'Don't you want to hear the rest of the song?' Of course I did, but first I wanted to know we could make a deal—I was that excited about what I had just heard.

That turned out to be a big mistake. I am convinced that from that point on, Stan thought I had no interest in the music and just wanted to make the deal. I was just another businessman with no appreciation of music. What he didn't realize was that I would have so much more pleasure listening to his music if I knew IRS Records would be able to sign it. It's why I prefer antique shops to museums. In an antique shop, at least there is a possibility of owning something you like—even if it is too expensive—whereas in a museum you can only look.

Stan was the singer and apparent ringleader of the band. Aside from the unique mixture of the instrumentation, there were his songs, which were more like short stories than songs: three or four-minute audio movies, partly sung and partly spoken, or more accurately something in between. Unlike many rock songs, where the words were often unintelligible, Stan's words were crystal clear. As the songs were virtually stories, the lyrics had to be clear. And it added to the unique flavor of the band.

Back while I was living in Beirut, my father had bought me a comedy album by Stan Freiburg that had one skit about a guy wanting to sing rock'n'roll who was told to stick a rag in his mouth as he was 'too understandable.' Stan Ridgway was definitely not that. His lyrics stick in your head. '*We'll do it tomorrow—sounds like a pretty good idea to me.*'

I became the band's manager as well as the record company, but most of the communication was through Stan. I can't say that I ever got to really know any of the other members. To all intents and purposes, it was Stan's band, though I felt there were internal issues within them, some of which were drug-inspired. Stan used to complain about some of this, but I can't remember the specifics. Meanwhile, the live shows were great if sometimes confused, but it was Stan's biting sarcasm and dark sense of humor that were the great appeal to me. At a Wall Of Voodoo show you never knew quite what you were going to get, but it would always be entertaining.

I filmed Wall Of Voodoo for *Urgh! A Music War* and booked them for the US festival, playing in front of four hundred thousand people, as well as shows supporting The Go-Go's, U2, and others, and toured them in the UK. I'm not sure exactly how to sum up the band, but perhaps it was a case of too many personalities in the mix, and I added yet another one, so it was never going to be smooth sailing. Add a few wires flapping around and you have Wall Of Voodoo. Just the same, the band produced some of the best music the label released. And this was a band that could have been one of IRS's biggest winners.

Ultimately, Stan's split with Wall Of Voodoo gives a pretty good idea of the dynamic we were dealing with. In 1982, when the single 'Mexican Radio' was almost Top 30 and destined to go higher, Stan called a meeting with me and his lawyer to announce he wanted to break up the band. Both the lawyer and I were horrified and spent the lunch convincing him of the stupidity of such a move. After dessert, Stan left, and the lawyer and I had a coffee, congratulating ourselves on having averted a stupid mistake. Stan had agreed to do the tour that was starting the next day, and to continue with the band until the single had peaked and gone as far as it could. Then, if he must, he could break up the band when they were at a high. Of course, both of us were hoping he wouldn't do that, and, if the single went much higher, maybe he would change his mind.

Several days later, I got a phone call from Stan in Texas somewhere, saying, 'Well, I did it.'

'You did what?' I asked.

'I told the band it was over.' He went on about how he had to be honest and couldn't lie to them. Needless to say, that honesty stopped the single dead in its tracks; radio jumped off of it everywhere.

In any case, IRS released two great Wall Of Voodoo albums, while in my opinion the best-of, *Granma's House*, is one of the top three albums ever released. The first release was an EP of the first song Stan played for me, 'Ring Of Fire.' That was followed by the *Dark Continent* album in 1981, and in 1982 the *Call Of The West* album, from which the single 'Mexican Radio' came. For 'Mexican Radio' we made a great video that MTV played heavily, and Michael Plen did his thing at radio, just like he had done for The Go-Go's. Wall Of Voodoo was going to be another big hit for IRS. In Canada, the single got to #17, and we were hoping for at least the Top 10 in the USA. Then Stan pulled the plug. I might have gotten off on the wrong foot with him but then Stan repaid me—he shot himself in the foot. Such is rock'n'roll.

That was not the end of Stan Ridgway, however. He went solo and continued to make great music. But he was never easy, even as a solo artist. He released his first solo album, *The Big Heat*, in 1986. The style was smoother but similar to his work in Wall Of Voodoo, and still in his storyteller style. One of the best-known *Rolling Stone* critics actually said the album was 'probably the most compelling portrait of American social life to appear on a rock'n'roll record since Bruce Springsteen's *Nebraska*.' In the USA, the album got to #131 in the *Billboard* charts, but for some reason it had more success in Europe. It was a #4 hit in England, did well in France, and gave Stan a minor hit in Germany with the single 'Camouflage.'

For the second album, we also expected most of the success to be in Europe, so Stan came to London to go over the album sleeve and media setup for the album launch. I had recently moved into new offices in the heart of London's West End, two blocks from the famous Liberty's store on Regent Street and two blocks from Dryden Chambers where I had first started. Actually, with the success of The Police I had bought the building aptly named Bugle House. That's where Stan and I met. I mention this because the entrance was right on the main street, with lots of pedestrians walking by. Stan had decided to call the album *Mosquitos* (1989), and he brought me his sleeve mockup. One look at it and I had to ask, 'What is it?'

'It's a mosquito's head magnified,' Stan said. 'Anyone would know that.' It looked like some indeterminate smudge to me.

I protested that no one would know it was a mosquito head, but Stan disagreed. So, I said, 'Let's see—come with me,' and we walked out onto the street.

I stopped the first passerby and said, 'Excuse me, sir, but can you tell me what this looks like to you?'

'Don't know—could be a bit of lint?' The next said it was 'fluff of some sort.' Another thought it was dust or dirt of some kind.

After a few more, Stan said, 'OK, I get it.' Not one person came close to realizing it was a mosquito's head.

At the beginning of 1983, my brother Stewart called me from his studio, where he was working on the *Rumble Fish* soundtrack for director Francis Ford Coppola. He needed a singer/songwriter to help him come up with a lead single for the movie and its soundtrack album. The film was very much in the vein of the Americana storylines that Stan Ridgway's songs often represented, so of course I said, 'Stan is your man.' They collaborated to create 'Don't Box Me In.' Stewart played guitar, drums, bass, and keyboards, with Stan on harmonica and vocals.

The end with Stan Ridgway was typical. He decided to launch himself as a new project called Drywall. The thought of starting from scratch for a third time was too much for IRS Records, though, so we parted ways.

CHAPTER 15

POLICE ESCORT

A central idea with The Police was to do things others did not—and also to ensure that we captured the moment. They were getting really *big*, so why not let the world see what we were seeing?

The Police started 1980 with another fourteen shows in the USA in early January before we were all off to Japan and the start of the band's first world tour. Japan was a 'must play' market, as was Australia, and we pretty much knew what to expect. As always, everything in Japan was well organized and efficient, with sold out shows but little opportunity to experience the 'real' Japan, except in Kyoto, where we at least got to see some ancient temples. Mostly it was hotels, trains, concerts, and lots of security. And, of course, the big Tokyo camera shops.

In Japan, Stewart bought a video camera to document events, Andy had various still cameras, and I stocked up on both. Always in promotion mode, I hired a small film crew to tag along with us to make a TV documentary. The BBC in London was interested, and sent along its top music commentator, Annie Nightingale, to interview the band at the various stops. They were already on a high from their UK success and were prone to pulling pranks and having fun, so throw a film crew into the mix and you should get some great, entertaining stuff. The world would see the sense of humor in the band, the intellect—and, let's face it, they were not shy.

As a manager, I always assumed part of my job was helping to create image, glamor, excitement—to feed the fans and the clamoring media. That meant taking advantage of every opportunity for photos and film incidents that would naturally occur. It also meant creating them whenever I could. For the band's first world tour, I tried to find unique concert venues that would provide unique visual images and might even give added historical importance to the band. The Police were always game—I could think crazy and probably get away with it.

Japan was pretty straightforward. Next came Hong Kong. It was my first time in the city and, as expected, the band got into the local scene, enjoying the restaurants and the local garb. All those cameras we had stocked up on in Tokyo started coming in handy. The band's show there was not in a huge concert hall, but it worked on film and, as it happened, it created an opportunity for a satellite broadcast back to the BRIT Awards in London. Annie Nightingale went into the band's dressing room after the show to present them with the 'Album Of The Year' award for *Regatta De Blanc*. It was the perfect kind of promotional stunt—a big award and a band in an exotic locale to receive it.

I didn't attend any of the shows in New Zealand or Australia, as I needed to work on organizing the more difficult shows to follow, which would really elevate the uniqueness of what we hoped to film. I had hired documentary-maker Derek Burbidge to film what was to become our 'Police Around The World' concept. Japan and Hong Kong were interesting places, but bands had been there before. The film needed something completely unusual, with great imagery. Where could be more appropriate than India and Egypt?

The problem was there had never been a rock concert in India, and only one that I knew of in Egypt. I didn't know any promoters in either country, and no one else I knew did either.

While The Police were in Australia, I went to London, to see if the British Arts Council could help. The council had been set up to promote British arts around the world, but it had never sent a rock band to India, so all the staff there could do was recommend I meet up with their counterparts in Bombay. The council in Bombay had no idea where to start, but they thought there might be one group crazy enough to help. They put me in touch with the Time & Talents Club, the most unlikely group of promoters that I had ever come across—or likely ever will come across again.

The Time & Talents Club was a group of little old Parsi ladies who were the wives of affluent Parsis in the city who ran charities and cultural events around Bombay. The following quote, from a recent article by Kunal Vijayakar in the *Hindustan Times*, describes the group so well that I had to include it:

> Goolu, Siloo, Sheroo, Dolly, Polly, Jeroo, Aloo. These names sound like they come from another world. You could actually imagine all of them sitting around cups of tea, Swiss rolls and banoffee pies or maybe chutney sandwiches and lemonade, cut glasses covered with doilies, counting out the threads of a silk cross-stitch pattern for the All Parsi Crochet Society. Frail powdered ladies with their pearls furiously swaying as they gingerly fox-trotted to the strains of 'The Isle Of Capri.' And you'd be half right. These are the ladies of the Time & Talents Club, and if I may say so, the pick of Bombay high society of the day.

At our first meeting, they were delightful, enthusiastic, and quite taken with the idea of promoting the first rock concert ever in India. They had never promoted any kind of concert before, let alone a rock concert, but they were keen to take it on and saw it as a great way to raise money for their charities. They were all in their sixties, and they were sweet and keen to the point I felt like I might be throwing them into the lion's den. They had no idea what a rock concert could entail. But I liked them, and they quickly made me comfortable that they had the right contacts to pull this off.

The only suitable venue we could find was the open-air Rang Bavan, which had a capacity of 3,500, but the public-address system was tiny. The ladies were used to quiet and sedate events, not the volume The Police played at. What was needed was speaker cabinets and power amplifiers big enough for a rock show. Their technician came up with the idea that if I could bring the speakers with me from London on my next trip, he could get a team of expert carpenters to build the cabinets to put the speakers in. After working out the details, I agreed. There was no other option anyway—apparently, there was no other PA system big enough for the concert anywhere in the country.

Meanwhile, the Time & Talents ladies showed me around the city and set me up at the Taj Mahal hotel. When I told them of my plans to film the band as Maharajas, they arranged for the costumes, complete with swords, turbans, and fancy coats. During this process, I learned that Parsis were a Persian Zoroastrian sect, different from Hindus or Muslims. When someone died, they put the body on a high platform called the Tower Of Death, where vultures would feed on the flesh. Once the bones were bleached by the sun, they were pushed into a circular opening in the center. The idea was *back to the earth from whence they came*, or something like that. It sounded a bit primitive to me, but it was an interesting take on death from a bunch of nice little old ladies. The Cramps would have loved it.

Driving around Bombay was a trip. There were beautiful buildings that had obviously seen better days, and streets teeming with people. Poverty next door to riches in a cacophony of confusion. At each stop light, children beggars would come up to the car for money. The Time & Talents ladies scolded me for considering giving money to one young beggar girl on the street. They told me the child had been purposefully maimed to gain sympathy, and giving money would only encourage the practice.

The last Police concert in Australia was on March 23. The band flew to Bombay the following day. The hotel I booked was the famous Bombay Taj Mahal Palace, and you could not get a better experience of Raj-era India than that—five stars, super service, great food. I arranged for the Maharaja suite to film in, as it had all the trappings of the visuals I imagined for the film. Playing in places no one else had played in was a good story, but if a photo is worth a thousand words, then showing the band looking like Maharajas would sell 'exotic' in overload. Of course, when we set up, there was no prodding necessary—the band all got into it, the film crew got everything on film, and I snapped away as fast as my cameras would let me.

The show itself was chaotic to say the least. As the audience had never witnessed a rock concert, when the band started soundcheck they all thought the show had started and fought to get in. Luckily, the show had sold out in advance, and the Time & Talents Club made a nice profit for their charities, but the capacity of 3,500 ended up at over 5,000, as fans came over the walls and broke down the gates to get in. The local police tried to stop the throng but had to give up. The roped-off area in the front for the little old ladies was soon swamped with adoring fans. I'd warned them, but no one ever listens until they see it for themselves.

In many respects, it was chaos, but The Police put on a hell of a show, and it was an emotional experience for everyone. Some people in the audience seemed absolutely delirious with emotion. The crew and I spent our time trying to keep it all together, so we didn't get to appreciate the event until it was all over.

Some years later, I learned that my first management act, Wishbone Ash, had performed a show in Bombay three years later, and had used the very same PA system that the Time & Talents Club and I organized. It seems we left our mark on Bombay rock'n'roll concerts well after that one crazy Police show.

§

The show after Bombay was in Cairo, at the American University, on Saturday, March 28. I left India ahead of some of the band to make sure everything was in order at the next step. I had met up with my 'fixit man,' who I'd arranged on my first trip to Cairo a month earlier, on my way to Bombay. Ahmed was the typical Egyptian in a secondhand suit that did not quite fit, but he had the suitable hustler instinct, so he seemed like the right man for the job.

When The Police's equipment arrived from Bombay, Ahmed and I went to pick it up at excess baggage, thinking everything was cool. Except there was no one there, and no equipment. We went to the freight section and were told that the equipment was there, but it couldn't be released as it was a Friday, and there would be no inspectors there to clear it until Monday. That the show was the next day didn't seem to matter to them.

Ahmed, figuring his fixit gig was over, said there was nothing to do— unless I knew some big shot in the government.

'I know Husan Tohami,' I said. 'Do you think he could help?'

Husan Tohami!? Ahmed's eyes grew wide with incredulity. 'You know ziss man? He is a god—he is vice prime minister of Egypt!'

I asked if he could get him on the phone, and, sure enough, he did.

Husan had been our next-door neighbor when my family lived in Ma'adi. After pleasantries—*how's your father, how's your mother*—the vice prime minister asked what I needed. I explained our predicament, and within minutes two carloads of gendarmes arrived, clapped their hands, and waved the equipment through. It was like magic. When I told the band, I could not help but add, 'Now that's what I call management!'

On the surface, playing the show was what we were there for, but in reality I wanted the photos and the film footage. Egypt was not a concert market nor a record buying market, so it was of very little (if any) commercial interest for a musical artist's business. But Egypt had super-visual and iconic images. I pictured Sting as Lawrence Of Arabia, galloping across the desert, with the pyramids in the background and the band on camels. Egypt could be a feast for the eyes, and it would look great on the documentary film. And that's what we got.

As a pure concert, the Cairo show was a comedy of errors. I first went to Cairo in early March, to reconnoiter the situation. I checked if there were spotlights, and, sure enough, there was one on each side of the theatre balcony and a central one in the back. The stage was big enough, and it had proper electricity, so all looked in order. What I did not think to do—and knowing Cairo like I did, I should have known better—was to look *inside* the spotlights, to see if there were any bulbs. On the day of the show, when I asked the electrician to turn on the spotlights, he just looked at me and said he couldn't. Why? There were no light bulbs in them.

'Well, get some,' I said.

'They have to be ordered from Europe.'

We ended up having to use the 'sun guns' the film crew had to make the band visible to the audience. But at least we had electricity.

Knowing rock'n'roll crowds, and having just seen what had happened in India, I warned the notables who had reserved seats in the front that it was a bad idea to sit there. I was rebuffed, of course. Then, almost from the beginning of the show, the area was rushed, the notables crushed. One man trying to protect his wife caught the attention of Sting, who put his foot out to try to stop the man pushing back some excited audience member. This caused a scene at the side of the stage, where all the policemen were stationed. Ahmed frantically told me Sting had just kicked Cairo's chief of police, and he was surely going to jail. I had to do something—quick.

I gestured to Sting, who ignored me, so I had to go onstage and whisper in his ear. 'You just kicked the chief of police and you definitely don't want to go to a Cairo jail, so you will need to apologize when you come offstage.'

Sting finished the song and then answered me: 'No.' I knew Sting, and this was a definite no.

By this time, the chief of police was at the side of the stage with a coterie of uniformed policemen, waiting to grab Sting at any moment. Just before the band reached their last number, I went onstage and said to Sting, 'Let me do the talking, and when I nod at you, just nod in agreement. Do it, or you are going to be in jail tonight.'

Sting agreed, and after the encore he was surrounded. I did all the fast talking I could, and then looked to Sting, who nodded in the affirmative, as he was prepared to do.

The chief of police looked at me and said, 'I do not accept that rude man, but you, a gentleman, I accept your apology.' He turned and left the stage. I was stunned that whatever I did seemed to have worked, and Sting was saved from an experience he definitely did not want to go through.

Even as a comedy of errors, the Cairo show was a historic moment, and it delivered the great photos and film footage I had hoped for. It also showed how well regarded my father was within the Egyptian government.

I said goodbye to Ahmed, who had come through for us, and we were off to Greece for another first. The Athens show on March 30 would be the first rock concert in the country since The Rolling Stones played there ten years earlier, before the generals took over the country. The city had its share of iconic scenery, but the main image was the number of police officers everywhere. There was an army of them, as if they were expecting riots or a revolution.

Greece provided a perfect end to the documentary film, as the band's next shows were in the more normal touring countries of Europe, whereas here The Police had made history: they had opened up Greece to rock'n'roll once again.

I had tons of photographs from those exotic places, too, and of course I did not waste them. In April, I made a deal with a British publisher to launch a monthly magazine called *The Official Police File*. The first issue went on sale in May; we kept it going until December of 1981, reaching a peak circulation of seventy thousand copies. I supplied most of the photos.

Meanwhile, The Police continued to tour all year, with many more notable moments to come. One of the bigger shows took place in Fréjus, France, and also featured Skafish and The Cramps. It was filmed for *Urgh! A Music War*. That was the show where Sting sent out his bodyguard, Larry, to remove a heckler from the audience. In July, there was the huge Milton Keynes Bowl gig in England, where I apparently pissed off Squeeze—and which shortly thereafter led to Jools Holland quitting the group.

Later in the year came the first Police concert in Mexico City, at the Grand Salon of the Hotel de Mexico. That was a scary gig—the audience of several thousand began bouncing up and down, and the floor did the same. Aware of Mexico's loose building codes, I was sure the floor would give way. I tried to get the promoter to do something, but he just looked at me with a helpless expression. That audience was not going to listen to anyone. That was Mexico for you.

Then came Argentina, where again, just like in Greece, the main concert visuals were of the local police pushing back the enthusiastic crowds. This was the time that the 'generals' were the government—the era of 'The Disappeared.' One does not have a lot of power in a police state, and the last thing you want to do is rub the police up the wrong way. As the audience surged forward, policemen would charge with the flats of their machetes raised, whacking at the legs of the crowd. As the crowd retreated, so did the police; then the audience would surge forward again, and the police would go whacking again. It was madness.

This time it was Andy's turn to run afoul of the authorities as he kicked a policeman who got close to the stage, and again I was forced to do some fast-talking management to keep him out of jail. In a country like Argentina, managing a band of strong individuals like The Police was a full-time job.

Argentina had its good points as well. The food was great, and the show did afford more opportunities for some iconic, image-enhancing photography, though this time it was more Stewart than anyone else. The Gaucho on horseback was the perfect image for him, as he was a fine horseman and polo player.

Finally, we celebrated the end of the year in London, in a huge tent we set up on Tooting Bec Common on December 21. Jools Holland played too, and, as something different, I booked comedian and magician Tommy Cooper to perform during intermission. Tommy was an icon of British comedy, but his act worked best on a TV screen, not on a huge stage, where his comedic nuances would be missed. The younger audience members didn't get him, and as he left the stage, he looked at me and said, 'After this, everything will be a comeback.'

⌒

From 1981 onward, the concerts The Police played got bigger and bigger, with sellout shows at places like Madison Square Garden in New York and Wembley Arena in London. When venues were not big enough, we just did multiple shows in the same venue. More followed: the band's first Grammy Awards in the USA, another BRIT Award (for 'Best British Group'), and finally #1 records in the USA, with 'Every Breath You Take' and the *Synchronicity* album. It seemed an accepted fact that The Police were the biggest band in the world. I don't know if that was factually true or not, but for sure they got the most publicity. They were everywhere— print media, TV, radio. Doors were open.

The first super-big concert The Police did in the USA was the Us Festival in Southern California on September 3, 1982. It was financed by Steve Wozniak, who had recently sold his share of Apple Computer and decided to spend some of it on a three-day rock festival. He brought in veteran San Francisco promoter Bill Graham to run it.

As I was supplying the headliner, I could also influence who else would be on the bill. I said yes to The B52's, Talking Heads, Ramones, and Gang Of Four. Oingo Boingo and English Beat came from IRS Records. The only act I said no to was Elvis Costello, but this was nothing to do with Elvis: it was entirely due to his manager Jake Riviera, who had been rude to me, to Squeeze, and to Jerry Moss. He'd crossed a line, and I did not want him on the same stage as me. This was one of those times where there had to be consequences for someone who went out of his way to be a prick.

In Rock'n'Roll World, Bill Graham was considered a big deal. So, I expected him to call to get me to change my mind. I didn't. Then Elvis's agent from CAA called to do the same. Again I said no. I actually said, 'If Riviera is there, The Police won't be.' I guess this created an impression with Bill Graham, because just before Oingo Boingo went on stage, Graham started yelling at me for no reason I could make out—'You Copelands think you are God!'—and stormed off the stage.

I turned to one of his staff to ask, 'What the hell is Bill angry about?'

The answer was, 'Don't worry about it—it's just Bill being Bill.'

The rest of the concert went well, except the temperature was hot—real hot: 110°F. Four hundred thousand people attended, and Woz was there the whole time, enjoying every minute of it.

ℰℛ

The Police's Shea Stadium concert on August 18, 1983, was a big deal for all of us. The Beatles had made the ballpark famous as a music venue, and for every other band ever since, playing there was like climbing to the top of Mount Everest. Only a few had done it, and now it was the turn of The Police. I was told the tickets had sold out in eight minutes; another report said five hours, but whatever the truth was, all seventy thousand tickets sold out quickly. It was a pinnacle of achievement.

At one point I was standing guard at the bottom of the stairs leading to the stage before The Police were to go on. The fire marshal was already hassling me about the number of people on the stage. Everyone and their mother was trying to get up there. The manager of Joan Jett, who had opened the show earlier, came walking up to me. Along with him came what looked like a bodyguard. I knew what he wanted, and sure enough he asked if Joan and her band could go onstage.

As politely as I could, I said there was no room: the fire marshal was there, and we were at our limit. He said he understood, but if there was anything I could do . . .

As he walked away, the bodyguard came up to me to whisper in my ear, 'I know you will take care of it.' He shook my hand as he said it and handed me a twenty-dollar bill. I just got tipped!

Security took over my position, and I went to get the group from the dressing room. As I entered the dressing room, I said, 'You won't believe what just happened, I got tipped twenty bucks to put Joan Jett onstage!' I thought it was extremely funny and waved the twenty-dollar bill.

'Where's our share?' they immediately asked.

Believe it or not, I doled out five dollars to each of them.

'This is great,' Andy said. 'It's like I am actually being paid for this gig.'

Soon after that, we all got onstage, and I waited to introduce the band. Given the go ahead as I walked out, flash bulbs started going off, and as I started the announcement, the place went berserk. The volume, the flash bulbs going off everywhere—it was intense. The roar was so deafening that I went to the side of the stage trembling. I could only think if my one minute had done that to me, imagine what an hour and a half would do to the group. I have introduced some big shows before, but never have I experienced one like that, nor will I likely ever do one again.

%

The band's show at the Miami Orange Bowl on October 28, 1983, was a similar setup in a huge open-air stadium. Before The Police went on, a security man came up to me saying one of my friends was at the backstage entrance saying there should be tickets for him. I had no idea who that might be. I walked to the entrance, and there I saw a big Rolls-Royce car with a couple of posh-looking guys and their girlfriends. When I asked them what they wanted, Lord Balfa-something said he was a good personal friend of Miles Copeland's, and Miles was to have arranged tickets for him.

'You spoke to Miles Copeland?' I said. 'And when did you do that?'

In a very posh English accent, he told me he had just spoken to Miles Copeland earlier that day, and we'd had dinner the night before, and it's all been arranged. That really pissed me off.

'I am Miles Copeland,' I said, 'and I don't know who the fuck you are, nor have I ever spoken to you.' He looked at me with a blank face, but before he could say anything, I added, 'If you want to get in, it will cost you each $100, and I will put you in the shit seats behind the stage where you won't see much. You, who are driving a Rolls-Royce, and if you think you should get in free when we have thousands in a sold-out stadium who have paid their hard-earned cash for tickets, you are mistaken. So, if you want in, pay up.'

An ashen-faced Lord Something was so embarrassed he gave me $400, and I put him in the shit seats, as promised. I then went into the band's dressing room to tell them the story.

'The nerve of some people—and the fucker was driving a Rolls-Royce!'

The band put on their last bits of clothing, then they came up to me and said, 'OK, let's have our share,' and I gave each of them $100. Then they headed to the stage, to another fifty thousand screaming fans.

ↄↄ

A couple of weeks later, when the tour reached Birmingham, Alabama, I went to see my father's brother, who we knew as Uncle Hunter. He was quite different from my father. He had a physique more like mine, but unlike me he had gone through bouts of drink. In fact, by now, he was an active member of Alcoholics Anonymous.

My father had always talked glowingly of his brother as the tough guy in the family who would come to his defense when he was being picked on. He saw himself, it seems, as the brainy weakling. I would hear stories of Hunter when they were young—how Hunter would dress up in sissy clothes and go to a rough part of town, hoping to be picked on by some bully. Then Hunter would beat the hell out of the bully. Then there was the time he was stopped late at night by a policeman for speeding, and the cop asked, 'Have you been drinking?' and his answer was, 'Of course I've been drinking, it's three in the morning!'

Anyway, Hunter's third wife had a seventeen-year-old daughter called Courtney Cox. During family conversations, Courtney told me she was hoping to become a model, so I volunteered to help get her started with some contacts I had at the Ford Modeling Agency in New York.

At the Ford agency they were worried about her height, but they said they'd put her in the teen division and see what they could come up with. I rewarded them with tickets to an upcoming Police concert. Ford delivered various jobs, including the famous video dancing with Bruce Springsteen, and Courtney then took a job as receptionist for Ian's booking agency, FBI. Ian then hired an agent who had connections in the movie business, and eventually Courtney was taken on by one of the big movie agencies in Los Angeles. From there, of course, she ended up as one of the stars of *Friends*, and she became super-famous.

Years later, when my brother Ian was dying of cancer, Courtney was there to help with the huge hospital bills. It is always nice to see when a big star is there to help a person who has helped them on the way up.

∽

There were many more big shows to come with The Police, and screaming fans became commonplace—to the point where one could easily lose perspective. Thankfully, they were not a drug band, and we were all old enough to take things in stride. Still, those were a crazy five years, and they're hard to describe unless you lived them.

By 1985, the steam must have been running out for Sting, and he began thinking about a solo career. Personally, I had always hoped for one last tour of The Police to really put icing on the cake. Just one more tour would have done it for me. Alas, it was not to be.

CHAPTER 16

BEAUTY AND
THE BEAT

In the first few years of the 80s, my record businesses in the UK and the USA were pretty separate from each other—but both were growing. In the UK, I hired a sales guy for Faulty Products to sell acts like The Cramps on Illegal Records, and acts we couldn't get A&M interested in. We also needed a stock guy in the warehouse to help. One night I went to some gig at a club and came across Steve Tannett, the guitarist who had been in Menace. When he told me he was now a forklift operator in some warehouse, bored out of his mind, I said, 'Come work for me in my warehouse—but I don't have a forklift.' So, Steve became the Faulty Products stock boy.

A few weeks later, Steve came up to my office and said, 'Your sales guy is passed out on the floor, and I think he slept there last night.' We went down and, sure enough, there was a passed out, probably drugged guy on the floor. Steve and I picked him up and put him out in the street and closed the door. I then turned to Steve and said, 'You are now the head of sales.'

Eventually, Steve rose to become the managing director of IRS Records in London. At one point he came to me saying he wanted to sign a band to the label. By then I trusted his taste, so I replied, 'If it's cheap, go ahead.' It was The Alarm, who ended up recording three albums for IRS. They were a great band who always seemed on the verge of making it big but never quite got there.

IRS added staff in the USA as well in 1981, ending up with a total of six. Having learned from previous label deals where all the promotion was handled by the distributor or mother company, like RCA did for BTM records, I knew that if IRS was going to succeed as a full-fledged record company, it must have at least some of its own staff to sell and promote its records, and not rely totally on the mother company/distributor, which in the case of IRS was initially A&M. This would especially be true when IRS was releasing records that would most likely be considered 'leftfield' and easily neglected by a mainstream company like A&M.

So, when A&M's RCA distribution arm eliminated its 'singles sales' staff on the West Coast, we were quick to pick up on the best people they might have let go. That brought Barbara Bolan over to IRS to become our first National Sales Director in March 1981. (Barbara continued in that position up to 1995, when she went to head the newly launched USA Virgin Records sales team; she then re-joined me in 2002, when I launched Ark 21 Records.) We still depended on A&M Records, but with Barbara on sales and Michael Plen on radio, we had the makings of our own team to work records, even if A&M chose not to.

As IRS moved into its second year, we released a second Cramps album, *Psychedelic Jungle*; The Payolas from Canada; Magazine, Alternative TV, and Henry Bedowsky from the UK; and Wall Of Voodoo and The Fleshtones from the USA. There were still no hits of the kind Jerry Moss and the A&M people could relate to, but the good news was that the second-year deadline that Jerry had set for IRS passed with no invitation to his office. I don't know if it was the huge success of The Police around the world or that IRS was beginning to show signs of success, but whatever the reason it looked like IRS was given rope for at least a while longer.

One thing's for sure: IRS Records was becoming known as *the* home of the new wave carving out a unique niche for itself in the USA. At least the underground was taking us seriously, which brought all sorts of strange acts who couldn't get a deal elsewhere to our door. Perhaps the most iconic musically, as well as business-wise, was The Cramps.

In my entire fifty years in the music business, I got into a fist fight only once. It was at a Cramps concert at Irving Plaza in New York City, August 18, 1979. The band were in the middle of performing, in their usual crazed, manic style, 'Human Fly,' which penetrated everyone—and me as well. Some jerk in front of me pissed me off dancing wildly and kept bumping into me, so I hauled off and whacked him, and he went to the ground. It was the music that did it. That was The Cramps. They could make anyone crazy.

I could easily say I loved The Cramps. Not as people, as they were not the kind you could get to know. There was the music, but more than that it was the image, posters, stage antics, and the general craziness all combined together that made The Cramps. One of the best descriptions of them I ever saw was this, from the Concord publishing website: 'With their unique image and fiendish brew of humorous retro-horror, sci-fi, B-movie lyrics mixed with their swampy, trashy, primitive stomps and banshee howls, The Cramps have influenced and inspired countless other bands in the garage, punk, rockabilly revival and early goth-rock genres.'

The problem was that The Cramps were *so* underground that there was no way I was ever going to develop a realistic business relationship with them. They trusted no one, especially someone as straight as me. Perhaps if I had covered my body in tattoos and cut my hair into a mohawk and had bones sticking out of my nostrils, they might have looked at me as someone they could relate to. But I suspect even then, all they would think was that I was an asshole. To them, I was the record company, and therefore I was automatically on the opposite side from them. It didn't matter that I helped set up their gear and drove them to gigs and put them on major shows with The Police and other big bands I worked with. I took them to Europe and released their records there. I put them up in my house in London. I would always be the enemy. And they could never believe that I liked their music, or them, or both. I did not take it personally as the more I dealt with them, the more I realized they saw everyone as the enemy.

The Cramps were led by Lux Interior (vocals), who had a death wish and descended into a wild animal persona at every show. He was not play-acting, and there was no hint of a twinkle in his eye, as I had seen in Johnny Rotten when I promoted the Sex Pistols. Lux was seriously real and seriously demented. He usually ripped off his shirt, dripping in sweat, his black leather trousers hanging a bit too low, drank beer from his shoe, and jammed the microphone into his mouth, mumbling the lyrics and screams. Sometimes he stripped down to his black speedo underpants.

Inevitably he jumped into the audience, who were usually as crazed as he was. The weird thing was, the more hostile the audience was, the more likely he was to jump into them.

One night when The Cramps were supporting The Police in Sheffield, England, the audience wanted to kill him, and what did he do? He jumped right into the audience, and it was at least a six-foot drop. Two security guys and I rushed to pull him out. Did he say thank you for saving him from certain death? He was back onstage, crazy as ever. Meanwhile, his wife, lead guitarist Ivy Rorschach (also known as Poison Ivy), played on expressionless and never said a word. Bryan Gregory on bass had long black-and-white locks all combed to one side of his head and usually some sort of fur for pants. The drummer, Nick Knox, dressed in black and always seemed to be pissed off.

For IRS Records, The Cramps were the ultimate underground act, and I was proud we had them on the label as they represented much of what we stood for. We released *Songs The Lord Taught Us*, *Psychedelic Jungle*, *Gravest Hits*, and various singles. 'Garbage Man' and 'Human Fly' were favorites. In England, they were on my Illegal Records label. I brought them to England for the first time, and then took them into Europe; put them on major shows, filmed them for *Urgh! A Music War*. I have no doubt that IRS was the only record company that would last through several albums with them. We made it to 1984, which was pretty good going.

The year before, I got a call from a lawyer who said he represented the group and was going to sue IRS Records for all sorts of supposed financial misdeeds. He was so threatening about things he did not seem fully aware of that I decided to go and meet him in his office to see what all the fuss was about. He had a small office on Sunset Boulevard, and almost as soon as I sat down to start the conversation, he announced he was going make his *name* by 'suing Miles Copeland.' It was kind of flattering, but also crazy, and more about him than any problem with The Cramps. I can't remember much of the meeting except leaving thinking he wouldn't last long with The Cramps. Most lawyers didn't. Whatever he was going to sue me or IRS for, he didn't. If he made a name for himself, I can't remember it.

Back in August 1980, I had tried to get them a lawyer I had met who represented Wall Of Voodoo. If he could deal with the Voodoo guys, I thought, perhaps he could deal with The Cramps. I invited him to see them perform in Santa Monica, for the *Urgh* filming, and I stood with him at the side of the stage while The Cramps performed. Lux had already begun his craziness—drinking from his shoe, ripping off his shirt—but the lawyer seemed OK. Then the drummer got angry at something and started yelling at the road crew. Then he threw his drumsticks, then a drum at some hapless roadie, and the lawyer looked at me and said, 'These people are horrible.' He didn't take on the band.

In that same year, Bryan Gregory left the group, and rumors started to circulate that he had taken up satanism. I have no idea if that was true, but one night while I was staying at a cheap hotel on Sunset Boulevard, in walking distance of A&M Records, Bryan came to see me with his girlfriend, Andrella. The front desk called to say I had someone to see me, so I went to the reception office to see who it was. Bryan was even weirder than usual—he had fur actually glued to his legs now, just like a satyr, and Andrella looked right out of the Addams Family: jet black long hair, white-white face, and long dress down to her ankles. They had a proposition for me, so we went back to my room to discuss. It turned out it was Bryan's new group: he wanted to know if I would sign them. I said get me a tape and we'll see.

The next day, I went to the small IRS office at A&M, and that night I went back to the hotel. I tried my key to the room and it didn't work, which was strange, because I had paid for the room in advance. At the front desk I saw my suitcase behind the counter.

'Hey,' I said, 'what is my stuff doing there, and why does my key not work?'

The clerk was a young guy, twenty-five-ish, and he looked embarrassed. 'We don't want your kind here.'

My kind? I was in my usual straight garb, nothing strange at all. As I complained, he just repeated, 'We don't want you here.' Finally, he let on that it was due to my 'friends' that had visited me the night before. The Cramps had gotten me kicked out of that shitty hotel!

That made me realize that The Cramps must have gone through life getting weird looks, being thrown out of places, maybe even beat up, so no wonder they looked upon everyone as the enemy. When I went into restaurants with them to eat on tour, every time people stared. On one US tour, we were asked to leave a truck stop restaurant for no reason. It's not like it was a nice place—in fact, it was one of those backwater places that a hobo could have walked into and got served. But not The Cramps.

✧

In spite of our often-termed 'weird' acts, someone at A&M must have pitied us, stuck in the original small shed we'd been in since we launched the label. Now, with more staff, we were given a bigger office—an interesting pairing where we were to share a suite with The Carpenters, probably the least IRS-like act on the A&M label. I remember the look on Richard and Karen Carpenter's faces when they came into the reception area and saw The Cramps there. At least Ivy told Karen, 'I like your music.'

It was not long before I got the call from Gil Friesen, president of A&M: 'Tell your staff to refrain from drawing mustaches on the pictures of The Carpenters.' I got the feeling *he* thought it was funny, but The Carpenters were a big seller for A&M, and it was not cool to insult them.

Even by the start of that second year, it was evident that other record labels had still not woken up to the scene, and I was rarely seeing any competition to sign bands. That of course helped our most significant signing to date: on April Fool's Day, 1981, when I signed the Los Angeles all-girl band The Go-Go's.

I first heard of The Go-Go's via a single release they did in the UK with Stiff Records. Though I'd never heard the song, the name registered—if Stiff saw something in the band, there must be something there. My interest was piqued when I was in Los Angeles during late December 1980 and early January '81, a time when one could not escape from the buzz about how The Go-Go's were one of the area's hottest underground acts.

I went to see them at the Whisky A Go-Go on Sunset Boulevard at the beginning of the year. I liked the band: good songs enthusiastically played, fun energy. I also liked that they were not a bunch of models selling looks over music. They were real. The audience liked them too: the Whisky was bopping. That they were all women seemed eminently promotable to me, and a definite bonus. An all-female band who played their own instruments and wrote most of their own songs . . . what's not to like? For a guy always looking for a promotable hook, they were ideal. Apparently, what I liked was exactly why no other labels were interested, and why there were no other label A&R men at the show to compete with.

The band had tried to get a deal with other labels but had been rejected because they were all girls. At least that was the view of the five band members and their manager, Ginger Canzoneri. Belinda Carlisle was the singer, with Kathy Valentine on bass, Charlotte Caffey on lead guitar, Jane Wiedlin on rhythm guitar, and Gina Schock on drums.

Charlotte liked to say that IRS Records circa mid-1981 was the home of all the rejects and freaks other labels ran from. It was where you went if you couldn't get a 'real' record deal: 'People at the record labels were like, *We don't want to sign you, you're girls*—sexist, ridiculous nonsense. IRS Records was the right place because Miles Copeland was as crazy as we were.' Jane once said, 'Miles is like P.T. Barnum, or Colonel Tom Parker—he's eccentric, and smart and strange.' A quote from IRS staffer John Guarnieri gives a picture of the label at the time: 'The IRS roster was full of bastard children: The Cramps, Wazmo Nariz, Skafish . . . The Go-Go's and IRS, we were both underdogs. I remember Miles saying one day, As go The Go-Go's, so goes IRS.'

Signing to IRS was considered a risk for The Go-Go's, as the label was yet to prove it could deliver a hit for anyone, but the reality was they had nowhere else to go. IRS Records was the only label willing to take a risk on them.

Even so, when I offered the deal and thought we were set to draw up a contract, Ginger went off to see if any other label would now be interested, now that IRS was in the bag. None of them were. Ginger called a band meeting after the band's next LA show and told them that the only offer on the table was from IRS. She then brought the band in to meet the IRS staff, and the yin/yang effect seemed to work. Or, as Kathy Valentine later said, 'Their earnestness made for a nice balance to Miles's forceful bombast.'

Once the band had agreed to sign to IRS, I sat down with their lawyer and manager, both of whom were women, and worked out a deal that was my most expensive undertaking yet, but for the band it was well under what they expected. The good news of the meeting was that I had limited resources, so I could not go beyond a certain point in advances or royalties; and The Go-Go's had no other competing offers, so we both were forced to be reasonable. We quickly agreed a deal on that April Fool's Day, then went to dinner to celebrate at Kelbo's, a lowbrow Hawaiian barbecue joint on Pico Boulevard.

When it came time to plan the recording of the first Go-Go's album, neither the band nor the manager had strong feelings about a producer, so when I suggested Richard Gottehrer, no one objected. I then approached Richard, who I knew from the Climax Blues Band days at Sire Records, to see if he would produce them. I respected his work on the *Blondie* album more than his work with Climax, but most of all I knew him as a songwriter. I wanted someone who knew his way around a song, but who at the same time was not stuck in the old school. Richard was the only person I knew who seemed to tick both boxes.

Richard was not interested in producing them, however, so he said no at first. After a bit of verbal bullying, he agreed to see the band perform before a final decision, so I sent them to New York. They won him over. Then we fought over the budget, which ended up at $35,000. Needless to say, Richard complained that it was too low—and naturally went over budget. When he called me asking for another $7,500, I had to tell him I could only pay him what we had agreed. Luckily for him, the record sold well, and he was repaid from his producer royalties.

When Richard delivered the album, the band were shocked that it sounded too 'pop' and not punk enough. They were so upset they cried. What would all their contemporaries in the LA music scene think? I had had the same first impression, and I remember screaming at Richard that I had given him a punk group and he had given me back a pop group. The band pleaded with me to have the album remixed, but then, the more I listened to it, the more I thought it might work. After many listens, I made the decision to go with the record as Richard had delivered it. When I called him to tell him so, he asked if that meant I would cover the $7,500 of his own money he had spent on it. It didn't. IRS was still making no money to speak of, and I was still financing everything. Meanwhile, the band refused to speak to him—until, of course, the album was a hit. Then they realized that by slowing down the songs, he had allowed them to breath and become commercial. Richard was a real record producer in the true sense of the word.

Beauty And The Beat was released in June of 1981. MTV launched in August, and as that was one of the few places we knew we could be guaranteed exposure for The Go-Go's, a video was a priority. Luckily, there was a small budget left over from a Police video from the *Ghost In The Machine* album, and we used that to shoot the band's first video, 'Our Lips Are Sealed.' Framed around footage of the band in a convertible, it was a pretty minimal video, but it showed the fun and personality of the band, and it worked for MTV.

By Christmas, *Beauty And The Beat* was climbing the charts, eventually reaching #27 on *Billboard*, which all of us saw as a great achievement. Reaching the Top 30 on the first album was great news, and it proved to A&M that IRS Records was finally on to something. After hovering at #27, the album dropped back to #31, and it looked like that might be it. I then suggested to the band and Ginger Canzoneri that they open for The Police on the *Ghost In The Machine* tour, which was due to start at the Boston Gardens on January 15.

I thought it was perfect timing. The band thought I was crazy. With a Top 30 album, they said, they could now headline shows on their own and make more money. My pitch was simple:

> Why preach to the converted? Of course, you can headline and play to hundreds of adoring fans, but with The Police you can play to ten-to-twenty thousand each night who will discover you and give your album the chance to go even higher in the charts.

I was sure that the radio play The Go-Go's were getting would ensure that The Police's audience would be receptive to them. It would not be like Squeeze and The Tubes, or like the experience The Go-Go's had when they toured with Madness in the UK and found themselves pelted with spit and bottles. That had been a depressing experience all round, so the thought of playing with a super-popular headline act like The Police caused some serious trepidation.

The *Ghost In The Machine* album started January off at #2 in the charts, so The Police band were super-hot, but The Go-Go's were also all over the radio. I crossed my fingers that what seemed like the perfect billing would work, and it must have worked: the album started a steady climb from #22 to #20 to #11 to #9 to #3, and finally, on March 6, 1982, to #1!

While I can claim that talking the group into joining The Police on tour was big a factor in the success of *Beauty And The Beat*, the real credit should go to Michael Plen, who fought the battle at radio from the beginning with the single release of 'Our Lips Are Sealed' in June 1981 all the way through to the #2 single position of 'We Got The Beat' and the album at #1 on March 6. It was a constant and dogged fight all the way, and it took someone with the never-give-up attitude that Michael had.

The initial strategy was to introduce the band to radio with 'Our Lips Are Sealed,' then follow up with what we all thought was the bigger hit, 'We Got The Beat.' Michael was a bulldog on both singles. It was like a steamroller going downhill—it was slow and steady, but nothing would stop it.

The plan worked like this: Michael would represent IRS and pitch the song to elicit the support of the large A&M radio team. As the single rose in popularity, the A&M team were all on it, getting radio stations to add it to their playlists and watching it climb the charts. When the single failed to get enough new stations in one week, A&M's head of radio assumed that it was over and pulled his team off of it, leaving Michael as the only radio man remaining to fight for it.

Michael would battle to get more stations the next week, and at the next meeting he convinced the A&M team there was still life in the single, and they would be back on it for the next week. That kept happening, over and over. As Michael tells it:

Radio perceived them as a novelty act because they were a girl band. American Airlines offered a deal: You could travel for sixty days, as long as you connected on flights, for $600. So, I bought a ticket and went from city to city, trying to convince radio stations to play The Go-Go's. My nickname is 'The Attack Hamster.' If I think a song has hit potential, I'll be a pest, the way a hamster will jump on your leg and you're like, 'All right, we'll play your record, get off me.'

We used to joke that radio stations added the record just to get Michael out of the building—and kept playing it to keep him from coming back. True or not, he delivered the group's #1—the first female group #1 album ever, and also my personal first #1, as well as the first for IRS Records. Also, on that day The Police's *Ghost In The Machine* was #6 in the same chart, having come down from #2 at the beginning of January. That was a pretty good week for me personally.

When the #1 happened, The Go-Go's were still on tour with The Police, and Sting graciously came into their dressing room with a bottle of champagne to celebrate. The Police, by agreeing to put The Go-Go's on their tour, also had a hand in the success. For me, as the manager of one happening band and the record company for another, it was huge—perhaps the biggest 'we are all in this together' feeling I would ever have. It was a win in so many ways. Thinking about it now, this is the week when Bill Graham saying 'You Copelands think you are God!' might have applied.

The #1 chart position was a high point for a number of reasons. It was a history-making achievement, yet to be broken: the first time an all-female group had achieved a #1 album in the USA, and they did it by playing all the instruments and writing all the songs. That made it a landmark beyond me—it was a landmark in the history of music. It validated the creation of IRS Records and my faith in the new generation of music that it was created for. (In the coming years, The Police would also hit #1, as would Fine Young Cannibals.) It validated Jerry Moss's belief in me and what I and my IRS team were doing. It validated my brother Ian and his FBI agency, who booked both The Go-Go's and The Police. It made the whole ball of wax seem worthwhile.

❧

In August 1982, The Go-Go's were on the front of *Rolling Stone* magazine. A few days later, the group's second album, *Vacation*, was released. It rose to #8 and was the band's only album to enter the UK charts, while the title track gave them another US Top 10 hit. In 1984, the third album, *Talk Show*, got to #18, and the single 'Head Over Heels' got to #11.

Unfortunately for IRS, The Go-Go's were like a shooting star that shone bright on the first album and went slowly downhill over the next two. It's hard for any band to follow such a quick success. Now add to the pressure of trying to make it, the pressure of trying to keep it, with all eyes watching you, and it's no surprise that they broke up in 1985. From #1, the only way is down. I also did not realize that from very early on, some of the band had drug problems. I even learned things from the documentary they did in 2020. I did know about Gina and how angry she got at the financial dealings of the band, but I never knew about Charlotte Caffey's problems with drugs.

The truth is that there is an inbuilt and sort of unspoken separation between artist and record company. At the beginning of the relationship, up until the first album went to #1, there was a kind of comradeship between band, manager, and label. Once the band got 'big,' I found Ginger more difficult; she wanted to appear to be making the decisions on her own, not with the record company. In effect, she wanted to prove her independence by doing the opposite of what I might recommend. I had to learn to tell her one thing, hoping she would object and do the opposite thing—which was what I actually wanted her to do in the first place. It was silly to have to think like that.

In the end, Ginger quit, and the band went to Irving Azoff's Front Line Management. The problem there was that Irving himself then left to become the head of MCA records, and the person who ended up as manager was really an accountant and not prepared to handle the internal problems that were developing within the group. As the record company, I was not aware of them, and I did not really see the members except when I went into the studio. On one occasion, I went to hear their latest recordings and Charlotte vomited all over me. That told me she was drinking too much; I didn't know it was more than that.

It might have been different if I was with them all the time, or at least in Los Angeles much more than I was. That was not possible, though: The Police, The Bangles, Jools Holland, and the other bands I was working with were all over the world, so I was all over the world as well. By comparison, The Police were older and had more life experience than The Go-Go's. 'Thank God this didn't happen to us when we were much younger,' Sting once said.

Typically, when a band goes from zero to super-seller, the band's lawyer wants to renegotiate the contract to get more money, more royalties, and anything else they can finagle. To create an atmosphere to make the label give more, there are accusations of improper accounting, and it all ends up in a legal battle. This happened with The Go-Go's. It was disheartening, but that's the price of doing business. When The Police broke big, we renegotiated their record deal, too, but never in a way that was threatening. My lawyer, Allen Grubman, had adopted a policy of saying, 'You don't have to hold back, as we are not trying to get off the label. Just pay us exactly what we ask for—*and no more*—and it's all good.' It was a strategy that I know Jerry Moss responded well to.

The Go-Go's lawyer adopted a more common strategy along the lines of: *We are going to fuck you so you'd better pay up*, and *Whatever you agree to, we are going to ask for more*. The result, of course, was that we held back. The lawyer had the band sue IRS, and IRS had to respond by suing the band. It was messy and stupid, and it sullied our success together. Then Belinda Carlisle called me on the phone personally and set up a meeting between me and the band, without lawyers and managers, and we settled all the issues. The band were paid what they were owed, contract improvements were agreed, and we all moved on. I can't remember the actual amount, but according to Kathy Valentine's book it was a check for one million dollars.

As time went by, I did become aware that disputes were building within the band. Charlotte, who had written the biggest hits and most of the songs, made a million dollars more than Gina Shock, the band's drummer. Most bands arrive at some accommodation on publishing, but The Go-Go's had not done so, and it was becoming an issue that would later lead to ugly lawsuits and eventually the band's breakup. One of the first things to happen in this situation is that the less-talented songwriters demand their songs be put on the albums, so they too can earn publishing royalties. This means that some good songs are not recorded, just to accommodate the lesser writers in the group.

Then there was another problem. By the time of the third album, Jane Wiedlin wanted to sing several songs as the lead singer. The band had a fairly rigid view that Belinda was the singer, and that's that. Jane

MILES A. COPELAND III

became disenchanted and finally quit the group. No one realized back then, though, that Jane was part of the glue that made The Go-Go's work, and her leaving loosened that glue.

All of this should have been dealt with by the management (or they should at least have let the record company know about it so we could help). It was not. This is one of the sad realities of the record business: all too often, the record company is looked upon as the enemy, when in fact the roles of artist, manager, and record company are intertwined.

As years passed, The Go-Go's came to appreciate what they had among themselves; animosities were healed, and the band reformed. They also came to appreciate the role I and IRS Records played in their success. In 2019, they asked me to participate in The Go-Go's documentary film, and of course my answer was *yes*. When I asked them to participate in the IRS documentary *We Were Once Rebels* in 2020, they answered the same.

ABOVE The Copeland siblings in Cairo, 1953: Ian, Stewart, Lennie, and me.

RIGHT My parents, Lorraine and Miles Copeland.

ABOVE In Damascus, aged five, with a monkey man.

RIGHT At Step Pyramid, Egypt, aged nine; outside Villa Tarrazi, overlooking Beirut, with the family mastiff, Ozzie.

OCT 63

LEFT During my high-school days in Lebanon, wearing a camel-hair robe given to my father by King Saud of Saudi Arabia.

BELOW Stewart, Ian, Lennie, and me in the mid-80s. Ian liked to play up his 'Arab roots.'

ABOVE The *Sniffin' Glue* crew—Mark P., Harry Murlowski, and writer Danny Baker—Dryden Chambers, London, 1976.

RIGHT The Cortinas with Mark P. (center) and me at Polydor Studios, 1977.

LEFT My longtime lawyer, Allen Grubman, and my father.

BELOW Andy Powell and Ted Turner of Wishbone Ash; the StarTruckin' 75 crew, ready to set off on the tour that changed everything.

OPPOSITE Me and Gene October of Chelsea, London, 1977.

THIS PAGE Billy Idol and me at the Roxy, London, 1975; with the members of Squeeze, A&M's Derek Green (top), and John Cale (right), who produced their first album.

OPPOSITE Sting and Jools Holland in France at one of the shows filmed for *Urgh! A Music War*; riding one of the motorbikes given to The Police and me by Yamaha.

THIS PAGE Peter Haycock and Robby Krieger play the *Night Of The Guitar*; Marc Moreland and Stan Ridgway of Wall Of Voodoo.

ABOVE The Police in Japan, 1980.

RIGHT Relaxing poolside with Sting, 1982.

ABOVE The IRS Records team at the time of our move from A&M to MCA; attending a staff meeting in Ireland, 1980.

RIGHT Carlos Grasso's original sketch for the IRS logo.

RIGHT Tony Brinsley, me, Mike Gormley, and the head of CBS ('Mr. Scary') with The Bangles, 1987; sightseeing with Italian superstar Zucchero; taking a canal-boat ride through Venice with my wife, Adriana.

BELOW Joining Sting at the mic to sing 'Every Breath You Take.'

ABOVE AND LEFT Sting and me on our trip to Benares, India, in 1998.

ABOVE Me and my brother
Ian at the Rock and Roll Hall
of Fame in 2003; in Shubra,
Egypt, with Saad al Soghrier.

RIGHT In the studio with Cheb
Mami and Sting during the
making of *Desert Rose*.

ABOVE With Puerto Rican singer Olga Tañón and Egyptian star Hakim; me and Iraqi musical icon Ilham al-Madfai.

LEFT My sons Miles 4th, Aeson, and Axton at Disneyland, California, in the 2000s.

ABOVE The Bellydance Superstars
at Château Marouatte; a family trip
to San Francisco in 2010.

LEFT Adriana and me after knighting
Sir Dominic Miller and Sir Mark
Hudson at the château.

CHAPTER 17

HALF FULL

. . . .

It would be easy to divide humanity into two types: those who instinctively or through experience see the glass as half full, and those who are predisposed to see the glass as half empty. In fact, there are grey areas in between, and that's where the vast majority of humanity resides. These are the people who are not sure about that glass, so they need someone to tell them one way or another. As a manager of artists, my job was often dealing with artists who needed telling. But the ones I was most successful with were the ones that did not need telling—in other words, the glass-half-full ones.

One artist who did not need telling, and who like me was clearly a glass-half-full person, was Jools Holland—or Julian Miles Holland, to give him his full name. I first worked with Jools, of course, when he was a member of Squeeze. During that period, his sense of humor and willingness to try things became evident, while his prowess as a keyboard player encouraged me to throw other things his way. Solo records such as 'Boogie Woogie '78'; sessions with other artists I was working with, like The Police at Madison Square Garden; Jools was always open to new ideas and experiences.

Even so, I never encouraged him to leave Squeeze. To me, as manager of the band, that would have been disloyal and destructive. But when he did eventually leave Squeeze in October 1980, I became his manager. This was the guy who had stood by me at that Squeeze band meeting in a way that I will never forget. Now, I embarked on an effort to find a way to repay that confidence, by hook or by crook.

Tour manager John Lay came with us as Jools's day-to-day manager. Jools's first move was to create a band to play the kind of music he was into, which he called The Millionaires. I will admit that this was not the easiest thing to promote, but that was his musical love, so we made records and did tours of America and Europe. I put him on support slots with The Police and whoever else I could, including the Police Christmas show at Tooting Bec Common in 1980.

The following year was largely devoted to launching Jools's new band and promoting the records. His pitch to attract musicians was typical of Jools's sense of humor: 'Do you want to be a Millionaire?' Then he added two female backing singers and called them the Wealthy Tarts. We did tours of the USA and England, filmed him for *Urgh! A Music War*, then issued his first album on A&M in the UK: *Jools Holland & His Millionaires*, produced by Glyn Johns and featuring lyrics by Chris Difford. When the A&M opted not to release the album in the USA, I put it out on my IRS Records.

The biggest opportunity came when the BBC agreed to do a documentary on The Police's recording of *Ghost In The Machine* on the Caribbean island of Monserrat, to be broadcast over Christmas 1981. I hired Derek Burbidge to film it, having worked with him already on the early Police videos, as well as the *Police In The East* documentary and the *Urgh! A Music War* film. When the BBC asked me which one of its presenters I wanted to host the Police documentary, I said I wanted none of them. The whole vibe we had established with The Police was of not doing things the traditional way, and using a traditional presenter would run counter to that. The presenter had to be unexpected, irreverent but polite, with a cheeky sense of humor, and musical in a way the Police members would respect, but at the same time be able to explain what the band were doing to the average person. Most of all, the presenter needed to be likable.

My gut told me that Jools had all of that, and when I asked him to do it, he simply said, 'If you think I can do it, I will—what will The Police say?' I had not told them yet, but I had a good idea that they would say yes. The Police knew I had good ideas, and this was probably one of them. I remember Sting saying, 'We like Jools, so OK.' The Police, just like Jools, were game to try something new. It didn't always work, but this time it certainly did.

However, as I had learned—and this would be reaffirmed over and over again in the future—TV executives are pussies. They are afraid to make mistakes and prefer to go with the proven route. Jools was not a presenter they knew, so of course they were not happy with the choice and tried to talk me out of it. I believed Jools was the right guy, so I said simply, 'It's Jools, or we don't give you the show.' Luckily for me, Jools, The Police, and the BBC, I was right.

The reality from the start was that Jools Holland was the one person in Squeeze that I found easy to work with. He, very much like The Police, was prone to say yes to any idea, even off-the-wall ones, before he might say no. That meant it was more fun for someone like me to put forward ideas, knowing they would not be dismissed out of hand. For The Police, I could say, *Let's go on a world tour and play Egypt and India*, and they would say, *OK, why not?* For Jools, I could say, *Let's pretend you are blind and do a Ray Charles on this gig. I will lead you out onstage, you wearing dark glasses, bobbing your head like Ray and holding a cane, so everyone will think you are blind. Then, a few songs in, you get up and walk towards the stage edge and freak the audience out, thinking you are going to walk off the stage.* Jools, game for a laugh, agreed, and he did just that. And the audience did freak out just before a roadie caught him and took him back to the piano.

He had a sense of humor, and he was willing to use it onstage. In Squeeze, Glenn or Chris would have been the natural choices to introduce the band, but they never did. I asked Jools to do it, and without hesitation he did—and with his usual cheeky humor. I got him to try some radio commercials for Squeeze's *Argy Bargy* album, released in April of 1980, and they proved to be winners—even better than I thought they would be. We launched the ads in the USA, and one can still hear in them today, via YouTube, the kind of disarming humor that Jools excelled in. He really was a very different person from his Squeeze bandmates.

This was the *Argy Bargy* ad:

> OK everybody, pay attention, this is an important message. I haven't
> got long—I wanted an hour, but people have been messing me about

all day. I am going to tell you that if you don't go out and buy this album, you will be making the gravest mistake of your life! You're saying to yourself, *What gravest mistake will I be making?* I'm gonna tell you what gravest mistake you'll be making. You will be missing out on listening to the most incredible band—no, no, not band—let's say the most incredible conglomerate of geniuses ever to wax their discs on record. I want you to go out and buy this record—I'm not going to tell you who it's by yet, I'm going to tell you some more about it! It's got the most fantastic guitar, fantastic keyboard, incredible drums, interesting bass, best lyrics you've ever heard since Bob Dylan, Randy Newman, and Marx put together ... I want to tell you that if you don't buy this you probably won't improve your life by any means whatsoever. And the name of the band—you're waiting for it, I'm going to tell you now, brace yourself—it's SQUEEZE, and the name of the record is *Argy Bargy*. Not 'aggy baggy,' as some people call it—people who call it that generally didn't go to school and are fairly stupid. Say *ARGY BARGY* on A&M RECORDS AND TAPES.

That was Jools off the cuff: no script, just a couple of takes and we had it. (By the way, 'argy-bargy' is an English expression for an argument.)

The *Police In Monserrat* show was broadcast on the BBC on December 1, 1981. It did a lot for Jools, and he took to the job like a fish to water. I later took him to the USA to host some of the IRS *Cutting Edge* shows for MTV. Then, Malcolm Geary, a producer working on a new music show for Tyne Tees TV in Newcastle, called me to see if Jools might be interested in co-hosting *The Tube*. I did not know Malcolm, so I am presuming he first called A&M Records and they gave him my contact phone number. Anyway, I agreed to meet, and Malcolm came to see me at my office in London to discuss the possibility.

Malcolm was not gung-ho by any means. Perhaps it was a negotiating tactic, but I didn't get the impression that he was committed to the idea yet. His real problem was that this was a big deal for him as a producer, and Jools had little experience, other than that one show with The Police. I saw an interview Malcolm did where he said it only took one look at the Police doc for him to know Jools was the man—not at all true. Malcolm was not a 'snap decision' kind of guy—this was national TV, and you don't want to fuck up. If you do, it could end your career.

For Tyne Tees TV, Jools would not be a safe decision. However, Malcolm had obviously seen enough to make him interested, which is why he was meeting me. There was also the problem that a new TV station, Channel 4, was launching on November 2, 1982, and his show would be one of the first and probably the highest-profile on it.

My point was simple: *Who else has what Jools has?* After much going back and forth, Malcolm conceded that Jools was the right person for the job. We made the deal, but then Malcolm asked for one more bit of insurance. Jools had to go to Newcastle for a screen test. I sent John Lay with Jools and called him afterwards to see how it went. John said he thought Jools had blown it with some off-color remarks about interviewing John Lennon's body and the like—Jools had been a bit more irreverent than usual. John was convinced it was a failure. The truth is that neither John nor Jools knew anything about Tyne Tees TV, and Channel 4 had not even launched yet, so Jools apparently wasn't taking it very seriously.

I had been assured that Jools would get the job, and that the screen test was more of a formality to keep Malcolm's associates in Newcastle cool, but that John Lay phone call worried me. It was a relief to get the call a few days later and hear that the deal with Jools was on: he was to be the co-host of *The Tube* with Paula Yates.

It is important to remember that cable TV did not exist in Great Britain at this time. There were three TV stations then, with Channel 4 to make it a total of four (two of the others were BBC, plus the independent ITV), so any show was bound to get a big viewership.

The first episode of *The Tube* aired on November 5, 1982. There were to be many funny and important moments over the next five years, as Jools recounts in his own book, *Barefaced Lies & Boogie-Woogie Boasts*. I went up to Newcastle every now and then, but mostly I just watched the show in the same way everybody else did.

The Tube had gaps between filming periods, which left time for Jools to pursue other ventures. In 1985, there was an opportunity to re-form Squeeze, with Jools once again joining the band. That led to the *Cosi Fan Tutti Frutti* album, released in August 1985 on A&M, with me once again as Squeeze's manager. For the next couple of years, Jools had to split his time between *The Tube* and Squeeze. Then, in February of 1987, Jools inadvertently swore on TV, drawing complaints from viewers, and *The Tube* was canceled. Even on an irreverent rock'n'roll show, the word 'fuckers' was a no-no.

The success of *The Tube* had put Jools on the map, and soon the BBC was on to me about having him do *Juke Box Jury*. Then, in 1988, Lorne Michaels of *Saturday Night Live* called, wanting to discuss the idea of Jools doing a new Sunday show for him. It was to be a freer show than *SNL*, and all about music—more in the jazz arena than pop arena—so I thought it would appeal to Jools. His co-host on *Sunday Night* was the musician David Sanborn, and the idea was that both he and Jools could play along with the musical guests that were on the show. To me, this would be a huge break for Jools: the chance to work with Lorne Michaels, a super-successful big-time TV producer, in the world's biggest market. The only problem was that Jools was already booked for concerts with Squeeze, and to his mind he was already pretty busy. I convinced Lorne that the only way to make it work was for Jools to fly over on Concorde each week, and Lorne agreed. I then talked Jools into doing it.

I will admit that I was putting a lot of demands on Jools's time, but this was the entertainment business—it is all about striking while the iron is hot. Working with Lorne would have led to more lucrative opportunities. You might make $100,000 doing a commercial for the UK, but in the USA it would be $1,000,000 or more. For me, as a manager, this was arriving at the big win that I owed Jools for him sticking with me back at that Squeeze band meeting in 1980. Lorne had launched the careers of some of the biggest names in film, and now it was Jools's turn.

Jools understood the importance of the show, but I don't think he was as thrilled about it as I was. Many weeks went by with Jools flying back and forth on Concorde. One day, he called to say he could not take it anymore. He was 'losing all his friends down at the pub.' It really was a plea to have a life again, and begrudgingly I had to agree and call Lorne Michaels to break the news. It was not a call I could look forward to making, but then again Jools was never driven by money, and I had to admit that the travel—even by Concorde—had to be a strain.

Lorne was shocked. He had never been turned down before. Maybe if Jools had carried on with *Sunday Night*, his potential in the USA would have been vastly greater. But c'est la vie.

∾

By now I was spending more time in Los Angeles—eventually living there as my base full time—so I turned over the day-to-day running of Jools's affairs to John Lay and his assistant, Paul Loasby. They were both loyal to Jools and they did a good job, and in the end the reality was that it was better for Jools and me to be friends than being in business together. In this business, proximity is everything, and I lived too many thousands of miles apart. I also had a life to lead—and, even for me, life cannot be all about making money.

Jools went on to do more TV: first with *The Late Show* (1992), which morphed into BBC2's *Later . . . With Jools Holland*, which airs in many parts of the world, nationally in the UK and on cable elsewhere.

In 2003, Jools received an OBE in the Queen's Birthday Honors List.

'What the hell is an OBE?' I asked him.

'You don't have to call me Sir just yet,' he replied.

CHAPTER 18

DIFFERENT
LIGHT

. . . .

In December of 1987, I was invited by a promoter to see Pink Floyd at the Sports Arena in Los Angeles. It was the typical Pink Floyd spectacle to a sold-out crowd of twenty thousand. After the show, I went armed with my backstage pass to the dressing room area and ended up talking to Dave Gilmour, the band's guitarist and leader. As people began to leave, I suggested that a group of us come back my house in Hollywood, and, to my surprise, Dave wanted to come along. We continued our conversation at the house, and it turned out Dave was very interested in the story of The Police and why they 'broke up.' He was thinking The Police would someday re-form, and he told me of his experiences with Pink Floyd.

According to Dave, he and Roger Waters used to leave all the early Floyd shows complaining that the band's drummer, Nick Mason, and keyboardist, Rick Wright, were, in their view, below par. When the band broke up in 1981, Dave launched his solo career with a fine set of musicians he was proud of. He built up to selling out the Hammersmith Odeon in London to some three thousand people—obviously not the Floyd's huge numbers, but very respectable numbers nonetheless. Then his manager suggested that since Nick Mason was in town, the fans might really go wild if he was invited to play with Dave at the end of the set. Dave's heart sank at the thought, but he agreed. When the time came, he introduced Nick, and the fans loved it. Nick sat on the drums and the final song started. Then a funny thing happened.

'It was like putting on an old comfortable shoe that fit perfectly,' he said. Dave realized at that moment that what the Floyd had was not about the individual musicianship—it was something that they had together that just worked. His point to me was that as good as Sting was, and as good as his current musicians were, he felt Sting would one day realize what he had in The Police.

I will always remember that moment of wisdom from Dave Gilmour. That 'something' that a band had was also the essence of The Bangles: a band that was greater than the sum of its parts. Take a piece of the jigsaw puzzle out and the picture is no longer complete.

I first saw The Bangles at the Starlight Club on Santa Monica Boulevard in West Hollywood in 1982, when they were performing as The Bangs, and I instantly wanted to take them on. They were refreshing and fun, and they had good songs. Contrary to what one might assume, I did not sign them because they were all girls—it was simply that I really liked them. I was not looking for another Go-Go's, but I was also not avoiding one. But I did realize that, as they were an all-girl band from Los Angeles, and also looked upon as part of the new wave, the danger was that they could be classed as a 'poor person's Go-Go's.'

I took on the management of The Bangles with Mike Gormley, my partner in a new company, Los Angeles Personal Direction (LAPD). Mike had been head of publicity at A&M Records when the first Police album was released. As often happened at record labels when cost cutting is in the air, the trend was to get rid of the #1 guy and upgrade the #2 with a bit more salary—and thereby save yourself a big salary. There's no point in firing a secretary and saving yourself $40,000 when you can fire an executive and save yourself $400,000. Mike was ready to move on anyway, and he became a valued partner in a growing business.

One of the first things we decided to do was to record an EP and release it through the Faulty Products setup, so as to create some distance between The Bangs and The Go-Go's. Then we got Ian and FBI involved to book live performances. Almost immediately, they were off for their first big dates all over America. Then came the problem with the name. I got a phone call from a group on the East Coast called The Bangs who said they would sue us if we used 'their' name—but offered to sell it to us for a price.

Thinking the price was too high, our band opted to add a few letters and came up with The Bangles.

The *Bangles* EP got airplay, especially with DJs like Rodney Bingenheimer on KROQ, plus good coverage at college radio. The name change delayed the release, and by the time the EP was ready, Faulty Products was learning the perils of independent distribution, resulting in me closing it down soon after. I had no option but to move the EP over to IRS Records, which released it again later in the year.

Luckily, between IRS, FBI, and LAPD, we had enough going on to get The Bangles on *American Bandstand*, the IRS *Cutting Edge* show we had on MTV, and concerts opening for bigger acts, as well as headlining shows at clubs. This was all with a view to at some point get a major-label deal for the band so we wouldn't have to put them on IRS Records. We managed to get that deal by August of 1983.

Peter Philbin, West Coast director of talent acquisition for Columbia Records, had been sniffing around The Bangles as early as March 1983. He approached me about signing them around June. I had been used to banging on the doors of labels to try to get deals myself, so Peter approaching me was a first. I was not aware at the time that he had already seen the band several times, but he convinced me he was keen to have them on Columbia. Mike and I were very ready to make a deal that would put The Bangles in the game—and with a really strong company.

The one problem with Columbia was that, unlike A&M Records and definitely not like IRS Records, at the top it was run by what we might politely call 'suits' who worked more by the numbers than by the gut. Peter was an artist guy, but he worked *for* the suits. Surviving in that world was not easy. But we were pleased when they put forward David Kahne as producer. He knew the group, having remixed 'Real World' for a Faulty mini-CD EP. It was pure coincidence that he had then taken a job at Columbia. In any case, we felt that it would not be cool to challenge the record company so soon, unless we had a good reason for it—and we didn't.

David Kahne had definite ideas about producing, and the band found out too late that he had no problem bringing in a session musician to play a part if he felt one of the Bangles was slow or, in his view, not up to the part. Columbia was paying for this, and The Bangles were not yet famous, so it was a matter of suck it up and try to make it work. Although The Bangles were hurt by the introduction of session musicians, the resulting album, *All Over The Place*, released by CBS in May of 1984, was mostly performed by them, and almost all of the songs were written by them—and it was a good album.

The second album, *Different Light*, was more of the same, and it was becoming clear that a pushy producer, right or wrong, was not going to work for much longer. I am not sure how, but around this time Prince got interested in Susanna Hoffs, The Bangles' main singer, and wrote 'Manic Monday' for her. At one point, he took her out on a date, but when we asked her about it she said nothing. David Kahne also brought the Liam Sternberg song 'Walk Like An Egyptian' for the band to record. That song, as great as I thought it was, had the same effect on Debbie Peterson, The Bangles' drummer, that 'Every Breath You Take' had on my brother Stewart: there was hardly any drum part, which meant Debbie didn't even play on the song.

'Manic Monday' became The Bangles' first big hit in the USA. Up to this point, I had had no problem with Columbia—things were going well—but then the US arm of the company said there were no more singles on the album, so they stopped working it. In London, 'Manic Monday' got to #2 in the charts, so, with momentum going for the band, the company wanted to put out a second single. I went into the London office and met with the managing director, Paul Russell, to discuss the plan. Paul's nickname was 'Mr. Scary,' which I found out was a pretty good description. I lobbied for what I assumed was the obvious second single, 'Walk Like An Egyptian.' Paul thought it too quirky and instead wanted to go with 'Going Down To Liverpool' from the first album.

'But it's not on the album!' I protested.

'A hit is a hit,' Paul replied. It was not a suggestion.

In the end, I had no option but to say, 'OK, but on one condition: whatever happens, you will release "Walk Like An Egyptian" as the next single. Even if "Going down To Liverpool" flops.' To my surprise, he agreed.

The 'Liverpool' single gained no traction, and within a week it was forgotten about. I went back to the Columbia offices to get Paul to honor his commitment. Our conversation opened bluntly, with him saying there was no point in putting out a third single. As far as Mr. Scary was concerned, our short meeting was over. It wasn't for me. I reminded him that—right there in that office—he had promised, come what may, that he would release 'Walk Like An Egyptian' as the next single. To my amazement, he said, 'I did promise you. OK, we will release it.' Mr. Scary turned out to be an honorable man!

'Walk Like An Egyptian' took off like a bullet, going to #1 in the UK and soon all over the world. When the US company released it, it went straight to #1 there, too, on the way to becoming the biggest-selling single of the year worldwide. It is hard to believe that a song that to me and others was an obvious hit had until now been blanked by the powers that be at Columbia.

By the time of the third Bangles album, and after the huge success of 'Walk Like An Egyptian,' we were in a position to solve the problem of bullying the group into letting session musicians play their parts by hiring Davitt Sigerson to produce. As far as I was concerned, David Kahne had delivered hits, but I knew the band were at the point where they really needed to feel they were in control of their own lives. Davitt had the 'artist friendly' vibe, and he was not likely to bully the band. But there is always a danger. The 'softer' the producer is, the less likely they are to push a band to correct mistakes. Sometimes it takes an outsider to do it.

When I heard 'Eternal Flame,' I thought it was a potential hit, but the song stayed at the same level all the way through. It seemed obvious that it needed to build towards some sort of a payoff at the end.

'Do you really think so?' Davitt asked. Yes, I did.

The next time I was in the studio, the build was there. 'Eternal Flame' became another #1 hit for the group. I can't say if Davitt would have done that on his own, or if the band would also have heard what I heard—all I know is the song changed after I talked to Davitt about it. In any case, it made 1989 another big year for The Bangles.

✂

People often compare The Go-Go's and The Bangles, but in fact they were quite different. This was especially true in how they treated photography and the general matter of image-making. In The Go-Go's, it was accepted that Belinda would be the front person, the lead singer, and probably get more press coverage because of that. Pretty much like Stewart and Andy's attitude towards Sting in The Police.

The Bangles set a rule of 'equality' from the start. That also extended to the stage. The rule was four spotlights, not one. For most road crews, this would not have made any sense, but it was a rule that the group insisted upon, and which sometimes meant no spotlight at all.

The Bangles' strategy was all based on the group mantra to not single out any member—especially Susanna. There was a fear that Susanna Hoffs would be singled out and eventually leave the others in the dust to go solo. I never felt any push from Susanna herself regarding a solo career—from what I could see, she had resigned herself to the rule as a fact of life in the band—but there seemed to be a real fear in the minds of Debbie and Vicki, the band's drummer and lead guitarist. Debbie and Vicki were sisters, and they were not shy about making their feelings understood. Michael, the bass player, was also no pushover, so it really was a group where all parties had to be considered, and each had their quirks and, more to the point, strong opinions.

The problem was that many newspapers and magazines wanted front covers showing one person, just like they have done for so many groups in the past, including The Police. Consequently, The Bangles turned down numerous front covers and major articles in the press. The situation was worst in the UK, perhaps because Rupert Murdock's papers were prone to go for attention-grabbing headlines and naked girls.

I had hired Tony Brinsley as the band's road manager for their 1989 tour of Europe, and it was Tony who faced the brunt of the band's displeasure vis-à-vis press requests. Some covers were turned down because they were overly sexual and inappropriate, but many were turned down simply because they wanted just Susanna up front. Tony was not happy about it, correctly thinking opportunities should not be missed. The situation became so bad that in the end the band made me agree to remove him from working with them.

It has to be said that the main pressure came from the press, not the band. Susanna was pretty and had an engaging personality, but she was not leading the charge to be out front. There was some frustration within the group regarding their choice of songs, such as who wrote them and if there was a quota. However, this was a group in which the songwriting talent was more evenly spread than it was in The Go-Go's, so the huge disparity in individual income was not so pronounced. Were song choices an issue? Yes. Was it a huge issue? From what I saw, no.

I also never felt the record company pushed for Susanna to go solo. No record company wants to see a change in a winning formula, and all too often the lead singer does not pick up where the band he or she came from left off.

∽

That Susanna eventually went solo was not my fault. It resulted from a long-time-coming disagreement I had with the group's lawyer, who had got it into her head that she and I would inevitably become an item. It mattered to me that a band's lawyer and manager could not be together— it would be an obvious conflict of interest—but that did not bother her.

I have no idea what conversations were going on between lawyer and group, but I saw the results. First, the band asked me to remove my partner, Mike Gormley, from their management team; then my brother Ian, their booking agent; and, finally, me. What that lawyer did not appreciate was that when you rock the boat, you don't always know what is going to fall out. A new management team took over, and shortly after that it was three members of the band's turn to fall out of the boat. The Bangles were no more.

Now that I have had years to reflect upon it, I realize that there was a method to the madness of The Bangles' 'equality' mantra. The secret of The Bangles' success was the unit. They had a combination that worked, like Dave Gilmour was talking about when he re-formed Pink Floyd. When I was fired and the new managers took over, they must have seen the age-old issue of dealing with a group of people and figured it's much easier to deal with one person than four, so they quickly decided to forget The Bangles and take Susanna solo. What they did not realize was the true dynamic of The Bangles, and that Susanna could shine because she was *within* that group.

I saw Susanna perform as a solo artist at a concert on August 3, 1991, on a bill with Don Henley, Little Feet, and Sting. When I saw her up there on her own, I thought, *You know what, those gals were right.* It didn't work.

The new managers had put Susanna in a predictable spot by not recognizing what The Bangles were. Stick a pretty girl onstage with a bunch of excellent (all-male) musicians, like that's all you needed to do? The disarming charm that she had within The Bangles was there, but it was lost in the nondescript surroundings of good musicians in a no-image band. Perhaps wild clothes and big production à la Lady Gaga would have helped, but that would have been out of character for Susanna. Needless to say, her solo project failed.

If The Bangles were more than the sum of the parts, the parts were interesting as well, as I discovered some years later, when I brought Vicki and Debbie to my Printemps des Troubadours songwriting retreats (see chapter 26). One of the lessons of those retreats was that as a song came together, one person might appear to be contributing little—it could be just one word or one chord—but that small contribution might be the key ingredient that made the whole thing work. That's why, from the very beginning, we established a simple rule: 'Three writers in the room, publishing split equally three ways.' Each was a part of a jigsaw puzzle—put them together and you had something special. That was The Bangles.

CHAPTER 19

RAPID EYE
MOVEMENT
. . . .

Writing a memoir where lots of things were going on at the same time is not easy. Nineteen eighty-two was one of those years, from The Go-Go's going to #1 on the *Billboard* charts in March, to signing R.E.M. in May, to signing The Bangles in June, to *The Tube* launching at the end of the year in England, plus constant happenings with The Police, Wall Of Voodoo, Lords Of The New Church, and more. But for many IRS Records fans, the signing of R.E.M. turned out to be one of the most significant.

My brother Ian knew the band members from his days working at Paragon in Macon, which is where I also met Bill Berry, as a limo driver, on my first trip there to meet Alex Hodges. Bill became R.E.M.'s drummer when the band formed in 1980. Ian was a fan from the start: he quickly became their booking agent and encouraged me to sign them, which I did in 1982, after Jay Boberg saw them perform in New Orleans and became their chief champion within IRS Records. IRS released an EP, *Chronic Town*, that year, and the first album, *Murmur*, in 1983.

The band played some major shows in 1983, including opening for The Police at the big Shea Stadium show. The Police thought they were boring, and frankly so did I. They were not ready to be on such a big stage and under such a spotlight. Perhaps it was the subtlety and the lack of image focus that failed to impress. For some reason, the band didn't even want to appear in their own music videos, which I thought was really stupid. Why do a video if you aren't even in it?

Their attitude towards their name was also peculiar. It came from 'rapid eye movement,' but the band didn't want that emphasized, so people used to refer to the band as *Rem*. In some ways, they were the antithesis of the IRS acts like The Cramps and Wall Of Voodoo, and certainly The Police. They also chose support bands like The dB's and Lets Active, whom Jay Boberg was into but I was not. (I can't remember one song by either of those bands, and they never sold any records.)

But R.E.M. were the darlings of many of the IRS Records staff. We tended to divide the relationships up between us, and Jay was definitely the R.E.M. person. I was never called in as there was rarely any problem with the band that Jay could not deal with. Basically, R.E.M. were nice guys—there was never a problem, no dramas, and I can't even remember any funny stories.

They were also the most unusual of bands for the label. They were steady, they lived up to their contract, they never tried to renegotiate their record deal, and they were never crazy in any way that I can remember (except of course not wanting to appear in their videos). Each album sold more than the last; it was a steady climb to the fifth and last one for us, *Document*, which was their first really big album. It reached #10 on the *Billboard* album chart, becoming their first platinum album, while the single 'The One I Love' reached #9.

That placed the band in an ideal position: just as their contract with IRS Records expired, they became free agents. The big record companies are always ready to pounce on a proven winner, and R.E.M. were proven. So, pounce they did.

Of course, we'd made repeated attempts to encourage the band to renegotiate their deal along the usual lines: *Give us some more albums in return for higher royalties and advances on your current deal and even the past albums*. But the band were content to keep to the contract. We even offered to give them their masters back at the end of the renegotiated term. Still no.

When the contract was over, the band's manager, Jefferson Holt, and lawyer, Bertis Downs, said, 'Make us an offer like every other label, and if yours is the best, we are happy to re-sign to IRS.' As the offers came in, it was obvious to sign them would take more money than IRS could come up with, so Jerry Moss offered to contribute three million dollars.

When it came down to IRS/A&M versus Warner Bros, Bertis and Jefferson came to show us the latest offer from Warner Bros. Basically, it said, *Whatever IRS offers you, Warner Bros will double it.* Obviously, I could not compete with that, even with the help Jerry Moss had offered. When I saw the final offer, I said, 'Here is my advice: leave this office immediately, go straight to Warner Bros, and sign the deal before they change their mind.' It was the best record deal I ever saw.

Some years later, when *that* deal expired, R.E.M. signed their second deal with Warner Bros, and it was the biggest record deal ever made. I know there were IRS staffers that were badly affected by R.E.M.'s departure, especially when they saw the huge success of the first Warner Bros album. For me, on one hand I was pleased that we had delivered an amazing success for them, and on the other hand I could not help but think, *So, now they are into making killer videos that they actually appear in?*

But, really, they were the one band on IRS that never shot themselves in the foot, as so many bands who looked like becoming bright stars did. In the end, R.E.M. were the brightest of stars.

ↄ

Around the time we brought R.E.M. to IRS, we also signed The English Beat. My starting point with this band would have to be centered around Dave Wakeling and a joke I came up with that if he were an amoeba and could divide himself in two, he would have. Why? Because The English Beat morphed into General Public, then split into three parts: Dave Wakeling, Ranking Roger, and Fine Young Cannibals. None of these formations made it to the third album.

Though they'd started as The Beat in England, when IRS signed the band we had to add 'English' in front, because there was already an American band using the name 'The Beat.' IRS released two albums: *Special Beat Service* (1982) plus a compilation album, *What Is Beat?* (1983). It looked like The English Beat might go on to be another hit band for IRS, with the first album getting to #39 in the charts. As their manager, Tarquin Gotch, says in his interview for the IRS documentary *We Were Once Rebels*, they could have been as big as The Police if not for the breakup. When Dave Wakeling broke up the band, he started General Public with fellow Beat member Ranking Roger. General Public released two albums: *All The Rage* (1984), which got to #29 in the charts, and *Hand To Mouth* (1986), which didn't do as well, so Dave broke *that* band up and went solo with his *No Warning* album in 1991.

Dave Wakeling was unquestionably talented, but he was also a 'shoot yourself in the foot when you are on the verge of making it' type. He also had a strange idea about me: 'He's evil but he's got a heart of gold.'

I guess we had to consider ourselves lucky that a byproduct of this was Fine Young Cannibals with his ex-band mates from The English Beat, bass player David Steel and guitarist Andy Cox. They had added singer Roland Gift and created the band in 1984—and, thanks to our English Beat contract, they were committed to IRS in America. The band recorded two albums, *Fine Young Cannibals* (1985) and *The Raw And The Cooked* (1989). The latter delivered the second #1 album for IRS Records and the first and second #1 singles for the label, 'She Drives Me Crazy' in 1988 and 'Good Thing' in 1989.

Fine Young Cannibals eventually disbanded in 1992. It was bad news for IRS Records that they lasted such a short time. Other than R.E.M., it seemed to be the fate of the label that our acts never lasted long. In the case of Fine Young Cannibals, it was due to an incident that happened to singer Roland Gift: his hotel room was broken into while he was in it, and it freaked him out so much that he went back to England and never wanted to come back to the USA again.

Perhaps, if that hadn't happened, the band would have recorded another hit album for IRS and the label would still exist today. The truth about labels is that their longevity has as much to do with the artists as to any moves the company staff might make. A label is only as hot as the acts it represents. One thing is for sure: IRS was great at signing great acts—unique, talented—but all too often they had some inbuilt self-destruct within them. We had more than our share of shooting stars. The English Beat were just one more example.

CHAPTER 20

7476 HILLSIDE

By 1983, I was spending so much time in Los Angeles that I decided to buy a house there, so in March of that year I bought a place in Hollywood, a few blocks from the A&M offices on La Brea Avenue. 7476 Hillside Avenue had previously belonged to the actor Raymond Burr, of *Perry Mason* and *Ironside* fame. It was big, set across almost three acres of land, with a swimming pool and two greenhouses, but it had a strange layout, and its main interior feature was brown: brown wooden ceiling, small windows with brown shutters, brown cork on the walls, brown wall-to-wall carpeting, brown woodwork, a huge master bedroom approached by a narrow staircase, and a small kitchen. That must have been why the price was as low as it was. But it was the first house I owned, and I could do with it what I wanted.

By now, I had also taken over the lease on 21 Marlborough Place in London, as the three Copeland brothers—Stewart, Ian, and I—had purchased a house for our parents in Aston Rowant, near Oxford, and they in turn had left Marlborough Place to me. So now I was a two-house person. As I was flitting back and forth between London and Los Angeles, and often on tour, I found a Scottish couple to be my live-in caretakers in Hollywood when I was gone. The husband, Don, had been a BOAC pilot, so I assumed he would make a good chauffeur, but he could not get used to driving with one foot. He had the irritating habit of putting one foot on the gas and the other foot on the brake, and he often pushed both down together.

Now that I had a chauffeur, I thought I should also have a limousine, so I bought a 1954 Packard Patrician that came with a license plate '1954 Limo.' I found a captain's hat for Don, who was happy with that as it reminded him of his days as a pilot. I thought this was all pretty cool until the limousine broke down in the middle of Melrose Avenue, right where everyone would be staring at me—which they did. Don and I had to push it to the side of the road, which of course had no parking—and, being a 1954 vehicle, it was super heavy. I had it towed to the house and never drove it again.

As I was slowly becoming an 'LA person,' living in Hollywood and spending more time there than London, Jerry Moss asked me to manage one of his signings, Beverly D'Angelo. Beverly had started her career in Canada, as a singer and recording artist, but had ended up in Hollywood as an actress. And it was Jerry Moss, so when he asked, I said yes. Beverly did sing great, but her film career was happening, and that left little time for music: the *National Lampoon's Vacation* films with Chevy Chase had pushed her into stardom, and she was making money as an actress, so there was not much incentive to embark on the long process of growing her music career.

Beverly was very well liked and connected in the film community. She seemed to know everyone, so when she said I should have a party and she would handle the invites, I thought, *What the hell*. Rock Hudson came; Lauren Hutton, Princess Leia from *Star Wars*, and a host of others were there, as well as actors I knew, like Mickey Rourke from *Rumble Fish* and Daryl Hannah from *Splash*. Sprinkled in were some of my IRS Records artists, like Stan Ridgway from Wall Of Voodoo, who got into a wild argument with Lauren Hutton and stormed out.

Over the next few years, the parties got bigger, so I moved them into the garden and what eventually became an annual 'Jungle Party.' Towards the end, there might have been as many as a thousand people there, and I keep running into people even today who tell me they met me at or at least attended one of them. One day, I walked into the A&M lot and the security guard said, 'Hi, Miles, great party last night!' I had always invited the executives at A&M, but this time it seems one of them had given his tickets to the guard, so I figured it was time for the parties to come to an end.

Beverly D'Angelo, meanwhile, was not unique—there were many in the film world who had either started out as a music artist or fancied themselves as one. Robert Downey Jr. took me to lunch one day to talk about me managing his musical career; nothing came of it, but it was a fun lunch anyway. With Daryl Hannah and her actress friend Hilary Shapiro, we went so far as to form a band, and we actually got close to recording an album. They were called The American Girls, but once again the film world was more lucrative than music, so Daryl would often miss the rehearsals. When her bandmates, who were actual musicians, came to me and said, 'Let's fire Daryl,' I realized that working with film stars, though it was a fun idea, was really a waste of time.

I had more success with a comedian. I'd started going to see shows at the Comedy Store on Sunset Boulevard, and one night in 1983 I saw Richard Prior followed by Barry Diamond followed by Eddie Murphy. They were all great, but Barry Diamond was outrageously funny. I laughed so hard I went up to meet him after the show. We soon became good friends and regular companions when I was in LA. I would see him perform at the Improv, too, but mainly at the Comedy Store. He was not a joke-teller; he played parts, going from a fighter pilot 'with nuclear fuckin' weapons' to a hobo living in a shoebox, to a gay Latino, to a black gangster, to a drunk. He was convincing on all his routines—sometimes a bit too convincing, especially his gay routine. His schtick was, 'I love everything about being gay: the colors, the clothes, the perfume, it's just that cock-sucking part where I say, *nooo*—check, please.'

I got him to make an album for IRS Records: *Fighter Pilot*, the only comedy album on the label. He performed all his routines over three days, and we edited them down to the best ones. Then my brother Ian got him to do the hold message on his answerphone at FBI. It was so funny— promoters would ask to be put back on hold just so they could hear the rest of his schtick, which was all in his 'drunken hick' voice:

> If you want Buck Williams, dat's a two-minute hold and fi' d'llas. If you want John Huie, dat's a fi'-minute hold and ten d'llas. If you want Ian Copelan', dat's a ten-minute hold and twenni-fi' d'llas.

I was convinced Barry could be a star. Comedy was not my field of expertise, but I was now living in Hollywood, and my track record of success with The Police, Sting, The Go-Go's, and IRS Records usually meant doors would open. Barry was brilliant, and, in my view, much better than all the other comedians I was seeing, so I started getting TV producers to come and see him. Every time I did, though, Barry would suck, and the producers would leave unimpressed.

Barry would only suck when it was important that he *not* suck. He wasn't trying to be a prick—he just couldn't help it. It was embarrassing, and I never managed to get a single TV producer to agree to book him for anything.

The end result was that I can't say I advanced Barry's career any, but he did have a big influence on me and many of my staff. We began incorporating 'Barryisms' into our conversations. Sometimes, Barry would walk up to a girl and ask her to buy him a drink or make some other absurd request. To him, it didn't matter—and the more absurd, the better. Next thing I knew, he was dating the girl.

One night, I was invited to a posh London reception put on by the famous beer magnates the Guinness family for a charity. I had been talking to a Guinness marketing manager about a sponsorship deal, which is why I was invited. I was dressed appropriately in a nice dark suit befitting the occasion, so I decided to try out the Barry technique. I noticed an attractive girl, probably in her mid-twenties, who turned out to be one of the Guinness daughters. In true Barry style, I went up to her and asked if she would loan me five pounds.

She looked shocked and said, in her upper-class accent, 'Absolutely not!'

Before she could say 'How dare you!' I said, 'Oh, are you short? I can loan you five if you need it,' and started reaching for my wallet.

This made her even more shocked. 'I don't need your money!' She was irate.

'No problem,' I said, and wandered off. I looked back from the other end of the room, and she was staring at me, like, *Who the fuck was that?* This happened a few times, so I had obviously piqued her interest. In the end, she came back over to me and said, 'Do you really need five pounds?' The Barry Method worked! And it had made a big impression on me.

❦

Since I was no longer spending so much time in London, I decided to find a young music scout who would be out there aggressively for me, looking for new bands. In 1984, I came across a brash kid called Richard Law. Richard was energetic and convinced he could spot talent to the point he was apt to think anyone who did not agree with him must be an idiot. Frankly, he was obnoxious, and I don't think anyone in the company liked him. But I was not looking for someone who would tell me what I *wanted* to hear—I wanted someone who would tell me what I *needed* to hear, so Richard worked. And I don't think Richard thought much of anyone else in the company, either. When he met Jay Boberg, he thought he was a nerd with no taste, and, though he never told me so, he must have assumed I was an old fart as well.

Richard's main contribution to the IRS story was introducing me to William Orbit. William was the main man in a three-piece unit called Torch Song with vocalist Laurie Mayer and an indeterminant member, Grant Gilbert, whose main role seemed to be to talk me into spending money on a recording studio.

Richard gave me a demo of the Torch Song album, which they'd recorded on a home eight-track setup. It was so good that I thought that was the album, but Grant insisted it could be better, so IRS ended up financing the band's upgrade to a 24-track studio, which became Gorilla Studios. When the new, 'improved' album was delivered, it was no better than the demo—in fact, I preferred the demo. To make the point, when the first single, 'Prepare To Energize,' was released, the A-side was the new 24-track recording and the demo version was the B-side. It made the *Billboard* dance charts in the USA and got play in the UK clubs—and on both sides of the Atlantic it was the B-side that got the most attention.

Although I was pissed off at spending out on the 24-track, 'Prepare To Energize' clearly showed the sound mastery and potential genius of William Orbit. I figured William should get into producing records—he was that good. The first opportunity was the first Belinda Carlisle album, for which William produced the remixed versions of her songs. Later, it was Sting's 'If You Love Somebody Set Them Free.'

Where William really delivered were on the two Strange Cargo albums for my *No Speak* instrumental series. 'Fire And Mercy' stands out as one of the greatest tracks we ever released, and was no doubt what encouraged artists like Madonna to hire William to produce music for them. They were all William: composer, sound engineer, and producer. With his genius, who needs a singer? Even so, I imagined combinations, and I tried to talk Stan Ridgway into using William to produce one of his albums. William was not well known at the time, though, and Stan didn't see what I saw. It took a visionary artist like Madonna a few years later to see William in the light I saw him. Madonna had gone through several well-known producers probably in search of a new sound but was not happy until she hired William in 1996. Together, they made her huge-selling *Ray Of Light*, which outsold her previous album four-to-one. That album was very much a departure for Madonna, and it was essentially a merger of her and William Orbit.

Before that, however, I did manage to get one band to take up my recommendation—my first management artist, Wishbone Ash. William Orbit produced *Nouveau Calls*, the gem of an album Wishbone Ash did for the *No Speak* series.

William Orbit is now one of the top producer/songwriters in the industry, with over 200 million sales to his credit, Grammy Awards, Ivor Novello Awards, BRIT Awards, and the like. For me, those Strange Cargo Records remain high on my personal playlist. As I said in the IRS *No Speak* promotion campaign for William, 'As a committed fan and at the risk of sounding overzealous, I have to say that not since the Pink Floyd has an artist had such a sense of space combined with power and delicacy.'

CHAPTER 21

ALL CHANGE AGAIN

· · · · · · · · ·

For the first half of the 80s, I could easily have imagined that the entire focus of attention in the music business was on the three members of The Police and the three Copeland brothers, fueled partly by what the media was telling us—and perhaps partly in our own minds as well. The Police were being hailed as the world's biggest band; my maverick record company, IRS Records, was happening, with the historic success of The Go-Go's; and my brother Ian's booking agency, FBI, had the biggest roster of new-wave artists.

The Police were all over the press, playing concerts in places never before played, and we'd even set up a charity, the Outlandos Trust. That had me hobnobbing with members of parliament in their various chambers in that iconic gothic building under Big Ben, dripping with history. In the USA, we were in with MTV like two peas in a pod with the IRS *Cutting Edge* monthly show and a tour sponsorship deal for The Police, while in the UK, Jools Holland was the host of *The Tube* on Channel 4.

In 1985, the three Copeland brothers were honored as 'Humanitarians of the year' by the AMC Cancer Research Center, and I was a keynote speaker at the Juno Awards in Canada and other major music events. I was on the front cover of *Marketing Week*; I did an episode of *Lifestyles Of The Rich And Famous*. Basically, we were pretty hot shit.

Back in 1983, I had been invited to deliver the keynote address at the New Music Seminar, which was held at the Hilton Hotel in New York.

The event had been attended by several hundred people in its first few years of existence, so, when I walked in, I was surprised to see an audience of almost two thousand. I can't remember all the things I said, but the most memorable part was when I had finished and was walking towards the door to leave, and a girl came running up to me with a tape—presumably an artist looking for a deal. Before I could take it, she passed out and fell to the floor in front of me. My first thought was to say, 'I didn't touch her!' Then I realized she had fainted when she came face-to-face with the person she thought could change her life.

This was perhaps the first realization that I was thinking of myself one way—just a guy working to get his clients and business happening—while other people were now imagining I was something else: a ticket to stardom, the guy with the magic touch. It was quite a shock.

When I look back on that period now and read some of the press I had forgotten about, I come to realize that in my first experiences within the music business, with acts like Wishbone Ash, I was merely a manager, and therefore only as interesting as the bands themselves, and even then only to the most avid fans who wanted to know every detail about their heroes. But in the punk era—or the new wave, as it became known in the USA—the media seems to have decided I was the instigator or influencer of the entire scene, and much more than a mere manager. Some of the acts seemed to think so as well, which is why some of them thought the CIA had put me up to it all and was financing me. In the USA, it became a joke that 'this punk, new wave thing that is happening—it's all your fault!'

The last half of the 80s was different. The focus of my attention was more and more on Sting, who had now gone solo. The Bangles, Jools Holland, and IRS Records remained important parts of my life, but the wild furor of the early 80s morphed into something . . . normal. The first time you have a #1 record, or the first time you hear your song on the radio, it's super-exciting. The first Grammy, the first BRIT Award—the 80s was a time of many firsts for me personally, as well as for the artists I was representing. But by the tenth Grammy, the hundredth concert in front of adoring crowds, another million records sold, more gold and platinum discs than I knew what to do with . . . it's still a high, but it's not the same. To put it bluntly, things settle down. I don't know if that girl who had fainted in front of me in 1983 would have done the same if she had run up to me in 1989.

e/5

The midpoint of the decade, 1985, proved to be a turning point for IRS Records, as we had a major decision to make about the future. It began with a meeting I had with Jerry Moss, where A&M put forward the idea of buying IRS and basically merging the two companies. When Gil Friesen heard about this, his comment to Jerry was, 'Miles would more likely be thinking of buying A&M than the other way around.'

In fact, that had not been my thinking, and I wouldn't have come close to having the money to do so, but what I *was* thinking of was a deal where IRS would sell to A&M but be given shares of A&M as part of the agreement. The idea was, if we were going to merge, let's make it a *real* merger, even if IRS was only a minor shareholder.

Jerry agreed to this in principle, and said he would come back to me with a proposal. Then, at the next meeting, when I thought we would hash out the final deal, Jerry withdrew the idea of exchanging shares. The reason, he said, was that A&M was a Subchapter S corporation, so giving shares to IRS was therefore not possible. That meant that the only offer on the table was an outright purchase for several million dollars.

At the time, I was not aware of all the legalities involved, but the A&M proposition did not fly with me. I was in no mood to sell out when in many ways all of us at IRS thought we were just getting started. I think Jerry and I misread each other, and we both came to regret it, but at the time the only option seemed to be to find a new deal that allowed IRS to continue to grow and control more of its rights. And that is what IRS did: we agreed a new distribution deal with MCA Records that would provide all of the services that A&M had given us and more—at least on paper.

So, in May of 1985, IRS Records left A&M for MCA, which was then headed by Irving Azoff. To make the point about what was occurring, all the staff and I put on white robes, and I as Moses walked from A&M on La Brea Avenue to MCA a few miles up the road in Universal City. It was a five-year deal that gave IRS full rights to its releases—unlike the A&M

deal, which gave A&M the right to continue distributing the IRS product it had released. On paper, it was a better deal, but MCA was not the same kind of company. It was more corporate. Whereas A&M might put up with some IRS eccentricities, MCA would not.

A perfect example came when Michael Plen lost his temper at one of the marketing meetings, and as a result Richard Palmese, the head of MCA's radio department, banned him from the meetings for the next year. The problem for all the IRS staff was that it took a lot more obvious action on a record to get the MCA promotions people on board. Frustrations became commonplace, and a growing problem.

In spite of a more unforgiving atmosphere, we had big hits with Fine Young Cannibals and Belinda Carlisle, but there were others that fell into the 'shoulda made it' file. There grew a serious resentment within the IRS staff. Finally, after much internal discussion, we decided there was no option but to go completely independent and reorganize the MCA deal, leaving all the promotional obligations to our own staff. The new deal gave us more profit per record sold, but it also meant we needed more than double the staff to sell and promote the records. It meant moving from a low-budget operation with latitude to be daring to one where making a mistake could mean having to fire someone or reduce salaries across the board. It was a fateful decision, and, looking back on it, I don't think it was a good one.

By 1989, the IRS overheads would become a serious strain, forcing us to look for other options. When our contract with MCA expired, we moved to EMI—a deal that saw IRS Records become part of the corporate world that we had in effect rebelled against from the start.

☙

Nineteen eighty-five year was also a big change for the members of The Police. For Sting, it began a period where he could do exactly what *he* wanted to do. He had the money and the prestige, so if he wanted to work with the top jazz musicians of the day—or opera, or country—he had the money and stature to do so. He chose to push the envelope towards jazz, but without abandoning the rock roots of The Police. My job was no longer one of balancing three equal musicians and interjecting my own vision into the mix—it was looking towards Sting's agenda and helping him achieve it, with my vision still there but subverted to his.

Sting going solo really came down to two things. First, he really wanted to have control of his songs. In The Police, he had to consider Stewart and Andy and their input. Stewart in particular, as the original founder of the group, had definite ideas, and they did not always coincide with Sting's. Going solo gave Sting the opportunity to have exactly the musicians he needed to deliver what he wanted, and as he asked. He really didn't want to have to argue to get what he wanted for songs that he clearly wrote by himself.

Second, there never was a conversation with me, Stewart, or Andy—individually or as a group—that specifically and clearly stated that The Police had broken up. None of us wanted to say that, and for Sting, even if he privately thought it, it did not make sense killing the golden goose publicly. When Andy launched his solo album, *XYZ*, he did say in various interviews that the band had broken up, but for the most part we all avoided saying it officially.

For Sting, though, achieving solo success that kept him at the standard of living he had become accustomed to, and in approximately the same limelight, would inevitably mean he did not have to think about The Police. Unlike other band front men who had gone solo and failed, like Mick Jagger of The Rolling Stones, Sting was well known as the one who wrote all the hits, sang all of them, *and* had the frontman look. He had received the lion's share of the media coverage, so, to many, he *was* The Police.

Sting's first solo album was *Dream Of The Blue Turtles*, closely followed by the film *Bring On The Night*. His idea from the start was to surround himself with the best musicians he could find and hone them into a unit that delivered what he thought his songs needed. They also had to be musicians he wanted to play with in concerts as well, and that he respected in their own right. The musicians he pulled together were Branford Marsalis, Kenny Kirkland, Omar Hakim, and Darryl Jones. They all had jazz credentials but were open to morphing into what Sting wanted to do—which was *not* to make a jazz album. However, working with players he respected, he would allow them the freedom to play, so the album naturally took on jazzy influences.

The project was obviously musically exciting for Sting, and that led to his idea of filming the band from their earliest days. The basic concept was to do the opposite of most music films, which are made at the end of a band, after years of problems, conflicts, breakups, drug dramas, and the like. Filming at the *beginning* would give a different take and presumably an interesting historic approach for a music documentary.

From a pure filmmaker's point of view, however, there was a serious flaw. At the start of almost any relationship, it is all sweetness and light. Everyone is on their best behavior at the beginning, just like in the average marriage. Reality sets in later, after foibles are discovered and dramas become highlighted. As the long-standing press motto goes, 'If it bleeds, it leads,' but that was unlikely to happen at the beginning, and where there is no blood, there is no story.

Even so, the film seemed like a good idea, and Jerry Moss at A&M agreed to fund a full-length theatrical release of what became *Bring On The Night*. The deal was separate from Sting's record deal, so I had no business problem with it. Michael Apted, who had a well-established reputation as a documentary filmmaker, as well as for theatrical films like *Coal Miner's Daughter*, was hired to direct it. That gave the project theatrical potential— this would not be a straight-to-video project. Filming started in May 1985, at the Mogador Theatre in Paris, where rehearsals were being held, and at a French château that was rented for the purpose.

From the very start there was great music, interesting characters, historically meaningful events, and the cool visual effect of filming in a French château. At the same time, it was all pretty tame and predictable. Everyone was getting along, and if there were any dramas, neither I nor Michael were seeing them. It was turning out to be a longform music video, and a pretty expensive one at that.

I can't blame any of the musicians, or Sting, as they were doing what they do and getting off on the music as they worked out each song. No one encouraged them to be pricks, or be angry, or challenge Sting, as that was not what the rehearsals were all about, and Michael Apted had not been hired to kick them into performing for a theatrical film. He was hired to capture the moment, and he did. The problem was that Jerry Moss was paying for a theatrical release, and Michael had a reputation to uphold.

It turned out the only one in the mix who could be a prick was me. I was an insider/outsider, and my job was to see things as they were. That's why Sting had me as his manager. So, when the rehearsals moved to the Mogador Theatre in Paris and I was sitting in the middle of the hall, looking at the stage set while talking to the clothing designer, I objected to the approach she was using. I never saw rock'n'roll as artsy-fartsy. Elvis, The Beatles, Elton, Prince, KISS, Lady Gaga—they all pushed the envelope visually in some way. Rock'n'roll has always been about flamboyance, exaggeration, and hype, not subtlety.

Looking at the gray stage set and the musicians dressed in gray, I thought they would blend into the background, so I said so. Colleen Atwood was a respected designer—and probably a great one, when directed properly—and I had no reason to be angry at her. It was just a conversation. However, when Michael Apted saw us having what was to me a small argument but to him might have seemed more, he came running with the camera crew, as if to say, *Great, we now have some drama*. He started gesticulating that we should heat it up, which we both did. My voice went up a notch, but it still seemed like much ado about nothing, so at one point I joked, 'Should I hit her?' For a second, Michael's eyes lit up, as if to say *YES!* Then he realized that would be a bridge too far.

For me, anyway, the scene ended up being more staged than real, with me as an actor more than a manager. But Michael must have figured he could use me again, so he kept an eye out for the next complaint or comment that might add some drama he could use. He was there for the conversation about business I had with Darryl Jones. It was a real conversation, and I had no problem 'telling it like it is.' That's what a manager is supposed to do, so the artist doesn't have to. Imagine how it would have looked if Sting had had to have that conversation with Darryl. The artist does not want to be seen talking about money.

In any case, when the movie finally was released, I became the star prick of the film, which the press seemed to delight in. For others, it just confirmed their impression that I was the typical businessman tough guy—anti-art, pro-money, probably heartless, and all the other nasty traits that a rock'n'roll manager is imagined to have.

Later, PopMatters.com wrote:

The two stars of the movie are Copeland and Marsalis. Copeland is straight out of *This Is Spinal Tap*. He is the business-first guy, and one of the film's best moments comes when he is arguing with the woman who designed the costumes for the band's first concert—grey and tan outfits that essentially disappear against the grey set. Copeland puts it bluntly: 'Well, I'm sorry—I'm just a peasant, man, but they look boring.' He is, of course, a total asshole, but he is right. He's not afraid to look bad, because he's actually being honest with the camera. His other great moment is spoken directly to the lens as he explains why Sting will be paid handsomely for these gigs while the infinitely more musically skilled jazz musicians will get paid crap. 'We've got Madison Square Garden sold out. Now, if you cancel the show, how many people are going to give their tickets back? No one! If Sting cancels, how many? Every one of 'em!'

For Jerry Moss, the film was released in November 1985, lasted a week in theaters, and grossed under two million dollars, so it was most probably a loss. For Sting, it was a nice historical piece about that band, and he comes across well. For me, I got some interesting press and a bunch of artists calling me to ask me to manage them. One act actually started the conversation with great enthusiasm: 'I just saw the *Bring On The Night* movie, and you are the only manager I want.' She liked what she assumed was my 'kick ass, take no prisoners' approach. Out of curiosity, I did meet her, and I found out what I usually feared from such artists. She thought a manager's job was to *make* the record company promote the artist's music. When she played me what she was convinced was a hit single, I said, 'You may be right that the song is a hit—I am often wrong—but I am not good enough to make a song a hit if I don't believe in it myself. If you are set on that song, then you should find someone else to manage you.' I never saw her or heard her music again.

The *Blue Turtles* Sting tour started strong on August 16, 1985, with five sold-out nights at the Greek Theatre in Los Angeles. A month later, Sting was on the front cover of *Rolling Stone* magazine. Then, in October, he was off to Europe. He did a lot of big shows in the *Blue Turtles* period—some in a package, like the Amnesty International Conspiracy Of Hope tour, and some on his own as a headliner. The biggest headlining show Sting ever did was at the Maracanã Stadium in Rio de Janeiro in November of 1987. It was before the stadium was reduced in size, so the Sting audience was reputed to be two hundred thousand people, which was huge. As usual, when he walked out onstage, the flash bulbs went off, and all of us were impressed with the sheer size of the spectacle. I guess it was a big deal, but there were so many shows like this, and by this time for me and indeed for Sting, most of them just became a blur.

CHAPTER 22

MY BRITAIN

Perhaps the most significant event for me personally around this time—which also reflected on my relationship with Sting—was the *My Britain* saga. It had a lot to do with Sting, but at the same time nothing to do with him. It was a TV program I did for Channel 4 called *My Britain*.

In early 1985, I got a phone call from Jools Holland. He was in Newcastle, filming for *The Tube*. I was due to go to see him the next day, and Jools wanted me to be sure to 'be nice' to one of the researchers of the show. According to Jools, John Cummins was someone I would like and should watch out for in the future—Jools thought this guy was destined to go places, but the people at *The Tube* were not treating him with the respect he deserved. Accordingly, when I got to Newcastle, John became my new best friend.

Jools couldn't have been more right. A few weeks later, John Cummins was appointed Commissioning Editor: Youth at Channel 4 headquarters in London. In other words, *The Tube* now reported to him. Not long after that, John came to my house in St John's Wood to introduce me to John Ranelagh, who commissioned political shows at Channel 4. At the time, there were nine commissioning editors at the channel who decided on all the programming. Of those nine, John Ranelagh was one of the few who was politically conservative, and he looked upon most of the other editors as 'indescribable lefties.' He had previously been a speechwriter for

Margaret Thatcher, and he later wrote a major book on the CIA—he was an interesting guy.

John Ranelagh lost no time grilling me about my political feelings, what I thought of England, did I believe in free enterprise—basically, did I think along the political lines that he did? It was well known that ninety-nine percent of the people in the music business were presumed to be 'lefties'—supporters of the Labour Party, 'socialism good, capitalism bad' kinds of people. It was in fact considered career destroying for a pop star to even hint at being anything other than a socialist. I doubt if many knew the real meaning of the terms socialism, capitalism, or free enterprise, but there was a definite political correctness about what one must believe depending on what side of the political spectrum one belonged to. For UK music artists, the political correctness spectrum was firmly to the left.

In any case, I must have passed the 'correct thinking' test, as John started describing a series he was creating for Channel 4. The shows were called *My Britain*, and aimed to highlight what various prominent people thought of the UK—what they liked and what they did not like. He had the leader of the Liberal Party, the Labour Party's shadow foreign secretary, the leading Communist, some bigwig in the Conservative Party, a big industrialist—all big shots in England, and all English. His problem was, he couldn't find anyone in the music business who would do one of the shows and espouse what he considered to be the correct 'free enterprise' values. I figured he wanted to take me on as some sort of advisor, to help him find a likely candidate. Then he hit me with, 'I want you to do the music business show.'

Surprised, I said, 'But I'm not English.' It apparently did not matter. For John, this was to be an important part for his *My Britain* series, and important for the youth of the country, who he felt were constantly fed the wrong message by the media—especially by the bulk of the programmers at Channel 4. If I was the perfect guy to deliver the right message, I was also probably the only one he thought he might convince to do it.

I could not help but be flattered, so I agreed in principle to consider his proposal. The next step was to meet the director who had been hired to film the show. That was Michael Jones, who it turned out had also been a Margaret Thatcher speechwriter. He was the one that came up with the 'short, sharp, shock' prison strategy that Thatcher announced in 1979. She loved it, then asked Michael, 'By the way, what does it mean?' Both he and John Ranelagh had some great stories about Thatcher, all of which ended up enhancing my view of her.

Anyway, Michael explained that the show would take two weeks, and they would set up all sorts of situations for me to comment on all over the UK. Basically, I would have my own film crew for the two weeks and be free to say what I wanted. It was assumed that I would say things about how capitalism and free enterprise were a good thing—the kind of thinking one would not normally hear from people in the music business. It was not an easy proposition to turn down, so I didn't.

This was going to be a big deal—primetime TV for one hour on one of the only four TV channels in the country—so I had to tell Sting, and of course my staff. Steve Tannett, who was now head of sales for all my indie record labels, was fearful. 'Whatever you do,' he said, 'you can't go out in the streets after it airs.' That was my first clue that this could be dangerous. Then I told Sting, and he put his foot down. He did not want me saying anything in such a high-profile place that could be interpreted as *his* views. Of course, all the big stars *were* capitalists, but they would never dare say so. But Sting insisted: 'If you do it, you can't be my manager.' That pretty much pulled the rug from under me. I had no option but to go back to John and say, no, I couldn't do it.

A few days later, Sting called up to say he had just sold his house and the new one was not yet ready, so could he stay with me for a few days in St John's Wood? Of course, the answer was yes, and on the first night, when we were sitting in the kitchen, there was a knock at the door. It was John Ranelagh and Michael Jones, here to talk me into doing the show. It was fate that Sting was there, as in reality he was the one who would determine if I could do it or not. John was very convincing: he said something to the effect that I had some very important things to say, and the country needed to hear them. Sting listened quietly, and, in the end, he said, 'I don't have to agree with what Miles has to say, but I will fight for his right to say it.'

I always knew Sting was no dummy, and that the 'politically correct' position of most in the music business was either naive or just plain bullshit. I have never heard any artist, manager, or lawyer say, 'Let's pay more taxes.' To avoid British taxes, many artists—like Rod Stewart, The Rolling Stones, and indeed The Police—took advantage of the 'tax year abroad' scheme. As long as one stayed out of the UK for all but sixty-five days, there was no tax to pay on foreign income. Artists were some of the most 'capitalist' people I had ever met. But Sting letting me say something nice about capitalism on TV? I will admit to being shocked, and I could not have had greater admiration for him.

Filming started in late 1985. Michael Jones had set up a number of interviews and situations to show Britain at the time and my view of it. I interviewed the clothing designer Paul Smith, who was just starting to build a reputation, at his shop in London; I interviewed Virgin's Richard Branson on his canal boat in West London; I spoke at the Conservative Party conference in Blackpool; I spent several days with The Farm, a seriously left-wing music group from Liverpool.

My basic message was that Britain had a lot going for it, but that an extreme leftist ideology had held it back. The most important message was that the music business, and the punks specifically, were all about 'free enterprise.' They started their own groups, or independent record companies, and they were exactly what free enterprise was all about. They did it on their own, and they hurt no one doing it. They got paid based on what they did and the popularity they achieved doing it. They were the very *definition* of capitalists.

That statement—as simple and true as it was—came as a shock to so many of those punks who were stuck thinking they were, or represented, something they were not. The Clash were capitalists, and so were the Sex Pistols—and so were all the bands I had ever worked with, pre-punk, punk, and post-punk. Even Mick Jones of The Clash recognized this when I talked to him, some days after the broadcast. I think of all those contract negotiations with artists and their representatives and the huge focus on what money they would earn, upfront advances, royalties . . . believe me, capitalism has been alive and well in the music business for a long, long time.

This would all sound rather silly to the average American. And Britain has changed so much since then that if the show was aired today, I am sure most of the UK would find it silly, too. But in 1986, when *My Britain* aired, it was a big deal.

The day after it aired—in prime time, no less—I had to go to Oxford Street in central London, and at one point saw a man come running towards me. As he dodged through the Oxford Street traffic, I thought, *OK, this is it, I'm going to be attacked.* When he got to me, he stuck out his hand and said, 'Thank you for saying what you did.' The response was the opposite of what everyone said I would get. I guess John Ranelagh was right. I got a lot of letters of support, and it was very gratifying.

In his review of the show in the Arts section of the *Times* on February 12, 1986, Christopher Dunkley wrote:

> 8:00 Channel 4: MY BRITAIN: Rich Anglo-American record producer Miles Copeland wonders why people as inventive and—as he says—greedy as the British reject the full logic of capitalism. Here is a program about ideas which does, at first, seem somewhat contrived in its determination to find pictorial means of expression. Yet it comes vividly to life when Copeland tours Liverpool with a coachload of teenage rock musicians and asks about their attitude towards money, public housing and so on. What he hears is a terrifying form of ill-digested neo-Marxism regurgitated as jealousy. It makes you think that perhaps those Tory scare stories about Trots taking over the teaching colleges might contain a grain of truth.

Several weeks later, I was glad to hear from John Ranelagh that Margaret Thatcher had watched the show and loved it. He had even managed to have it screened in the White House for President Reagan, who John told me also loved it. That was even more gratifying. A year or so later, John left Channel 4 and took a programming job for Norwegian TV. He had the *My Britain* show aired there as well.

The next year, I heard from Michael Jones that the show was to be aired again on Channel 4. It was actually listed on the broadcast schedule. Then, just before it was supposed to broadcast, he called again and said, sorry, it had been pulled. Why? Because those leftie commissioning editors thought it would 'influence the upcoming election.' Now that *really* was gratifying!

∾

For anyone marketing or selling anything, TV exposure is usually top of the list whether it be the thirty-second commercial, or product placement, or better yet a full TV show. Luckily for me, my relationship with MTV was growing out of mutual interest—they needed product, but few would give it to them; I needed exposure for my artists, but few would give it to me—so I suggested IRS could do a TV show for MTV that would feature up-and-coming acts.

It did not take long to convince them. Perhaps it was my commitment to not only have IRS and FBI acts on the show but to draw from the whole new music community that convinced them, or maybe it was because I agreed to fund it myself, provided they gave me some advertising time so I could get some funding to pay for it. Probably the latter. They got a free show—they had nothing to lose. I got my own show, and IRS became the only record company to ever have its own show on the channel.

Then I went to Carlos Grasso, art director at IRS, and told him we had a show on MTV, so get it together. As usual, it was a great opportunity for IRS, but at the same time I was throwing my team in at the deep end. None of us had ever made a TV show before. And that was the start of *Cutting Edge*. It lasted five years on MTV, and it was the first to give TV exposure to many music stars of the future, from R.E.M. to NWA. It became one of the lasting legacies of IRS Records, and is remembered by many to this day.

∾

A few years later, in one of my stupider moments, I was talked into going into the film business. I suppose, spending more time in Hollywood, I should have expected it. The culprit was an engaging ex-IRS Records employee by the name of Paul Colichman. Thankfully, his idea was not going for the big time, but more in the tradition of IRS Records looking for off-the-beaten-track films, new directors and actors, and ideas major companies would most probably not be interested in.

The first film fit that idea to a T. It was *The Decline Of Western Civilization: The Metal Years*, directed by Penelope Spheeris, who was to become one of America's premiere female film directors. For the half-a-million-dollar budget, it was a success; it enhanced Penelope's career and added a lot of fun stories to the mix. Much of the filming happened in my house in Hollywood. Ozzy Osbourne was filmed cooking in the kitchen, KISS in the living room, and the singer of Wasp drunk out of his mind swimming in the swimming pool. I didn't swim in that pool for a month after.

Paul was a good hustler, and he knew his way around making films. In all, some twenty-five films were made, all in the one-to-three-million-dollar range. I even had an acting role as a TV evangelist in *Bank Robber*. The best film was *One False Move*, which was another example of the original concept of the company. It was the first feature for director Carl Franklin, and the first film starring Billy Bob Thornton. The company also made Bobcat Goldthwait's first film, *Shakes The Clown*, which was about miserable clowns. On paper, it looked very IRS, but it was not one of our high points. My wife, in fact, hated that movie.

The good news was that each film made money, and most of them were interesting movies. We even got awards. The bad news was that the money made was never enough to cover the costs between the films, so inch by inch over its eight years of existence, the company lost money. The biggest problem was that I didn't have time to learn the ins and outs of the film business, so I depended on Paul to run it. When I realized that fact, I decided it was time to change the relationship. My deal with Paul was seventy-five percent to me and I fund it and twenty-five percent to him. I suggested we switch roles, and it looked like the Allen Grubman motto, 'It's about the money,' was correct again. Paul left and the company dissolved. All I got in the end was credit as executive producer on twenty-five films and some amusing stories to tell.

However, Paul and many of the directors and actors that got their start with IRS Media went on to become successful. Paul now runs a major LGBT media network called Heremedia. Penelope Spheeris and Carl Franklin went on to be top directors; Billy Bob Thornton, Bill Paxton, and many others became staples of the film business. So, like IRS Records,

IRS Media can claim to have discovered great talent and helped launch careers, but financially I can't put it on my 'win' list.

At the same time, I learned a lot. The biggest lesson was that for all the lies and hype one found in the music business, the film business was the same, except that the price tag was ten times bigger. Losing a few thousand on some wacko music project was not a big deal, but in the film business such an idea could be a million dollars. As the risks were greater, one's propensity to go by instinct alone was severely dampened.

I still kick myself over *Mr. Christmas Dinner*, which was eventually released as *Lucky Stiff*. It was a super-funny comedy script that I talked Showtime into financing. Their first thought was that we needed a 'name' director to give it credibility, so they pushed for Anthony Perkins, who had made his name in *Psycho*. Admittedly, he qualified as a 'name,' but he was *not* a funny man. He was basically a horror actor. I should have squawked, but I was new to all of this, and I figured Showtime was financing the project, so I trusted they knew something that I did not. In short, Anthony turned the funniest comedy movie script I had ever read into a horror movie. Of course, it flopped—big time.

Mr. Christmas Dinner was also the first time I met Sharon Stone, who had auditioned for the film. She was not known at the time, so she was rejected out of hand. The crazy thing was, she was rejected even before she did the audition. If we had only known! Funnily enough, I did meet her again some years later, after she had become a big star, when she was playing the lead in a Miramax film, *The Mighty*, and I was releasing the soundtrack on my Ark 21 label, with Sting singing the title track. There was a scene set in a museum that had a great suit of medieval armor, as part of the plot involved a young disabled boy played by Kieran Culkin imagining the days of King Arthur's Knights of the Round Table. Years later, I came across that very same suit of armor, made by Peter Fuller, one of the world's great modern armorers. I bought it, and now it resides at my place in France. Funny how what goes around comes around.

༉

This period also coincided with my dabbling in the London film world. London was like a small town: if you were in one part of the entertainment business, you morphed into other parts as well. Jools Holland and I had cameo roles in the movie *Eat The Rich* for producer Michael White, who I had done *Urgh! A Music War* with. Also in the movie were Paul McCartney, Lemmy from Motörhead (who did much of the music), and half the entertainment world in London. We hobnobbed with the likes of Jennifer Saunders, Dawn French, and Leslie Ash, who hosted the second season of *The Tube* with Jools; there was Paula Yates and Bob Geldof, of course, and various other music personalities. All this while flitting back and forth between the UK and America.

In 1987, Jools inadvertently used some 'no-no' words while filming an episode of *The Tube*, and that forced the termination of the entire series. In the USA, I finally had to pull the plug on the IRS *Cutting Edge* show on MTV. Its five years had been great for the profile of IRS Records, but MTV never helped cover the costs, and it became a growing financial drain.

The biggest loss turned out to be IRS's bulldog radio promotion man, Michael Plen, at the very end of 1986. That meant IRS started 1987 as, in effect, a different company. The more I look back on the history of the label, the more I realize what a mistake that was. As the principal owner and leader of the company, I have to mostly blame myself, but I also blame Jay Boberg. The break came when Michael asked for a small ownership share of the company, and to make that happen both Jay and I would have had to give up shares. When Jay refused, that left me no option but to refuse also. If I could do it all over again, I would have forced the issue, but, then again, neither I nor Jay realized at the time how difficult it would be to replace Michael. We did fill the position, but we never replaced the man.

CHAPTER 23

THE SHOK OF THE NEW

. . . .

If there were acts that were inexpensive yet interesting in some way, I was likely to be up for signing them. That word was out, and all sorts of strange, wonderful, and completely nuts acts were offered to me, IRS, Faulty, and to Ian's FBI. Some wanted management, some wanted a record deal, but all wanted in on the game in whatever way they could. Tapes would arrive in the mail, staff would be lobbied, I would be stopped in the street; I even had waiters at a restaurant bring my food with a tape. When I bought a car in Los Angeles, there was even a tape in the cassette deck. I actually signed that band: Dada. There was no escape.

Dada were a three-piece band in the mold of The Police. The guy I bought the car from turned out to be the singer/guitarist of the band, Michael Gurley. Things started well with the first album, then on the second album Michael got tendonitis and we had to cancel all the live performances, which pretty much killed the record. By the third album it was now the turn of IRS Records to have problems, resulting in *El Subliminoso* being the last album released on the label. Dada became yet another act to put on the 'shoulda happened' list.

In the early days, the philosophy was not so much about selling lots of albums and making money as it was getting involved with music that I personally liked. But since funds were limited, it also had to be about *not* losing money. The main marketing strategy was based around live shows, because in the first few years of IRS there were very few radio stations that would play the music, and not much press either. MTV did not join the effort until August 1981, with the *Cutting Edge* show debuting in March 1983. As the company grew, acts were often brought to my attention from the staff, and out of sheer politeness one had to pay attention. One wants everyone in the company to think they can contribute, and one never knows where the next exciting, hit act might come from. I remained the chief signer, but I also had to be open to company opinion and input as well. Sometimes, it meant IRS agreed to sign an artist that we shouldn't have.

The one that comes most to mind is a heavy-metal act brought in by Barry Lions, who became IRS's national radio director after Michael Plen. Shok Paris looked like every spandex-trousered, long-hair band that we used to refer to as 'old fart' bands. Definitely not the typical act one would find on IRS Records. The only reason the band was signed was to accommodate Barry, who for some reason believed in them. I saw my first job as trying to find an image and story that would make them unique or at least different enough to validate the signing. We figured Barry could get them on radio, but they had to somehow seem relevant to a label like IRS. Easier said than done.

When I met the band at the IRS offices, my first question was, 'Tell me about the name. Why Shok Paris?' Never being much of a speller, I actually thought it was *Shock* Paris. The answer was as limp as the band turned out to be. They had put various names in a hat and pulled out Shok Paris.

'So, the name doesn't mean anything? Is that what you would tell a journalist if asked? Doesn't make much of a story, does it?'

I figured it was at least an interesting name, so why not create a story around it that might give a journalist something more to write about when we got them interviews? I suggested they should say they chose the name because they 'hate the French!' I argued that 'we all know you can't say you hate anyone ethnically, racially, or for religious reasons, but no one is going to be freaked out if you hate the French.' It's like saying you hate cabbage—no one is going to be offended. 'Then, onstage, you could smash French champagne bottles, destroy a model of the Eiffel Tower; basically, *Fuck the French* would be your motto.' Perhaps silly, but I was making a point. It would at least be memorable, and definitely fodder for journalists to write about.

The band sat there, silent, stunned, looking at me like I had two heads. I could have been speaking to a blank wall. When I said their band photo sucked and made them look like every other heavy-metal band, they lamely protested. To prove it, I stuck their photo to the far wall of the office along with several other similar photos of other heavy-metal bands and said, 'OK, now which photo is yours?' They couldn't pick theirs out. I had made my point.

The strange thing is that a few years later, when George Bush took the USA to war and the French government declined to offer its support, there was all sorts of anti-French feeling that the band could have capitalized on. Remember when 'freedom fries' replaced french fries? It once again goes to show the importance of timing.

Needless to say, Shok Paris were not a success for IRS Records, and they soon disappeared from sight. The story of 'Fuck the French' persisted, however, and it was used to prove just how nuts I was. Whereas I used the story as a lesson in not wasting any opportunity to get press coverage. A band's name was part of the image, so why not make it work for you? Stewart did that in choosing the name The Police. Names like The Damned, Lords Of The New Church, The Clash, Grateful Dead, Rolling Stones, and of course Sex Pistols had an automatic image vibe to them. My idea was this: *Put yourself in the shoes of a journalist tasked to write about you—you are not famous yet. The journalist has done twenty reviews that week, all basically saying the same thing and is bored out of his mind. Hell, give the poor guy something to write about! Make it up, exaggerate, the journalist will thank you for it!*

That's probably why I went for the crazier acts. They were more likely to get attention or have a photo or a story that the media would go for. The more outrageous or newsworthy, the easier to promote. That's what Malcolm McLaren did with the Pistols. The only difference was, Malcolm saw press coverage as an end in itself, and mainly for him personally. I saw it as a way to promote the music and establish the artist.

As time went on, the A&R (signing) policy of the label became more and more a group policy than mine personally. As mentioned earlier, Steve Tannett in London brought in The Alarm; Paul Orescan in Canada brought in Candi; Carlos Grasso went to South by Southwest in Austin, Texas, to check out bands and came back with several tapes of bands he thought we should consider. Sometimes it was a good and smart thing; other times it moved IRS out of its established niche. But when I heard Timbuk 3, I immediately wanted to sign them.

Timbuk 3 was Pat McDonald and his wife Barbara plus a drum machine. They were even more economical than Stewart's concept of The Police. Timbuk's third member didn't take up space, complain, or take any fee. It was a small box that fit into a suitcase. Their first album was nominated for 'Best New Artist' at the Grammy Awards in 1987, and it looked like they were going to be a very good signing for IRS Records.

Ever since my college days, I'd been into lyrics that had a touch of sarcasm and humor in them as they dealt with social issues, so of course I was a big fan of Bob Dylan. At IRS Records, it was Stan Ridgway and Pat McDonald. Of course, I would have to put Sting, Chris Difford, and Simon Wilson of 29 Palms into the pot of great lyric writers, but Pat stands as the one that gave me the biggest bit of insanity I had in the business.

Pat McDonald was what we politely call an 'art monster,' but in my blunter and more private moments I would have to characterize him as a severely blinkered muso stuck in silly ideas that verged—at least to my mind—on insanity. He had it burned into his skull that letting a song be used in a commercial—of any sort—was the ultimate sellout. He would rather kill his mother than let a song be so used. On one hand, you could admire his 'not in it for the money' mentality, but on the other hand it was, 'Are you fucking crazy!?' Yet for all that, I always thought of him as a super-brilliant songwriter—a master of the lyric. In later years, I would bring him to my castle songwriters' retreats more than any other artist I worked with. And I liked him.

On the first album that IRS released in 1986, *Greetings From Timbuk 3*, there was a killer song called 'The Future's So Bright I Gotta Wear Shades.' It was fun on the surface, but it was actually about nuclear war. It was clever, and it was also perfect for Ray-Ban sunglasses, prompting the company to offer one million dollars to use it in a commercial. One can imagine a Ray-Ban commercial would likely be very cool and image-enhancing, and that it would enable Timbuk 3 to sell millions of albums.

The good news was that the IRS deal with Timbuk 3 was for both music rights and song rights, and the contract allowed me to grant rights without having to consult the artist, unless we needed to do so on moral grounds. When I called Pat with the good news, he gave me the bad news. He started pleading with me to turn it down.

'But Pat, you will get $500,000—think of that! You can buy a house!'

It's not like Pat and Barbara were rich—far from it. But Pat pleaded so hard that I ended up agreeing to turn down the deal—a decision I've regretted ever since. The same happened a year later, when Ford motor cars offered $800,000 for the same song. In all, I turned down close to three million dollars on that one song alone. Then Clairol wanted to license 'Hairstyles and Attitudes' for $450,000. Again, Pat pleaded. I turned it down, bought a plastic piggy band, sealed shut the slot where you put coins in, and mailed it to Pat for Christmas.

Pat had very definite ideas about his songs. Sting used to call his songs his 'babies,' but he still knew which ones were his best and which were not. To Pat, they were all the same. When it came time to do a best-of album, I had a long argument with Pat: 'This is a best-of, which means it has your best songs on it.' Pat hated that name, as it would imply that his other songs were *not* his best. It was like he was afraid he might offend them. That's how the title became *Some Of The Best Of Timbuk 3.*' To me, that would imply that some of the best songs were left off the album, so not putting one's best foot forward. But that was Pat. One could argue with him, but that meant phone call after phone call until one was worn down, so giving in was the only way to get out. *Some Of The Best Of* is not a good title. With Pat, it was always two steps forward, one step back.

In later years, at the many songwriter retreats he attended, Pat wrote songs with Cher, Peter Frampton, Keith Urban, my brother Stewart, Imogen Heap, and so many more. I still regard him as one of the most gifted songwriters IRS ever signed. Years later, Pat McDonald started his own songwriter retreat, and he wrote me a long letter saying he now understood the problems I faced, as he was now having to deal with the same sort of things. That was nice—like he was finally learning that there are two sides to every story. However, he still won't admit that turning down all that money was a bad idea . . .

c/s

Nineteen eighty-seven was the year that The Bangles were voted 'Best International Group' at the BRIT Awards; Sting released his *Nothing Like The Sun* album; I launched IRS Media to develop low-budget movies; R.E.M. released *Document*; Sting and I launched Pangea Records as a home for soundtracks and other projects that personally interested him; Animal Logic formed; Stewart released *Equalizer And Other Cliff Hangers*. Torch Song (featuring William Orbit), The Alarm, and The Truth had new records out on IRS too. It was becoming usual to have a busy year, but this one had a few landmines. One of them was Andy Summers.

With The Police never having publicly or formally broken up, I was still the de facto manager of Andy Summers (and Stewart). So, when Andy came to me for help with the launch his solo career, I was obligated to deliver for him as an individual, just as I had done for the entire Police group. I was working with Sting on launching his solo career, just as I was Stewart, and there was no question I would do the same for Andy.

Andy's first request was a record deal. One of the first things I did was go to Irving Azoff at MCA. Irving was aggressively looking to build MCA into a more important label; signing a member of The Police would be an attractive proposition. The deal was made without having to play music or lay out facts or make promises of any kind. I presume Irving thought, *How bad could it be? A high-profile member of one of the biggest bands in the world, and a manager who knows what he is doing.*

MCA offered a decent advance and royalty, and I had delivered the first step of the process. Andy then went off to record the album. I would go to his studio from time to time, but Andy was confident in himself; he did not want any input from me, and I was not invited to give any.

When Andy finally delivered the album for me to take into MCA, my first comment was that there was no single, and that this would create a problem. On top of that, the vocals needed work. I suggested he record some more songs, to allow us to replace some of the tracks on the album. That did not go over well. Andy disagreed with all my comments. Andy would listen to Sting, but for some reason I didn't have the ability to make him listen to me. He wanted me to take the album to MCA to see what *they* thought, which I promptly did.

The product manager for Andy was a woman whose name escapes me, and I'm probably doing her a favor not to mention it. We listened to each song in her office, and at the end she looked at me and said, 'What are we supposed to do with this shit?' She didn't like the songs, she heard no single, and she didn't like the vocals either. It was pretty much exactly what I had told Andy, except worse.

'I know Andy can do better,' I said, 'and I've told him so, but I need you to tell him what you just told me.'

My hope was that an MCA meeting might convince him to work more on the album and fix the problems both MCA and I saw. The objective was to help Andy have the hit album he wanted, since the album he'd delivered was far from that.

A day or so later, I brought Andy into the MCA offices to meet the product manager, to let him hear firsthand the problems the label had with the album. I was walking in as the idiot who didn't see how good his album was, but I hoped to walk out as the manager who'd given good advice to his client.

As we walked in, Andy's first words were, 'It's great isn't it? There are lots of singles.'

To my shock, the A&R lady agreed with him. 'We all love it.'

The rug was pulled right from under me. Not one hint of any objection or problem from MCA. I walked out of that meeting still an idiot.

When I was back at my office, I called MCA to ask, 'What the hell happened? Why didn't you tell Andy what you told me?'

The answer I got was, 'How can I tell Andy Summers his album is crap?'

'Because that's your job!' I retorted.

MCA began setting up the album for release in July of 1987. I got a letter from the marketing department that said, 'Due to the esoteric feel of the album, as opposed to broad commercial pop appeal, we are concentrating on musician-oriented publications.' That gave me a good indication of how the album had been received within the company.

MCA released the album, *XYZ*, and then, as I could have predicted, the label had forgotten they even had it by the beginning of the second week. The few reviews it got were all bad; they all mentioned the vocals, and they went even further than I had done. The gist of the comments was: boring arrangements; repetitive, inferior vocals; unmemorable songs. One reviewer even said he found some copies in a dump, listened to one, and then put them all back in the dump.

The point is that Andy could have done better, had he listened. As far as I know, he never made another vocal album again. Perhaps he read some of the reviews. The shame was that he was a brilliant guitarist with some songwriting talent, and with a different approach he might even have pulled off the vocals. Collaborating with songwriters might have given him better songs to choose from. As I heard so many times, if you want ten great songs, write a hundred. The songs on *XYZ* did not apply that rule.

Perhaps the most frustrating thing was the missed opportunities. One thing we learned from our experience with The Police is that you never know where a hit is coming from. The Police missed 'Roxanne,' CBS missed 'Walk Like An Egyptian,' and who would have imagined an audience of four people in Syracuse on that first US tour would have opened such a huge door for The Police?

As a small record company, representing what many considered fringe acts, I was always looking for a break to get exposure, so IRS and I personally kept our eyes out for movie soundtracks. Consequently, we chased movies we heard about, and movie companies approached us when they heard of our interest. Early IRS soundtracks included *Bachelor Party* (1984), with songs by The Alarm, Jools Holland, R.E.M., The Fleshtones, and Oingo Boingo; *Intimate Creeps* (1986), with tracks by Intimate Strangers, Stan Ridgway, and Jane Wiedlin; *The Texas Chainsaw Massacre 2* (1986), with Lords Of The New Church, The Cramps, Concrete Blond, Stewart Copeland, Timbuk 3, Torch Song, and Oingo Boingo; *She's Having A Baby* (1988), with Dave Wakeling; and *Leaving Las Vegas* (1995), with Sting and The Palladinos. Stewart launched his soundtrack career at IRS with *Rumble Fish* (1983); the TV show *The Equalizer* (1985–89); *Out Of Bounds* (1986), with Belinda Carlisle, American Girls, Intimate Strangers, Lords Of The New Church, and Adam Ant; *The Leopard Son* (1996); *Boys And Girls* (2000); and so many others.

When I got a call for Andy to do a soundtrack for *Revenge Of The Nerds*, however, he seemed insulted that I'd offered the film to him. I guess he was reacting to the title, which he saw as indicating that I did not hold his music in high regard. He said something to the effect of, 'I am surprised you would offer something like that to me.' The film went on to be a hit, though, and it is now considered a cult classic, often listed among the Top 100 funniest movies ever released.

I can't remember exactly how much later Andy and I parted ways, but if memory serves it was around April of 1988. His final words were, 'If you don't like my music, you shouldn't manage me.' He was right. But he should have said, 'If you can't make me listen to good advice then you are not the right manager for me.' Then he would have been absolutely right.

The Andy situation was sad for me. An outside journalist might say something like, 'Miles Copeland never learned the fundamental rule of artist management: *Always tell the artist what he or she wants to hear.*' One will never be penalized for telling someone they are great or that their work is genius, but tell them it needs work, or even that it is crap, and you will almost certainly be fired.

If my lawyer, Allen Grubman, wrote my gravestone, I am sure he would say, 'Here lies a putz who was too naive and principled to tell a lie.' Or more likely, knowing Allen, he would cut to the chase and just say, 'Here lies a putz.'

The truth is that, having often been accused of only caring about the money—a standard criticism of anyone on the business side of things—I would say my problem was *not* caring enough about money. If I had cared more, I would have been a better liar. I have also been accused of 'telling it like it is,' and that is true too—and a good reason why I lost the management of several artists I cared about, one of whom was Andy.

e/3

Another Police offshoot was Animal Logic, a three-piece band formed by my brother Stewart, bass player Stanley Clarke, and songwriter Deborah Holland, who was also the singer. The simplest way to describe the band is to say that the frame was better than the picture. The musicians were superstars in their field: Stanley Clarke was often referred to as the greatest bass player in the world and my brother Stewart the greatest drummer. The singer, however, was a gifted songwriter but a mouse by comparison. Onstage, it might as well have been two lions and a mouse. That mouse was Deborah, who didn't have the convincing persona to compete with those two, and at shows the audience would wave at her to move over so they could see Stewart and Stanley. She was too nice and normal, so she was placed in a near impossible job. It was hit or miss trying to pull it off. Mostly it was a miss.

Animal Logic appeared on *The Tonight Show* and *Letterman*, where it was easier for Deborah to hold her own as the cameras boxed in the view. On tour, it was a different story. They toured South America, Europe, and the USA, but gaining enough momentum to overcome the inherent mouse/lion problem really depended on a hit record.

I thought I made a great record deal with Virgin Records in Europe for the world outside of North America, but I realized afterwards it was really a bad deal. I use this lesson when I give lectures on how to do smart deals. Like most record deals, the advances escalated from the second album on. That second album triggered a hefty advance. So, why was it a bad deal? Because the first single Animal Logic released was moderately successful, as was the second one. So, the debate at the record company was, 'Do we release a third single?' At this point, the accountants stepped in and said, in effect, 'If the third single doesn't happen, then for sure we won't pick up the expensive option on that second album, so why risk the money?' And so Virgin never released the third single.

The point is this: if that second album had been . . . let's say *free*, there's no question the record company would have released the third single, and that might have been the one that broke the group into success. In other words, the good deal on paper turned out to be the thing that scared the record company into pulling the plug.

Virgin opting out of the second album left it to IRS Records alone to pay for and release it, which obviously put a serious dent in the funding. We had all counted on that funding to make the group viable. In the end, two albums were recorded, and then the band came to an end. When it came time to promote the second album, Stanley Clarke had a bunch of soundtrack commitments to honor, so he could not tour and was not available for much of the promotion. That put the final nail in the coffin.

CHAPTER 24

I NEVER PROMISED YOU A ROSE GARDEN

. . . .

In 1988, a promoter I was friends with invited me to Rod Stewart's birthday party in Los Angeles. I didn't know Rod, but I was told he had this great house in Beverly Hills and lots of interesting people would be there, so I went along. At one point I saw a beautiful girl sitting alone on a chair, so I went up to Rod's manager, Randy Phillips, and asked, 'Who is that?' He said he thought she was from South America somewhere, probably Colombia, and she was single.

In true Barry Diamond style, I went up to her, got on my knees, put my hand over my eyes, and pretended to be some sort of mystic seer. 'Don't tell me, you not from here... you are from the south... yes south... ah, I see, Colombia!'

Adriana looked at me like I was a crazy person and said, 'No.'

I put my hands back over my eyes and muttered, 'Yes... more south... ah, Brazil?'

'No' again.

'Uruguay?'

'No, Argentina.'

The ice was broken, and we kept talking. I then told her I was a 'gardener to the stars' and I could build her a rose garden, which she didn't believe for a minute. Of course, she refused to go out with me because I was in the entertainment business—smart girl—but by the end of the night she'd agreed to let me take her to tea and given me her phone number.

I left shortly after for the month-long Amnesty International's Human Rights Now! tour around the world, and from each country I would telephone Adriana. Japan, India, South Africa, Rhodesia, Ivory Coast, every stop. We were married two years later.

I did make one mistake, however. On one of our rare arguments, I said, 'I never promised you a rose garden.'

'Yes, you did!'

☙

The Amnesty International tour was a big deal—we were going around the world with our own jumbo jet plane carrying Bruce Springsteen, Sting, and Peter Gabriel as the main headliners, while Tracy Chapman and a few others were on the bill as well. The famous promoter Bill Graham was with us, but I never got much chance to talk to him as he stationed himself at the rear of the plane. Sting and I were right in the front, with Bruce and his manager John Landau right behind us. Apparently, John and Bruce had had a run-in with Bill, which is why Bill was at the back of the plane.

Peter Gabriel was one of the nicer people on the tour, and he always put on a great show. I tried to talk to him at various times, but I was probably too intense for him. He had that 'deer caught in headlights' look—he was probably thinking, *Who is this maniac with his crazy ideas?* Tracy Chapman was a nonstarter from the get-go. The lights went out when she entered a room, and I can't remember her saying 'hello' or 'good morning' on the entire tour. My favorite people, and Sting's as well, were Bruce Springsteen and John Landau. Bruce had a humility about him that was very disarming. He seemed to admire Sting and his band and would say his own band was really a 'bar band,' but Springsteen knew that what he had worked. It reminded me of when Bruce Allen, Bryan Adams's manager, called me once after Bryan had supported Sting on a few shows. Bryan was a very successful artist in his own right, and Bruce said, 'Tell Sting he fucked up my artist.' Apparently, Bryan was so impressed with Sting's musicians that he decided to upgrade his own band, which Bryan's fans didn't go for.

All of the Amnesty shows were huge, playing to audiences of fifty to eighty thousand people. The tour took in places like India, South Africa,

215

Japan, the Ivory Coast, Zimbabwe, and Argentina, as well as Europe and the USA, so it was important for me to be on the whole tour. But the one concert that left the most indelible mark was the one in Costa Rica on September 6, 1988.

Costa Rica is a small country in Central America, and it's rarely on anyone's concert touring circuit. I have never had any other concerts there before or since. The reason it was on the Amnesty schedule was due to the president of the country having just won the Nobel Peace Prize. When we arrived at the small airport, we were whisked through and taken to a bus to take us to meet the president at his official residence. On the way in there were huge crowds of onlookers welcoming us.

Bruce Springsteen, sitting behind me and Sting, said, 'You know what is going to win these people? "La Bamba."' Of course, none of the entourage, including Bruce, had that song in their set so, his comment was thrown out as a sort of challenge for all the bands to hear.

When we got to the presidential residence and were ushered in, everything seemed organized for about three or four minutes, with the usual pleasantries back and forth, meeting the president, shaking hands with the local dignitaries and the like. Then the meeting room doors flew open, and in came the president's daughter and her friends, and the sedate atmosphere became more like the backstage door at a supergroup's rock concert. The president was pushed aside, as were his staff and the startled dignitaries, and whatever security there was totally lost control. It was nuts, so we had no option but to get the hell out of there as fast as we could.

The next day, at the concert, there was an audience of around seventy thousand people, all seated, enjoying the festival atmosphere of good music. Tracy Chapman went on and did her usual pessimistic, downer show, which I had long since stopped watching. Then Peter Gabriel did his show. Of course, neither of them did 'La Bamba.' Then Sting went on and did his show, and once again no 'La Bamba.'

Bruce Springsteen closed the show. I had never been a big fan of his music, but as a person he was a great guy, and I got so that I *wanted* to like him. Sting and I were both at the side of the stage, watching his performance. Bruce did his usual set, but about three-quarters of the way through he looked over at me and Sting, as if to say, *I told you guys: you had your chance, now watch this.* He looked back at the audience and went straight into 'La Bamba.' Like magic, the whole audience went wild— everyone was immediately on their feet. From that moment on, Bruce Springsteen owned that show—none of the rest of us existed. It was an amazing thing to see, and one could not help but understand in that moment why Bruce had become such a big and beloved star.

❧

The second big tour of the year for me was the *Night Of The Guitar* tour. It was my concept from beginning to end—a pet idea that had been brewing in my mind, and now finally I had a chance to make it happen. It was going to be a fun tour with some real legends, so Adriana and I attended all the dates.

Going way back to the beginning of Wishbone Ash, I had always been a fan of the electric guitar as *the* iconic sound of rock'n'roll. When I started in the music business and saw 'Eric Clapton Is God' painted on a wall, it was Eric Clapton the guitarist, not the singer, that it referred to. In those early days, when it came to the guitar, Andy Powell, Ted Turner, Laurie Wisefield, and Peter Haycock were *my* gods. Indeed, my favorite tracks from both Wishbone Ash and The Climax Blues Band were always the more instrumental ones, which of course always featured the guitar. Live, when it came to The Police, the same was true. Perhaps it was the freedom of no lyrics that made it possible, or maybe the fact that there were no lyrics freed the brain to think what it wanted, with no word to direct thoughts one way or another. Perhaps that is why I related to artists like William Orbit, and later all the Arab artists like Cheb Mami and Hakim—even Zucchero, whose lyrics I didn't understand—so that I was free to think as my brain took me.

Anyway, this led me in 1988 to come up with an all-instrumental series of albums called *No Speak*, which IRS art director Carl Grasso cleverly promoted as 'Music Too Good For Words.' The germ of the idea came from several directions. Films and television shows often looked for music that had no lyrics as it would not interfere with a story line. The same was true of commercials, plus what seemed to be a growing market for 'ambient music'—the kind of music one might play at a dinner party. It

217

was always meant to be a tangent for the label, to enter a potential market where we would not face stiff competition from major labels. That was the challenge IRS faced more and more as time went on.

The first releases were instrumental albums by the Wishbone Ash guitarists and Climax's Peter Haycock, plus William Orbit and my brother Stewart. Then I looked further afield to favorite guitarists I might talk into contributing at least a track or two for compilation concepts. That led to Alvin Lee of Ten Years After, Leslie West of Mountain, Robby Krieger of The Doors, Jan Akkerman of Focus, Steve Howe of Yes, Steve Hunter from Lou Reed's band, Randy California of Spirit, and the recording of the two *Night Of The Guitars* compilation albums.

When it came time to promote the albums, the obvious way would be by a concert tour, if I could get enough of the guitarists to agree to participate. Thankfully, they did agree, and we did our first tour around the UK in November 1988, followed by a second one on the Continent. The tours featured a house band, with each guitarist doing three songs, followed by a finale with all of them onstage. I was the host introducing the show. For a guitar aficionado, the shows were obviously a super treat, with big names all together in one show. They really were 'Guitar Gods,' and even if one was not a big fan of one of the players, a few minutes later another player would take over.

It's funny what one remembers of the players. Leslie West was a bear of a man—loud and gruff but a real sweetheart. An imposing force on the outside, a teddy bear inside. Jan Akkerman hated the Germans; he could not forgive the World War II occupation of Holland. Robby Krieger was remarkably quiet and unassuming. Having been a member of the hugely successful Doors, one would have imagined a wild man. Alvin Lee was just a good guy. Randy California idolized Jimi Hendrix and could play exactly as Jimi did. It was an interesting mix of characters.

As one can imagine, they were great shows, and an obvious opportunity for filming—which I took full advantage of. The funny thing was that when I went to MTV the following year to see if they would broadcast the film, I was told that the days of the guitar gods were over, and no one would be interested. The new wave—which I had been partly responsible for—was now the dominant music on MTV. It's like I was responsible for killing what I had once been promoting. Meanwhile, I was convinced there was still interest, though, and finally MTV consented to give me a 'death slot' to air the program.

The death slot was late evening on a Sunday. The following Monday, when I called MTV to see how the show had done in the ratings, I was told there must be a mistake—they would have to get back to me. It seemed the show had rated #1 for the entire month, and that couldn't be right.

The next day, I called again, and they had to concede that indeed, the show got more viewers than any other show that entire month. Once again, I had proved that I might be crazy, but I am not *that* crazy . . .

CHAPTER 25

THE SULTAN AND
THE BURLEY MINDER

. . . .

I once was asked, 'Aren't you a bit young to have founded the CIA?' Well, yes, I am—but I didn't found it, my father did. Having the same name, I should have guessed that someone, sometime, would put two and two together.

Almost from my arrival in London in 1969 to his death at the end of 1990, my father was forever being called to appear on some TV news show about this event or that happening somewhere in the Arab world. He was often asked to review books for various journals and newspapers as an expert on terrorism, intelligence, the Middle East, the CIA, KGB, MI5, or whatever. He often said things on TV that, as he put it, 'made it hot for them.' Of course, he never let on who 'them' were. So, he kept all his intelligence and journalist contacts up to date; he was, after all, in the business of knowing what's going on.

Sometimes he dragged me along. At one point, I went to lunch with him and the US senator Jack Kemp, who my father seemed to think might run for president. After the lunch, I said, 'Forget him, he's an idiot.' I met the leaders who eventually took over South Sudan during their fight for independence—in Washington, when they were trying to elicit support from the US government. One of the most interesting characters he picked up was a notorious Saudi arms dealer called Adnan Khashoggi.

Adnan was a super-rich Saudi who seemed to insert himself into various schemes to do things like bring about peace between the Israelis and Palestinians. I came to suspect that these were actually my father's schemes, and that he was merely using Adnan. He would compose letters and reports and credit Adnan with having written them. In typical CIA style, he saw Adnan as a convenient front.

Adnan was by no means an imposing figure. He was short, squat, and balding, and if he had any charisma or class it was only because he was rich. I can't say I was thrilled about the association, but I was busy doing what I was doing, and I hoped some of these activities might actually lead to something good. Peace in the Middle East might be a stretch, but you never know. I hoped that was what my father was thinking, too.

Anyway, in the late 80s, Adnan was reputed to be the wealthiest man in the world (he was not). He had a huge, 285ft yacht on the Mediterranean that he named after his eldest daughter, Nabila, which he normally parked in Monaco. That yacht, by the way, was used in a James Bond film and later sold for $29 million to Donald Trump—who in turn sold it at a loss, at $20 million, to try to save the Trump Casino.

Adnan held a huge birthday party for his second wife, Lamia, at one of the big Monaco hotels and invited all sorts of notables to come, plus every model in the region. My father had been meeting Adnan in Monaco, so he called me from there to ask if I would like to attend the big do—and to invite anyone I wanted to come with me. Adnan would send a Learjet to pick me up and take me back to London.

I called Sting and invited him. At this time, there was a rift between Sting and his then wife, Frances Tomelty, but it was by no means public knowledge. I was not sure of all the details either, but when Sting invited Trudie Styler to accompany him to Monaco instead, that pretty much confirmed that a change was coming to his personal life. Trudie had been Frances's best friend and neighbor, so it was all a bit messy, and the less I knew the better.

On the morning of the flight to Cannes airport, near Monaco, my father called me again to ask if I minded 'Superman' joining us on the flight. Since it was now just Sting, Trudie, and me in an eight-seat jet, that seemed OK to me, so I said yes. When we arrived in Cannes, a helicopter was waiting for the three of us and took Sting, Trudie, and me to the Nabila yacht— Christopher Reeve was driven by limo instead, and we never saw him again.

221

The yacht, said to be the biggest in the world, was typically ostentatious and over-the-top. One thing about Adnan Khashoggi: he liked to show off his wealth. At dinner later that evening, his wife, Lamia, was dripping with jewelry. It was a typical Monaco big-money event with all the 'beautiful people' one could think of, but I can't remember much about it except for the tons of young models everywhere. They all looked like they'd been paid to be there simply as ornaments; they knew it and, not surprisingly, they didn't seem comfortable about it. In fact, they *were* paid to be there. I'll bet ninety-nine percent of the guests had no idea who the birthday girl was.

My main memory is of arriving back in London: just before we got out of the airplane, Sting said, 'You go first and take Trudie,' like she was with me and not him. The paparazzi were there in force, waiting for Sting, and it looked like the situation was going to be all over the news. I led Trudie, arm-in-arm, to the limo, and on the way, just as a paparazzi stuck his camera towards Trudie's face, I smacked him to the ground, which apparently also smashed his camera. The next day in the newspapers it was 'Sting's Burley Minder Attacks Journalist.' I was the burley minder.

℃℃

In 1989, IRS Records moved to EMI. I can't lie: the motivation was purely financial. Going independent from MCA had proven to be a mistake that left the company few options. IRS needed money, and the only realistic option was to sell to a major. R.E.M. had signed to Warner Bros; Fine Young Cannibals had disbanded; Belinda Carlisle had moved to MCA Records. There was still meat on the IRS bone, but not enough to make the company the hot property it had been only a few years before.

Of course, moving to EMI, we hoped for the best. But being owned by a big company meant that I, Jay, and the rest of the staff had to answer to a power above us. No longer was it an option to sign what I wanted or do what I wanted without thinking of the financial consequences. I developed a strong friendship with Jim Fifield, the head of EMI, who was a genuine music fan, and Jay did likewise with Jim's number two. But that didn't make much difference to the accounting people at the annual 'presidents' meeting.

All the various label heads would meet the head of finance, who would

222

give everyone a profit target to meet, including Jay and me, along with the message, 'We don't care how you achieve it—fire people and lower your overhead, or have a hit record—but if you don't make this profit number, neither of you get your annual Christmas bonus.' When the Christmas bonus was $250,000, that put a big incentive towards making the profit.

This way of working distorted our whole approach to what IRS Records was and had been. When we saw one of our fellow label heads ship out tons of albums at the end of the year, knowing full well that many of them would come back as returns in the first quarter of the next year, our first thought was, *That was stupid*. Then we learned that the Christmas bonus was based on albums shipped, not sold. The label heads figured they would worry about the returns next year; for now, it ensured their Christmas bonus for this year. Of course, if all the label heads met their targets, that would in turn mean the top EMI corporate people would get their bonuses as well. It didn't take much reading of the newspapers to realize that Jim Fifield's Christmas bonus was in the millions. No wonder he was called 'Lucky Jim.'

All of this gave us insight into the corporate world that IRS and I personally had never faced before. From that standpoint, it was an education that I am glad I got. However, it reminded me of a lunch I had had in London back in 1987 with the chairman of EMI Records, who told me he was surprised that the sum of the executives' salaries exceeded the profit of the company. In effect, EMI was structured to make the executives lots of money but the shareholders the minimum they could get away with. All the talk of making money for the shareholders appeared, to me, to be bullshit.

&

During this period, one of the most interesting groups IRS signed was Concrete Blonde. One can never forget a person like Johnette Napolitano, the band's leader. I first met her when she was the assistant for the artist-relations person at A&M Records, then she quit, only to turn up a few years later in Concrete Blonde.

Johnette was the loose wire while her guitarist/producer/co-writer Jim Mankey was the calm one, so they were a sort of yin/yang pair. Then there was Harry the drummer, who would come into the IRS offices in LA every few months and go around to all the offices and ask, 'Got any new product?'—like he wanted to hear the new records we were releasing. The problem was that when he walked out, he had picked up multiple copies from each office, then went straight to the used record store (Aaron's, I seem to remember) to sell them. One day, an upstanding salesman called to say, 'Better check your staff—we are getting a lot of IRS Records promos over here.'

I put the group on some tour dates with Sting (six big shows in March 1991) and made the mistake of going into the Concrete Blonde dressing room when Johnette was angry about something. She threw a plate of food at me. One could say she was mercurial. Then, of course, there was the usual artist dispute with the record company that went around in circles between lawyers. One night, Johnette called to say, 'Let's settle all this between ourselves.' She suggested we meet for breakfast at a place that sounded like it was pretty deep into the dangerous part of Los Angeles. The next morning, when I was getting ready to go, my wife Adriana saw me put a knife in my shirt and asked, 'What are you doing?' I explained that Johnette was so unpredictable that perhaps it was a setup, and maybe I was going to be assassinated by some gang members. I needed the knife for protection.

When I got close to the restaurant, I realized it was in fact *not* in a dangerous area, but I still I drove around the block to see if any suspicious types were hanging around, ready to come and get me. There was no one. Then I went into the restaurant, which was also pretty deserted, except for some elderly types. Feeling safe now, I sat down with Johnette. We had an entertaining breakfast, settled everything, and we left.

Another time, Johnette got really pissed at me when I left a concert early—according to her, my white hair was like a beacon that everyone could see. I had to promise to never leave any of her concerts again. I still have the black rainhat I used to take to the shows so she wouldn't see me if I had to leave early.

One day, Johnette was pushing IRS to do a video for the song 'Joey,' from the 1990 album *Bloodletting*. She was in London at the beginning of the year after recording the album there, and after her video request was turned down, she went to the IRS office at Bugle House. With a stapler in hand, ready to throw, she asked Steve Tannett, 'How much will it cost to repair that window?' It was one of my expensive antique stained-glass windows. Steve didn't want to report the smashed window, so he relented, and the video was made. And Johnette was right: the song became the band's biggest hit. MTV put it into good rotation, and by the beginning of November it had got to #19 on *Billboard* and #1 on the modern rock chart.

Needless to say, the Concrete Blonde relationship was always up and down, and before long there was another dispute, this time inspired by another record company's interest in the band. By now, I figured it was time to bail; if Capitol Records was interested, perhaps I could settle things by offering to step aside for a fee, leaving the band free to make the deal. I'll be honest: I didn't have much regard for the MD of Capitol at the time, and I figured he didn't know what he was getting into. But if he wanted Concrete Blonde and was willing to pay IRS $100,000 for them, he was welcome to have the band—and he deserved what he would get.

The MD was the same guy that I had once suggested should take advantage of the iconic round Capitol building to develop a big merchandising business. All those tourist shops on Hollywood Boulevard would have sold tons of them. He declined with the lamest reason I have ever had a record person use: he was afraid that promoting the image would attract terrorists to blow up the building! What an idiot. Anyway, Capitol paid IRS the $100,000, and Concrete Blonde switched labels in 1993. The band delivered one album to Capitol then promptly broke up.

The Concrete Blonde relationship may have been up and down, but the music was consistently great. They made some of the best records on the IRS label, mainly because inhibitions were not part of Johnette's personal makeup. She was the real deal.

⁊

By 1991, Sting was my main management focus. He had also become one of the world's most important artists. I can take some of the credit for that, but it was mostly Sting. I say 'important' because he was more than a ticket seller. He had social influence, and he was seen as the ideal spokesman and representative for worthy causes. Whenever there was any charity or big event looking for superstars, it was Bruce Springsteen, Sting, and U2 at the top of the list. That was not always a good thing, as few people appreciated it when an artist said no to someone's pet cause. The easiest thing was for the artist to say yes, then call the manager to get them out of it. Better for me to be the bearer of bad news than the artist. Believe me, the amount of times Sting was hit upon was beyond *anyone's* ability to support, so I was often the bearer of bad news. I am sure it did a lot for my image as a tough guy and even a nasty guy.

By now, as with every artist, many of the concerts Sting played felt like more of the same, but there were some unique ones as well—or, as I prefer to call them, 'learning experiences.'

Five years after the Amnesty tour, there was another chance for Sting to perform with a supergroup that had an iconic, legendary status. It was a supergroup that also had never figured into my and certainly not Sting's thinking. In April 1993, I got a call from the manager of the Grateful Dead, asking if I would be interested in having Sting open for them at eight stadium shows. At first, I was surprised by the call. I would not have thought of such a coupling myself, but when he went on to say that the Dead always put on a big act as a way to give their fans their money's worth, and that they also paid decent fees, I said that if Sting agreed, we would do it.

I had seen the Grateful Dead once in the 70s and had bought their first album back then, but I was by no means a fan. I did know, however, that they had built a reputation for never playing the same show twice, having a fanatical and huge following, and doing huge business in merchandise. Whatever they were doing, it worked, and the more I looked into it, the more interested I got. Then I called Sting. He must have thought, *Here is Miles, being crazy again*, but he too was intrigued. In the end, he said, 'OK, let's do it.'

The run began with three sold-out shows at a sixty-thousand-seat stadium in Las Vegas in May of 1993. For me, these shows were an education. I learned that forty percent of the audience went to all three shows, forty percent went to two shows, and twenty percent to only one show. The reason was that the Dead never planned what songs they were going to perform in advance, and they never played the same show twice. At the Vegas shows with Sting, over the three days they only played twenty percent of the same songs on every show. The audience knew this, so the big fans would have to see all three shows to have fully 'seen' the Grateful Dead in Las Vegas.

I thought this was genius. It meant of the 180,000 tickets for the three shows, they would only need half that many fans to sell out. It was like the record business, where you sell a song as a seven-inch single, then the same song as a twelve-inch, then as a remix, and then on colored vinyl—selling the same song to the same people, multiplying the business with the same fans.

The other thing about the Dead was their realization that after twenty or so albums, they were unlikely to have any more hit records. As Jerry Garcia told me, if they sold a hundred thousand copies of any album, that would be a huge win for them. So, they let it be known that they were happy for people to record the shows and send tapes to whoever they wanted. Since they didn't sell records anyway, they weren't giving anything away, and it helped build their mystique as a 'for the people' band, not a 'for the money' band. When I walked out into the stadium and saw the area reserved for fans that wanted to record the show, I was amazed at the sophistication of the setups.

Those shows with the Grateful Dead were an interesting experience on several levels. There was no question that Jerry Garcia was the musical brains behind the band, and indeed he was the only one that Sting related to musically. Garcia kept saying, 'There's another way.' I was not sure if he meant that to apply to the way the Dead did business or to something to do with music.

The music itself was surprising, too. At the first shows, the crew offered Sting and me headsets to hear what the band members were saying to each other—conversations that did not go over the public address system to the audience. On one show, the keyboard player kept saying, 'This fucking keyboard is out of tune!' and he kept tinkering with it as the band played on. No one seemed to care if he was out of tune.

After the Sting performance, the Dead walked onstage and sound-checked for five or so minutes, and just as I was thinking they were going on too long, I realized they had already been playing a song for a few minutes. To say it was informal would be an understatement. Perhaps it was good that a large part of the audience was stoned.

227

I did talk to Sting about altering his show each night, as he had enough songs by now to do at least two different shows while still playing the key hits that the audience would expect. It was one of the times he said no.

Three years later, on March 13, 1996, Sting played Moscow, which was memorable largely because there was an overwhelming vibe that something bad might happen at any moment. We had machine-gun-toting security guards at all times: at the concert, at the hotel, and while traveling. At the hotel, armed guards set up in the hall outside the bedrooms. It was not a place to relax.

The concert itself was held at the Kremlin, and it was completely different from all the other shows we ever did. In America, like most places, the audience comes dressed informally, ready to have a good time: T-shirts, shorts, even tracksuits. In Moscow, the audience came dressed like they were going to a ball. People were incredibly well dressed. At one point I walked around the theater, and in front of me I saw our road crew watching the audience come in. One of the crew commented that it was the best-looking audience they had ever seen. They were drooling over the women.

In June of that year, we did another strange show. It was a concert for the Sultan of Brunei in his tiny principality in the South Eastern Pacific. It was only interesting because it was a strange place to go: we had all heard rumors about the place and its fabulous wealth, so we were curious . . . and it was lots of money, plus all expenses paid. The support bands were The Gipsy Kings and Bryan Adams. We weren't the only ones making big bucks. Meanwhile, the audience was to be no more than one hundred people. It was a pretty crazy gig.

At the concert itself there were about thirty incredibly beautiful girls sat on tables near us, but none would speak to any of our entourage. One would have thought they would at least speak to Sting or Bryan Adams, but no. We were told that indeed they were models and were paid $10,000 to be there, but if the sultan chose any of them, they would get $100,000 for the night. Each of those thirty girls was hoping to be chosen, so talking to one of us would kill that possibility for them. We had no factual evidence of this but it seemed highly plausible, and it explained why none of the ladies would talk to us.

The day after the show, the sultan's son invited us to see him fly his helicopter at the sultan's private airport. It was kind of pathetic, but there were hundreds of cars lined up on the tarmac. Apparently, the sultan had a standing order to buy a hundred cars each year from Rolls-Royce and Mercedes. Only the top marks, of course; there must have been a thousand cars just sitting there. Sting said the experience made him feel like a pauper.

No rundown of Sting concerts would be complete without mentioning the annual Rainforest Foundation concerts. Sting and Trudie held one each year at Carnegie Hall in New York to raise money to protect indigenous peoples in the Amazon Rainforest. They got bigger and more impressive each year. It was Sting and Trudie's thing, so I did my best to keep my distance from the actual organization of the shows. One thing I've learned about charities is that they can be a thankless task; before you know it, money you think you are raising for a good cause ends up where it is not supposed to. I figured I would do my part buying tickets, helping when asked, and attending the shows. Each event had huge stars, from Elton John to Bruce Springsteen, Paul Simon to Billy Joel, James Taylor to Don Henley, and all sorts of New York notables came. Even Donald Trump came once. It soon became one of the most important social events of the year, and it was responsible for a lot of good works in Brazil.

I would have to say it was a valiant effort that needed to be fought, but so many forces were against it. Money interests, political interests, greedy people, hungry poor people—this was a charity that was probably destined to fit the 'two steps forward, one step back' formula. Knowing Brazil, one can only imagine that there must have been times when it was one step forward, two steps back.

CHAPTER 26

A CASTLE FOR A SONG

. . . .

In the summer of 1991, having sold IRS Records and with money in the bank, I decided the UK company should invest in a property that would be a fun place to visit and could serve to solve a continuing problem with the artists I represented. That problem was songs—or, more precisely, getting enough of them to find a hit. I was thinking of a remote place that would discourage hangers-on and paparazzi from showing up, but not too remote to prevent people from coming at all. It should preferably have some kind of mystical vibe that could inspire creativity, plus enough space and privacy.

A medieval castle with towers, moat, and battlements would seem the perfect type of place. Walt Disney understood the image a castle can create, and a castle became the singular image of Disneyland. And if it's good enough for Walt, it should be good enough for me. Also, a castle would also hearken back to my days in the Middle East, picnicking at the famous crusader castles of Krak des Chevaliers, Beaufort, and Aleppo.

From long experience, I knew how easy it was for recording artists as well as songwriters, especially successful ones, to develop their own cocoon, often without even knowing it. I figured it never hurt to jolt people into looking at things differently and becoming exposed to new ideas—to remove the blinkers, so to speak. It's like Jon Bon Jovi said to me at one of the retreats: 'At home, no one can get to me—my handlers keep everyone away from me. Here, I am just one of the guys like everyone else, trying to make music like I did in the old days.'

This idea came into focus when I started going to Nashville and seeing how the writers there operated. What I discovered was how collaboration between writers was organized and commonplace, and virtually ingrained into the system—the complete opposite of my early experiences with bands like Wishbone Ash, and something I had seen little of in Los Angeles. So, I started seriously thinking of ideas to find ways to make interesting collaborations happen. My first move was to open a music publishing office in Nashville. But, as usual, the biggest move was a completely left-field idea.

In 1991, my wife, Adriana, took a month-long sculpting course near Nantes in northwestern France. I would visit her on the weekends and kill time during the day when she was doing her classes by renting a car and visiting nearby villages and sites. One day, I passed by an estate agent, and in the window was a listing for a castle that looked really appealing, and the price was so low that I walked in and asked about it. The guy must have thought this was his lucky day—an American looking to buy property—so he immediately said he could show it to me. He locked the office and off we went.

The castle turned out to be great inside, with beautiful tapestries on the walls, stained-glass windows, majestic carved gothic fireplaces, but the outside was a turn-off. There was a trailer park across the street, and on the other side a builder's yard. No privacy, and no mystique for sure. But the inside . . . *wow*. So, I asked what other properties he might have.

Over the next few days, we went from property to property, until he took me to one that was nearly perfect. Lots of land, impressive entrance, plenty of space, mosaic floors, gothic architecture, but it was more expensive than I would have been comfortable with. That evening, Adriana asked what I had been doing, and why was I not bored out of my mind? I told her I had seen a castle for sale, and I was tempted. She agreed to skip a class and come see it with me the next day. On the way, she told me that as a little girl, growing up in La Pampa in Argentina, she had dreamed of one day living in a castle, so we both started getting into the idea. When we toured the place, she said, 'The hell with sculpting, let's buy a castle!'

When we decided we might actually do this, we figured we'd better make sure we were buying the perfect castle. We scouted the Loire Valley and then went south, to the Dordogne area. We looked at over fifteen castles in all. Some were too small, some had no electricity or plumbing, some had no land, and after a while we were getting depressed that nothing worked for us. At one point, an estate agent took us to *Les Milandes*, a castle that had once been owned by Josephine Baker. It overlooked the Dordogne river and sat on forty acres of land, but there was a village outside its front gate. We had lunch in the village, and we noticed how many of the local shops were selling merchandise relating to the castle: cups, T-shirts, Josephine Baker paraphernalia. The owner had tours going through it, and when I said we really didn't want to buy a property with tours, he said, 'Don't worry, you can stop all the tours.'

'How popular do you think that is going to make us with the townsfolk?' I asked. He just looked me as if to say, *Fuck them, I want to sell the property*. Aside from the fact that it would always be Josephine Baker's castle, though, neither of us relished the idea of being hated by everyone in the village.

Finally, the estate agent said, 'I do know one place that should be perfect, but the owner is strange. He was some kind of Danish art dealer, and he bought the castle without telling his wife. When she heard about it, she secretly came and took out all the contents, curtains and all, and burned them in a nearby field. Now he lives there alone in the place with hardly any furniture. I warn you: he drinks a lot. It is for sale, but if he doesn't like you, he won't sell.'

The agent gave us directions, and we scheduled a meeting the next day. On the way, the closer we got, the more things were looking good. Beautiful rolling hills and woodlands. Fields of sunflowers. Cows munching freely in pastures, picturesque villages and no throngs of tourists. The castle itself was on a hill, and as we drove up the long driveway, we started thinking this might be the one. At the entrance to the outer walls, we met up with the estate agent and the owner, a Mr. Rasmussen, who had obviously been drinking. He was indeed strange, but Adriana must have charmed him, so it looked like we might be able to make a deal. By the end of our tour, we'd decided this was the one: if the price was right, we would buy it. Its name was Château Marouatte.

We worked out a fair price and agreed to buy it, except for one more thing: throw in that old Ford tractor and we have a deal. He agreed. Then the agent told us we had to wait one month because, under French law, when a foreigner buys farmland, it first has to be offered at the same price to all the locals, and they have one month to decide. If no one wants it, it's yours. So, we waited the month, and the only farmers that showed up were ones who wanted to sell us *their* properties. At 270 acres, I figured we had enough space, so no sale. We bought Marouatte in December of 1991. I say we because it was actually bought by our UK company, Firstars, to develop the songwriting events I had been planning.

Prior to the final purchase, I asked the agent what facilities there might be to have someone there while we were elsewhere.

'No problem,' he said, 'it's easy to get a *guardian*—all you do is give them a place to stay and they watch the place for you.'

It turns out it was not that simple, and I could not find anyone. Thankfully, Rasmussen said he would stay until we found someone. It was early December, so we agreed. We flew to London to try to figure out what to do.

As luck would have it, I had only been in London for a few days when Andy Powell from Wishbone Ash called me to say that drummer Steve Upton had quit the band and his wife had locked him out of his house, and the rest of the band were worried that 'he might do something.' He reminded me that back in 1974 sometime, I had joked with Steve that if he ever wanted to come over to my side of the business, he could count on me for a job. Steve was always the 'together' one in the band—he handled the business side.

'If you were serious,' Andy continued, 'now is the time to offer him that job.'

Thinking this might solve my castle problem, I immediately got Steve on the phone.

'Hi Steve, how are you doing?'

'Don't ask,' he replied, and then began his tale of woe until I said, 'Steve, I may have a job for you.' He said he'd do anything.

'How's your French?' I asked.

'Bon jurr, mon suer.'

'That's good enough for me,' I said. 'You're hired.' I then explained that it was in France, and his job was to live in a castle and keep an eye on it while I was gone. It would be free accommodation, phone, water, electricity, and a salary to live on.

I guess Steve was as desperate as I was, because he said, 'I'll do it— when?'

'How about tomorrow?'

I bought two plane tickets, and we flew to Bordeaux and rented a car to drive to the castle the next day. Steve would be the castle's guardian for the next fifteen years.

Of course, when the word got out that we had bought a castle in France, all of my friends, especially the French ones, thought I had gone mad. One might go to Bordeaux or Toulouse on a concert tour, but never to the Dordogne. As one French promoter told me, in a thick French accent, 'Za Périgord ez verry beautiful, but it ez no wherre!'

☙

With a suitable venue now acquired, the concept of an annual songwriters' retreat—to bring together my publishing, recording, and management artists with the top songwriters and producers who would help them come up with hit songs—could now be realized. To fund it, I teamed up with Jerry Moss and his publishing company, Rondor Music. Like me and indeed like every other record company and music publisher, Jerry was always looking for ways to get more hit songs, and he thought the songwriters' retreat idea sounded like a good one. Together, we went to the open market to find artists and record companies looking for songs. The formula ended up being quite simple: one songwriter from Jerry's company, one from mine, plus an artist looking for that elusive hit song.

The first retreat, in October 1991, had only nine writers; the next thirteen; within a few more events, we ended up with eighteen and then twenty-one. The first retreat was simply about writing the songs; nothing was recorded. Chris Difford and Glenn Tilbrook from Squeeze came along. The thinking then was that people would record their songs when they returned home, but after a few months, we realized it was not working—I never heard any of those songs again. For all future retreats,

234

we decided to record the songs at least as demos, so that we had a record of them.

As technology changed and improved, we adapted as well. At one point, we set up three recording studios with three engineers, so every song could be recorded well. Once a song had been written, each songwriting group chose one of the three studios, and they were given three hours to put it down. It is remarkable how the urgency of having to record a song in three hours actually worked. In so many cases that demo was actually better than the final recording that happened later in some fancy studio in the USA or UK.

It was often the strange combinations that worked the best. The first #1 written at the castle was a collaboration between an A&M new-wave singer from Los Angeles, Sally Dworsky; a country singer from my company in Nashville, Paul Jefferson; and Jan Layers, an invited bass player from a Belgian Group called Soulsister. Aaron Tippin cut the song, 'That's As Close As I'll Get To Lovin' You,' and it went to #1 in the US country charts at Christmas of 1995. One of the most successful was 'The Reason,' written at the castle by Carole King, Mark Hudson, and IRS Records artist Greg Wells; Celine Dion covered it and released it on the thirty-one-million-seller *Let's Talk About Love*. That song put Greg Wells on the map, and he went on to become a superstar songwriter and producer.

I met Greg in 1994 through Tina Clark, another well-respected songwriter who came to me at the previous year's retreat about a Canadian artist she was excited about and wanted me to sign. It was Greg Wells, with a project he wanted to call Silas Loader. It was an unusual pitch: he wanted to play every instrument, engineer, and produce. A virtual one-man band operation from start to finish.

When I saw him do what he said he'd do in the studio, I came to realize that the real story of Greg Wells would not be the album he made: it was Greg the musician, songwriter, producer. When the concerts I booked him on gave me a good idea that playing live was not going to be his thing, I looked to his other talents and talked him into coming to the songwriters' retreats.

I had to practically bully him to come, but then, as predicted, he ended up playing on everyone's sessions. He was the go-to guy almost every time: *Hey, Greg can you put drums on my track?* He would do one take, then go to the next studio, where a guitar was needed. Keyboards, bass—he could do the lot, and he wasn't just good, he was great at all of them. In the mornings I would team him up with writers, so his week at the castle was writing songs from 11am to around 3pm, then running between studios from 3pm to midnight.

Greg's big break was teaming him up with Carole King and Mark Hudson on 'The Reason'; with that, his reputation was launched. To date, he has been involved with the sales of over 125 million albums, producing and writing and co-writing songs for such stars as Katy Perry, Mika, Adele, Keith Urban, Aerosmith, and many others.

ↄ

One of the side effects of the retreats that actually became almost as important as the songs written at the castle was the long-lasting collaborative relationships that built up between songwriters meeting there for the first time. At one point, a relatively unknown Australian guitar player living in Nashville doing country music who I was co-managing at the time, Keith Urban, teamed up with Charlotte Caffey and Jane Wiedlin from The Go-Go's. It was a strange match—two punk girls from LA with an Australian country artist—that eventually led to Keith's first #1 single, 'But For The Grace Of God,' which pretty much changed his life.

Keith came to the castle twice, but the funny thing was that he initially resisted it (more on that in the next chapter). The same was true for Greg Wells. Both were glad they did. Being jolted out of their cocoon and injected with new inputs worked—and was the central concept of the retreats from the start.

I should also make clear that I am not a believer in fate or Ley lines, or reincarnation or any of the supposed mystical or religious connections between things. Aliens didn't build the pyramids, and there's no such things as ghosts, werewolves, or witches. When visitors come to the castle and swear they've seen or heard a ghost in their room, I have to say, 'Please be true—if we can prove that, I can up the rent!' But, I have to admit, there is something strange and 'fate-like' about something I discovered in the process of validating this crazy idea of a castle songwriter retreat in the depths of France. It was the story of the troubadours who it turned out were the first Western songwriters back in the twelfth century. What's more, it was the songwriter, *not* the singer, that was honored. Richard the Lionheart, King of England, and many others in royalty fancied themselves as songwriters, and it became a good way to advance oneself into the upper classes. Meanwhile, the actual musician, the '*jongleur*,' was less well regarded—being a *jongleur* was considered a menial task. Then I discovered that the center of this troubadour thing was southern France, and that four of the seven greatest songwriters actually came from within a forty-minute drive of Château Marouatte; and the greatest of all the troubadours, Arnaut Daniel, came from nearby Riberac, only twenty minutes away. What a fantastic coincidence!

My discovery of the troubadours inspired me to call the retreats 'Printemps des Troubadors' ('Springtime for Troubadours'). Then, as a way to reward and inspire writers and add a mystique to the events, I created the Grand Order des Troubadours de Marouatte, whereby if a song written at the castle got to #1 or sold ten million copies, the writers would qualify to be inducted into the order in a flamboyant knighting ceremony, with all the trappings of the age of chivalry. If my wife was not there to do the knighting, my mother or I would do it—dressed of course like a king or queen, with as much pomp and circumstance as could be dreamed up. As of 2020, there are twelve knights of the order, each with a banner hanging in the Hall of Troubadours. I am proud to say I knighted Lady Carole King myself.

Many stars—and wannabe stars—came to the retreats over the years. Great guitarists came, like Peter Frampton, Jeff Beck, and Keith Urban; Carole King came three times, and one night we caught her arguing politics with Ted Nugent. That is one conversation that I wish had been recorded. Pat McDonald of Timbuk 3 came many times; my brother Stewart several times; Timothy B. Schmidt from the Eagles, Paul Young, Dominic Miller and Vinnie Calautti from Sting's band, Jon Bon Jovi, Cher, Soraya, Belinda Carlisle, Olivia Newton-John, Paul Thorn, Paul Carrack, Zucchero—over 250 different writers and artists in all.

For one event, I decided to go international and really mix it up to see what would happen. I invited Ragheb Alama from Lebanon; Hakim from Egypt; Necmi from Turkey; Amina from Tunisia; Khadja Nin from Senegal; Khaled, Rachid Taha, and Faudel from Algeria; and Najma Akhtar from India. It was like a chemistry set of talent to mix in unexpected ways, to see what would come out. One of the songs written there became the lead song on Oojami's first album, and a staple song for bellydancers around the world to dance to. A Najma/Ragheb duet became a huge hit all around the Middle East and India. Had it not been for the events of 2001, I would have done many more of these international retreats.

The September 11 terror attacks on New York and Washington scuttled the winter retreat that year and even the next year's retreats as well. The songwriters' retreats faded into a kind of legend status. Jerry Moss and Herb Alpert had sold their publishing company to Universal in 2000, and I closed my Nashville office. It was a good idea, though, and it inspired others to copy it.

Over the coming years I often had people tell me that the songwriters' retreat was one of my best ideas. It would have all ended in 2000, though, had it not been for Marc Emert-Hutner at the American Society of Composers, Authors, and Publishers (ASCAP). In 2008, Marc called me from the ASCAP offices in New York to ask if I would consider starting the retreats up again, and what did I figure it would take? ASCAP would do all the inviting, pay the running costs, and send staff. It was intended to create opportunities for the songwriters signed to ASCAP, but also to reward success.

The ASCAP retreats became an annual event from then until the lockdown of 2020. A wide range of artists and writers have attended, including Ellie Goulding, Mika, and Adam Lambert, who is now the singer of Queen. The first #1 was 'Somethin' Bad,' written by Brett James, Chris DeStefano and Priscilla Renea, which was taken to the top in the US country charts by Miranda Lambert and Carrie Underwood. All three writers have been duly knighted and joined the Grand Order des Troubadours.

As a sort of joke, I created another order, the Grand Order Of The Walnut, walnuts being to the region what olives are to areas further south. The idea was if a song was released that had the words 'Marouatte Castle' or 'Château Marouatte' in the lyric, it would qualify the writers to be inducted into this most prestigious order.

I got a call in 2016: 'Miles, get ready for a walnut induction.' Britney Spears had cut 'Man On The Moon,' which was written at the castle by Jason Evigan and Ilsey Juber, and had 'Château Marouatte' in the lyric. ('Just sing it,' Evigan reportedly told her, when Britney asked, 'What is Château Marouatte?') We held the ceremony the next year, and it was so over-the-top that all the writers started putting Marouatte into their lyrics, as they too wanted to be 'Walnuts.'

One of the secrets of the event was its isolation: no hangers-on, no diversions, only what was in the grounds of the castle. Even the cell phones had bad coverage. As Cher said at one point, 'If there was a phone in my room, you would never have seen me.' Paparazzi were never allowed; no press or film crew ever attended. The point was to keep it quiet and totally focused on the task at hand, which was simple: writing hit songs.

CHAPTER 27

GO SEE THE SHERIFF

. . . .

In 1993, about a decade after I stopped working with The Cramps, they crashed into my world again—like you could never escape from them. It had to do with one of the most obscure rockabilly artists they covered . . . and one of the strangest songs they ever recorded.

According to his biography on Wikipedia:

> Hasil Adkins was born in Boone County, West Virginia, on April 29, 1937, where he spent his entire life. He was the youngest of ten children of Wid Adkins, a coalminer, and Alice Adkins, raised in a tarpaper shack on property rented from a local coal company. Born at the time of the Great Depression, Adkins's early life was stricken by poverty. His parents were unable to provide him shoes until he was five years old. Some reports say he attended school as few as two days of first grade.

The Cramps were influenced by early rockabilly artists, especially obscure ones few had ever heard of. Hasil Adkins was one of those artists, and perhaps the strangest. At one point, he did a whole album dedicated to chickens and called it *Poultry In Motion*. One of his songs, 'She Said,' was perfect for The Cramps—it was just as crazed as they were. The song tells the tale of the frightening aftermath of a drunken one-night stand. The lyrics don't make much sense, so it's probably good that they were largely unintelligible anyway. From what I could make out, they are as follows:

> Why's don't I tell you what it is?
> I wen' out last nigh' and I got messed up
> When I woke up this mornin'
> Shoulda' seen what I had inna bed wi' me
> She comes up at me outta the bed
> Pull her hair down the eye
> Looks to me like a dyin' can of that commodity meat

Then comes the chorus: '*Oo hee hoo ha ha, oo hee hoo haa haa.*' It was basic and barely decipherable, but it worked well onstage, and it was one of The Cramps' most popular live songs. It worked especially well when Lux stuck the microphone deep into his mouth when he sang it.

Sometime in late 1993, I got a call from Henry Padovani at the IRS Records office in Paris, saying he'd been approached by an advertising company that worked with Peugeot, who wanted to license a Cramps recording for a television commercial. The song was 'She Said,' and they wanted it for one of their 1994 cars. The Cramps were signed to IRS Records, so we controlled the recording rights to the song, but we didn't own the music publishing rights. We needed both to be able to grant the license. The composer was Hasil Adkins. How Peugeot or their advertising people came across it I will never know. It was by no means a radio hit, not even an obscure one. Somebody at that advertising agency must have been a serious Cramps fan, or crazy, or perhaps both.

When Henry called, it was a last resort. If I could not find Hasil or his publisher soon, we would lose the commercial. He had tried in France with SASEM, the big performing rights society that represented everyone, but drew a blank. No one in Europe had any idea who Hasil was or who he might be published by.

Henry hoped I might be able to find him. That proved more difficult than any of us thought. Hasil had virtually disappeared from view for many years. Even in his heyday, he was pretty obscure. No one was even sure he was alive, and no publisher claimed rights to the songs. I called the two big writers' societies that handled the vast majority of songs in the

USA, ASCAP and BMI, and even they could not give me an up-to-date contact for him. Eventually we got several addresses, but the zip codes did not match. There was an address in West Virginia with a zip code from Wisconsin; there was an address in West Virginia with a zip code in Virginia. So, I told Alletta, my secretary, to send a registered letter to every combination of the addresses and zip codes we had and hope for the best. The message was, 'Call collect, I have money for you.'

A week later, Alletta said, 'Miles, it's him!' It was Hasil, calling from a payphone in Boone County, West Virginia. The voice sounded like an old codger from deep in the sticks of some backwoods part of the country—which is exactly what he turned out to be. I told him I was interested in his songs and asked if he had a publisher or a representative. He didn't. How about a lawyer? 'Na, don't like lay-ers, don't like lay-ers,' was his reply.

I did not want to lose the commercial, and time was ticking, so I suggested I would come to West Virginia to meet him so we could discuss a deal. In all my years of touring, I had never been in West Virginia, so I thought it would be a bit of an adventure. Besides, Hasil sounded like a character. He gave me what seemed like an address, and I had Alletta book me a flight to Charleston, West Virginia.

Needless to say, there are no direct flights from Los Angeles to Charleston. When I got there after changing planes in DC, I rented a car and headed off to the town of Madison in Boone County. Stupidly, I was wearing a suit, so I must have stood out like an outsider, and I got some pretty weird looks as I drove to try to find Hasil. As I got deeper into coal country, with big trucks passing by, I could not help but think I was in *Deliverance* territory. Strange-looking people sitting on porches, watching this city boy drive by.

I went up and down the two-lane road in the middle of nowhere where his place was supposed to be, until finally I gave up and entered the gates of the next coalmine I came to. The young guy I came across knew exactly where Hasil lived: 'Down the road 'bout mile … de gulch on right … can't miss it. Wh't in hill you lookin' for that crazy kook?' He definitely thought I was crazy, too.

Sure enough, about a mile down I saw a shack, but I could not imagine anyone living there, so I drove on. I found no other possible place, though, so I came back and ventured down the 'gulch' the guy at the mine had told me about and up to a corrugated shack. Knocked at the door, and this old codger answered. It was Hasil, even older than I had imagined him.

We sat in his living room/bedroom, which had yellowed newspaper articles pasted to the wall. He did not appear to be drunk, but I could smell alcohol in the room. I asked him about his music and what he had been doing—basically, the pleasantries before getting down to business. He told me he had been to LA many years ago, and almost had a deal but had to come back, 'cuz his ma was sick. He had missed his big chance at making it. It was a sad story from a guy that life had passed by, and I thought to myself that I might change that. I said I would like to sign a publishing deal with him and had brought a contract with me. He looked embarrassed and said he couldn't read it; didn't know how. 'Can't write, neither.'

I knew that if the contract was to be legal, I would have to have it witnessed by a lawyer. When I asked if he knew one that we could go to, he ranted on a bit about lawyers but then said there was one back in Madison. Apparently, that lawyer had put him in jail. That was good enough for me. I got the name, and for the address he said the town was small, so just ask. Then we talked money. I said I could pay him $20,000, including $5,000 cash, and give it to him right there. He lost not a second and replied, 'Make that twenni'-fi' and we got us a deal.' I was so impressed that I said yes. Of course, he had no bank or bank account, so I told him I would work out how to pay him with the lawyer.

I drove back to Madison and found the lawyer in a one-story wooden house in the center of town. He was nice enough and happy to help, but he found it strange that Hasil would have suggested him. I then heard the story that he had represented the husband of a lady that Hasil had been flirting with; when the man complained, Hasil pulled out a gun and shot the man in the mouth, blowing out his cheek.

'You can't just go around and shoot a man in the mouth!' he said, like he had to validate doing what he did. In fact, though, he did: he apparently got grief from the locals for having arrested their local star.

I told him that I wanted to make a deal with Hasil, but as he could not read or write, the contract would need to be approved and witnessed by a lawyer representing him. That was all fine until he asked me how much money I was to pay Hasil. I said $25,000.

'*What!* Well, you'd better go see the sheriff.' This was a lot of money in Boone County, which I later learned was the last county in the USA to have a communist party—and it got votes!

I went to the sheriff's office, which was just across the street, and told him what I was up to. He was exactly what one would expect to see in a town like that: large, overweight, with what looked like a cowboy hat and of course a gun strapped to his waist. When I said I was to pay $25,000, the sheriff said that was crazy: every girl in the region would show up claiming Hasil had impregnated her; bill collectors from all directions would show up. Basically, that was insane. I suggested I open a bank account for Hasil and make a deal with the bank to only allow him to withdraw $1,000 a month. The sheriff cooled down and thought that would work. Then I went to the nearest bank and made the arrangements to transfer $20,000.

I went back to the lawyer, who looked through the contract and approved it, then I went back to see Hasil, gave him the $5,000 cash, and had him put his *X* on the contract. Then back to the lawyer to witness it. Mission accomplished.

I headed back to Los Angeles, and the next day I called Henry in Paris to grant the license. Peugeot released the ad in Europe to promote the 1994 model 106 KID. The ad showed a naked man running into a lake, then driving the car, then being stopped by two policemen. It was a strange choice of song, but I was not complaining. It was found money for IRS Records, The Cramps, and for Hasil, too.

As we were now officially the publishers of the whole Hasil Adkins song catalogue, it made sense to record all the songs so that we had copies of them. Part of the deal we made with Hasil was to get him a telephone, so that there would be an easy way to communicate with him. Using that phone, we arranged for my young publishing manager, Dan Graeff, to head to West Virginia to bring Hasil to LA.

Daniel set off, and the next day he called from the airport in Charleston in a state of disbelief as to what I had gotten him into. I had warned him what to expect, but apparently what he found was far worse than I had said.

First, when he drove to Hasil's shack, Hasil had no recollection of my conversation with him to arrange his trip to LA. Dan had to get him out of bed and sweet talk him into the car to drive to the Charleston airport. Hasil came with nothing but the shirt on his back.

Dan's next problem was that Hasil refused to get on the plane unless he had a drink. The drink was vodka, and lots of it. I said, 'Go ahead buy what you need.' On the plane, Hasil insisted on more drinks, and Dan bought as many vodka shot bottles as he could. When he got to Washington to catch the plane to LA, Dan called again. Same problem, and Hasil was now seriously drunk.

'If that's the only way to get him on the plane,' I said, 'give him what he wants. Just get him here.'

When they arrived at LAX, I picked them up, and Dan was visibly worn out. Perhaps shellshocked would be a better word. Hasil was completely soused, but more than that he smelled and looked like an impoverished hobo. Dan and he must have made an interesting travel duo on the trip. We drove to the motel we had booked for Hasil, making sure the hotel security and front desk did not see him, and put him to bed.

The next morning, Dan picked up Hasil and brought him to our office studio across the street from Universal Studios, where the IRS Records engineer Scott Gordon was waiting to do the recording. Hasil arrived with a serious case of the shakes, something I had never seen before. He was in no shape to record anything. He could hardly walk, but at least he had clean clothes on. Dan had called my secretary from Washington, telling her to buy men's underpants: Hasil was not wearing any, his butt was showing, and everyone was staring at them at each airport they passed through. If she could find pants and a shirt, all the better. I am sure that is one of the stranger calls she ever got working for me.

The thought was that if we were to record Hasil, he should be sober, so Dan was not to give him any more vodka when he picked him up that morning. When I met them at the studio, however, Hasil was in such bad shape that there was not going to be any recording. He really needed a drink, so there was no option but for Dan to go out and buy a bottle of vodka. In fact, he bought several, just in case. The drink stopped the shakes, so finally we got down to the recording.

Normally, the recording would be done track by track: drums, then bass, then guitar, and finally vocals. Hasil could not record that way. In his slow, backwoods drawl, he explained that he had to record all at once, like a live performance. The story was that when he first heard his songs on the radio, the DJ had said only one name, so he thought Hank Williams must have played everything. So, we recorded Hasil as a one-man band, playing drums, guitar, and harmonica all at once. Over the next few days, a total of fourteen songs and various bits of songs were recorded. I think it was an emotional experience for Hasil, and at one point he broke down and cried.

For all of us there was a feeling that this was sad, but at the same time we were going to make this guy more money than he had probably ever seen. Scott Gordon, the engineer recalls:

> I remember meeting Hasil Adkins for the first time. He needed a drink badly. We got him a bottle of vodka and the shakes stopped. He drank straight from the bottle and would go through a fifth or more on each four- or five-hour session. We set him up in the middle of the IRS studio on Lankershim. We mic'd up his guitar, harmonica, a kick drum, a hi-hat, and a snare, and a vocal. I didn't get how he would play everything at one time. Somehow, he managed with his feet on the kick and the hi-hat while he played guitar and sang. When there was a break in the guitar part, he would just use his hands on the snare drum to play a drum fill. He played everything all at once. I recall a lot of flailing around, a lot of false starts, laughing, coughing, guitar and vocals mostly out of tune. Very rough—he was drunk the entire time.
>
> I remember on the first day of recording, you came in the room, saw how drunk wasted he was, and offered up anything at all that he would like to eat, anything. All he was able to articulate was that he wanted gravy. We were all perplexed as to what sort of gravy he wanted. The best we could figure was that he liked the gravy from KFC. So that's what you got for him, along with some chicken and mashed potatoes. But mostly gravy.

That must have been one of the strangest recording sessions Scott had ever done for me. I had met him when he was the assistant on the Animal Logic album with my brother Stewart and Stanley Clarke. He then did the Robby Krieger's *No Speak* album, which was his first actual producer credit. Scott was great at making things work with the least bit of gear, so naturally I roped him in to organize the recordings at our songwriters' retreats, and he became the chief engineer there for many years.

☙

A few months later, I had a phone call from Hasil that was hard to decipher because he was so drunk, but the gist of it was, I was a crook, keeping him from his money. Apparently, shortly after, he did the same thing with the bank, but in person. He had gone in screaming and embarrassing everyone, so they notified me that they had had enough and were letting him take out all the money and closing the account.

I never heard from Hasil again. In the end, he made over $40,000, and I'm sure what the sheriff said would happen did happen. When Dan got there to bring him to Los Angeles, he already had a new mobile home and more cars on the lot. I released those recordings later that year on an album titled *Hasil Adkins: The Best Of The Haze*. It had a total of fourteen songs and was just over fifty minutes long.

Some years later, I heard that Hasil Adkins died, on April 26, 2005. I assumed it was from alcoholism, but apparently a teenager had hit him with an ATV; he died several days later. May he rest in peace.

☙

The Hasil story was so strange, interesting, and unique that when Dan Graeff called me the first time from the airport, I told him to make sure to write down a record of the trip as it was bound to be eventful. Luckily, he did, and here it is.

April 5, 1994, 7:30pm Charleston | Boone County, WV
On the flight up to Charleston from Atlanta, I happened to be seated next to a salesman who had lived in West Virginia his whole life. He was the type of person who believes he can, and likes to, start conversation with anyone. So, I figured I'd ask this guy about where I'm going. I pointed on the map to Boone County. All he could say is, 'You're going up there?' He didn't even ask why. We didn't speak for the rest of the flight.

247

Upon arriving in Charleston, I'm immediately struck by the fact that every other block has a church. Church Of Jesus Christ. Gospel Church. Evangelical. Revivalist. Church Of The Lord.

And no one cusses.

The next morning, I leave at eight for the drive up to Madison. This is strangely beautiful country, and the surreal backwardness of it all makes it all the more interesting. I drive back by what I think is Hasil's place and turn around to have a second look. On the way back I drive by a makeshift sign that reads: *Haircuts $10 Perm Special $25 He is Risen.*

After beating on Hasil's door for half an hour (which is padlocked shut, by the way), I walk the perimeter of the shack and its surrounding area. I begin to take in where I've been placed. The infamous 'Hunchin Bus' (spray painted on the side) that I'd read about, sat there, chock full of shit—weird shit. Mostly mannequins, some with missing heads, all sitting in the seats. Four cars were parked where they broke down. A forty-foot trailer home with all the shades drawn (what for fuck's sake is in there I can't imagine), and plastered on all sides of the shack are handmade placards which read, 'Praise His Holiness the Lord.' I don't know whether they're salutations to Jesus or an indication of who lives here. Still no sign of Hasil. Find a phone, call Alletta.

Becky's

I head up and out of the gulch where the shack is located and back up to the road. I end up at Becky's, a sort of makeshift roadside diner made from a double-wide. I get a coffee and collect my thoughts. Alletta and I have already discussed different ways of finding Hasil. We've both called him numerous times, to no avail. Now I'm just settling in to wait it out. Suddenly, a kid no older than eighteen stumbles in. It's the same guy who was hitchhiking that I drove by six times on the road while searching for Hasil. I figured he's here to kick my ass for not picking him up all those times I drove by. Instead of asking me why the fuck I didn't pick him up, he asks Becky for a 'pop.' She denies him, telling him she 'don't give no credit no more.'

A closer look reveals a strange, generally confused look on his face, a denim jacket that is torn to shreds and written all over it with some inbred tongue that is indecipherable to me. He splits as quickly as he arrived. Becky lets out a long sigh and says, 'He ain't right. There's something bad wrong with that boy.' She went on to tell me that he thinks he's Elvis, and that he usually hitchhikes around the county in a white leather jumpsuit. 'I used to pick him up and give him a ride until my son put a stop to it before he killed me.' She added that, 'He's good looking when he combs his hair.'

Phone rings: it's Alletta to tell me Hasil is home and waiting for me. He is Risen.

Driving to Charleston, | Flight to Atlanta

I pity the poor bastard that has to sit next to 'Haze' and me. I can call him Haze now instead of Hasil, such is the nature of my now nine-hour relationship with Hasil 'The Haze' Adkins. You see, ol' Haze don't smell so good. Sort of like the smell of rancid toilet water combined with the stale cigarette smoke embedded in trousers that probably haven't been washed in years. Add to that the smell of cheap vodka straight that oozes from his skin, and that's just the beginning. Every ten minutes or so, Hasil leans over a bit too close for comfort and implores me to, 'Get me a drink, man.' I remember the stories of him shooting a guy in the mouth, of him breaking a guitar over the head of a music critic. It really feels like anything can happen here, and none of it good.

At about the halfway mark, he then begins the ranting: 'I need that drink. . . . You don't know, forty-five fuckin' years on the road . . . people talkin' all the time . . . tearin' at me . . . you don't know!'

This is precarious for me, as I don't know the point at which he passes out or gets violent, as he apparently legendarily does. Either option is precarious and might get me fired by Miles before my career even starts, because I can't get him out of West Virginia, let alone to LA.

'I need that fuckin drink man.'

I quickly realize that when he adds *fuckin'*, it's serious. Thankfully, we're almost at the airport by this time, and I tell him he can get a drink on the plane—it's free, even. It works. The airport is small, as is the plane, so we're onboard relatively quickly. Now all I have to do is placate him until I can get drink service on the plane . . .

It was hard keeping him calm, but thankfully there weren't that many on the flight, and the drink service came quickly. This is when I started steadily feeding him miniature Smirnov bottles, one at a time. Again, I have to do the math on how much is enough to keep him docile and how much will cause him to pass out. It isn't easy. He nods off midflight. I begin worrying about how I'm going to get him from one side of the sprawling Atlanta terminal to the other, where the long-haul flight terminals are located.

Atlanta | LA

I've not calculated his vodka dosage well enough, because halfway from waking him up on landing, to getting to the gate area where our flight to LAX departs, he's getting pissed off at me and starting the incomprehensible ranting. He just sits down and demands a 'fuckin' drink, *now*.'

Everyone who hasn't already noticed this bizarre pair made up of a Slick LA Dude and a Drunk Wild-Eyed Hillbilly, now does. I don't give a shit. I pull him up onto his feet; he's utterly filthy, so touching him is like handling a leper. He obliges because I tell him that just at the top of this escalator is a bar. I don't know that to be true. Thankfully, it is. However, before I can start plying him with alcohol, I have to call Miles to see if he thinks I should keep plying him with vodka, because truly I can't guarantee how this is going to go, at all. I call the office from a payphone and Alletta picks up. I tell her to get Miles for me, no matter what. The whole time, Hasil is on simmer to my left with the muttering madness.

'Get him a bottle, for fuck's sake!' Miles tells me. Cool.

After several vodkas, it's time to go. He's definitely more docile, so that's good. All I have to do is get him on the plane. We find the gate and board without a hitch. Once we're in our seats, I realize too much time has passed. We really need to get airborne. We finally push back. It takes twenty harrowing minutes to get off the runway. What a time to be stuck on the airfield. Hasil is calm now, but I fear that any moment he'll explode with, 'I need a drink.'

Near catastrophe averted. Hasil was ready to launch if he didn't get his third vodka of the flight. The problem is that I don't have enough cash to keep endless vodka going for the whole flight if necessary. I call Alletta on the seat phone and tell her that I need her to meet us at the airport with cash. Otherwise, I won't have the cash to get my car out of the LAX parking. She asks if I need anything else, and I reply, 'Yes, underwear for Hasil.'

Sick of people . . . third vodka of the flight down. This is in quick succession, so much so that this fucker gets kookier by the minute. He keeps yammering on about how he hates people and is now worried that he might barf. I made him give me his word that #4 would be it. He downed it in less than a minute.

Now he seems to be sleeping. Just in time to calm the splintering nerves of the flight crew.

'Is he sick?' they ask.

'No. He's just Hasil Adkins. Wanna Hunch?'

‿

Around the same time as the Hasil Adkins adventure, I happened to start a conversation with a local publicist by the name of Anastasia Pruitt at an ASCAP reception in Nashville. I was actually on the search for someone to open an office with me in Nashville, but I was not looking for someone who was already established in a management or road-management position. I was far more interested in someone who would think of how to promote an artist, rather than how to get them from point A to point B.

Being a publicist, Anastasia was in line for what I was looking for. The more I talked to her, the more I was convinced I had found someone with the chutzpah and positive energy to take on a new challenge. I talked her into becoming a partner in a new Nashville publishing and management company. She was married to a successful doctor and therefore set up, so it was an easy, equal partnership from the start.

The first act Anastasia brought me was Junior Brown, a kind of rockabilly meets country artist with the right kind of quirky that interested me. He had invented a guitar he called a 'guit steel,' which combined an electric guitar with a lap steel. He was just the kind of iconic American that

Europeans might go for, so we brought him to France to do some gigs and film a video at the castle (which, by the way, seems to have disappeared).

Junior Brown was an interesting cat, and definitely an original. He proved that at London Heathrow Airport. During the normal security pat-down to board the plane, Junior Brown decided the inspector was delving into his private parts and made one hell of a scene.

'Get your fuckin' hands off of my balls!'

Thank God I was not there, but Anastasia was, and it pretty much freaked her out. When she called me later and told me what had happened, she said, 'I want you to know I had to do some pretty fast talking to keep Mr. Brown out of jail.'

'Welcome to the management business,' I said.

We also took on Peter Frampton, who was living in Nashville at the time. His *Frampton Comes Alive* album had been a huge hit in the 70s, and he was known as a great live performer, so I decided *Frampton Comes Alive II* would be a good bet for IRS Records. He came to the castle songwriting retreat in 1994 to start writing songs for the album, which we recorded at the Filmore West in June 1995. I enthusiastically presented it to an EMI/IRS marketing meeting in early October, and it was released at the end of the month.

A US tour started soon after, but before we got halfway through, Peter's wife had dangerous complications with a pregnancy. Peter rushed back to Nashville, and the rest of the tour was cancelled. That was bad enough. Then Anastasia called me: 'I hate to tell you this, but Peter needs to cancel the European tour as well.' A lot of work had been done to set up that tour, and IRS was counting on it to make the album a hit. Without the tour and the artist to promote it, the promotion people moved on to other projects. Who could blame them? Two steps forward, three steps back. By April of the next year, IRS Records had terminated.

In late 1993, Anastasia called me in Los Angeles and said she had found the 'country Police.' She was so enthusiastic that I had my secretary, Alletta, book me a flight to Nashville. There, Anastasia had set up the three-piece band in the foyer of the new office we had just rented, and they played a short set. Anastasia was right: Keith Urban, the singer/guitarist front man, was similar to Sting. He was good-looking, a good singer, and a great musician. In fact, he was one of the best guitar players I had ever seen—similar in style to the Dire Straits guitarist Mark Knopfler. In fact, when my brother Stewart played with Keith at one of the songwriters' retreats a year later, he told me he had played with both but considered Keith the better player.

Keith, however, was not as convinced as we were that he was great. He was better with melodies than with lyrics, and he usually teamed up with lyric writers to create songs, but he apparently did not know he was as good a guitar player as he was. When I invited him to the castle retreat in 1994, Anastasia called to say Keith was refusing to go, insisting he was 'not good enough.'

'Just get him on the plane,' I said, 'and I will do the rest.'

Anastasia actually drove him to the airport and made sure he got on the plane. And, as noted before, it changed his life. He later sent a fax to Anastasia, thanking her for making him go.

Our last signing in Nashville was Waylon Jennings. I later recorded him for an Ark 21 release, which ended up being the last album Waylon ever recorded. He was a grand old man and a treat to work with, but he was not of a mind to go out and kill for an album release. He had been there done that, so while it was nice to say you had a Waylon Jennings album in the catalogue, it was not going to be much of a moneymaker for the company.

The Nashville office had delivered some great writers, all of whom I invited to the Château Marouatte songwriting retreats. I have to say I learned a lot from those Nashville writers, and including them in the mix became one of the secrets of why those retreats worked so well. But the Nashville office also had its issues. Keith Urban went through a period of drug problems, Anastasia got divorced then married producer Tony Brown, and frankly it became one more expense that looked like it would absorb cash for more years than I was willing to commit to. We closed the office in 1998. Of course, Anastasia went on to become one of the stars of the Nashville music business.

೪↗

Around the time we opened the Nashville office, I had another thought: *Let's start a label that only has the absolute most outrageous acts on it and call it Shock Therapy Records.*

I meant *really* outrageous. As I remember it, the inspiration came from a band in Florida called Genitorturers. The leader/singer was a beautiful blonde female surgeon named Gen whose day job was doing autopsies at the local morgue, as well as taking donated organs from the newly deceased and sending them to various hospitals all over America. At night, onstage, as the lead singer of her band, she was an entirely different person. During each show, an audience member was invited to the stage, made to drop his pants, and had his scrotum nailed to a wooden plank. This was not a stunt like Cat Iron had done back in 1975—this was real!

That sounded outrageous enough for me, so I sent one of my staff to Orlando, Florida, to check it out. Of course, that staff person had to have a thick skin and know how to deal with shock, so it had to be Nick Turner, ex-drummer of The Lords Of The New Church, who had joined the company to work on new technologies. The internet was relatively new at that point, but we knew something was happening and that it could be important, so Nick was tasked with figuring out how we could use it to help promote our acts.

The stories that came back were even more shocking than I had anticipated. Apparently, there was an X-rated show that was even worse than the scrotum thing. There was no question that Genitorturers had to be the first act released on Shock Therapy Records. I never even saw the band perform, but I didn't need to. I signed them anyway.

We released *120 Days Of Genitorture* in May of 1993, its title was a reference to *The 120 Days Of Sodom* by the Marquis de Sade. During the recording of the album, Gen was called to get organs from a guy killed in a motorcycle accident. She found the body with no head. When she asked where it was, she was handed the helmet—the head was inside it. Another time, she was called to do an autopsy on a guy who had died of lung cancer. The studio engineer was a smoker, so Gen asked him to tag along, and he went. When she cut open the lungs, they were black. The engineer never smoked again.

There was one problem with Genitorturers. They were so outrageous we never found another act that could follow them, so Shock Therapy Records ended up being a one-record company.

CHAPTER 28

KEITH MOORE, ZUCCHERO AND THE END OF IRS

. . . .

One of the things I don't remember doing in this period is worrying about money. Thankfully, I did not have expensive tastes, and I did not spend much time with people who did. It didn't occur to me to have a Rolls-Royce or buy fancy bottles of wine or get into racehorses and the like. And, of course, drugs were anathema to me.

I don't think Sting worried about money, either. Which turned out to be a mistake. The Police, and later Sting, used an accounting firm in London run by Keith Moore, a man who seemed like the typical English gentleman—not particularly colorful or flamboyant, with a steady lifestyle that would not trigger suspicion. None of the band or I had any reason to suspect anything untoward was going on. Then, in October of 1994, Keith was arrested and charged with embezzling millions of pounds from Sting's bank accounts. In October of the following year, after a four-week trial, he was sentenced to six years in jail.

In early 1994, Sting had phoned my house in London, telling me he had received an anonymous letter from someone who worked at Keith Moore's office. A whistleblower was warning Sting that Keith was stealing from him—and it was a lot of money. It was a shock, so I immediately drove to Sting's home in Wiltshire and read the letter. Sting was concerned that others might be involved, so we went down the list of possibilities. First was his lawyer, Christopher Burley, which I said would be way out of character. It was obvious that there were legal implications, and we both agreed that since Christopher was highly unlikely to be an accomplice, I should meet him as soon as possible and work out what to do.

I met Christopher early the next morning, and after his initial shock we quickly worked out a plan of action. The major concern was a leak, so I agreed to go to Keith Moore's office immediately, to take all the books as evidence and close the place down. That would stop anything being destroyed or removed.

Moore's office was a self-contained, one-story building at the foot of Holland Park Road in West London. Keith's office was immediately to the right on the ground floor as you walked in. That day, when I walked through the front door and into Keith's office, it was almost like he was expecting to be exposed. All he said was, 'It's all over.' He was in the shit, good and proper.

Once all the documents were secured, I could not help but ask Keith, 'What on earth were you thinking?' I had known him for a long time, Sting even longer. Fifteen years in all. He offered feeble excuses that I don't think even he could have believed. It seemed like Keith wanted to be a sugar-daddy investor, some kind of bigwig hero, but since none of the investments made sense, even that didn't seem plausible. I would have been happier if he had used the money for himself—one could at least have understood that. He did use *some* for himself, but mostly it was tantamount to flushing money down the toilet. The only thing one could conclude was that he was sick.

One would expect in a story of an accountant stealing large sums from his client that the accountant would have spent the money on some sort of lavish lifestyle for himself. Perhaps a clandestine one—a Walter Mitty life—a villa in the South of France, fancy girls, fancy cars. Keith did buy a new Jaguar XJS with Sting's money, but he then gave it to Sting as a 'gift,' a sign of his appreciation. As far as I know, that is the only fancy car he bought. He did get Sting to sign a £680,000 check, telling him it was to pay his taxes, when in fact it was to pay Keith's company tax. But lavish lifestyle? Not that I could see. One can only imagine the fun he *could* have had, spending seven million pounds that was not his.

Keith did purport to have used some of Sting's money to make 'investments' on behalf of his client—without telling his client, of course, but presumably investments that he thought would look good when they paid off. In that scenario, one would think the investments would be something like a promising internet startup that could become a billion-dollar company, a spread of interesting stocks, or maybe even a promising local restaurant that he could actually see and have dinner in. You would also expect share certificates or contracts of some sort, or a clear paper trail to show an ownership share of the venture.

What you would *not* think of is investing in an Indian restaurant chain twenty thousand miles away in Australia—where you never saw the restaurant, never met the chef, or indeed never had any paperwork to prove you (or your client) owned a share of it. You would also not think of investing in a scheme to convert Russian military aircraft into jumbo freight planes. How did he even find out about such an 'investment'? There was also some scheme to build ecological gearboxes. These kinds of 'investments' sounded crazy, yet they were precisely what Keith used Sting's money for. His rationale for the Australian restaurant 'investment' was: Sting likes to eat. What Sting would do with a Russian jumbo freight plane or an ecological gearbox, I have no idea.

Add it all up, and Keith stole seven million pounds from his client. Towards the end, he was doing it at a rate of £250,000 every month, right out of Sting's bank accounts. On my mission to retrieve as much money as possible, I first looked at where any supposed assets might be. I will never forget the blank look on Keith's face when I asked for backup papers to chase the supposed 'investment assets.' Luckily for Sting, Keith turned out to be a pretty stupid crook. He had apparently been able to take money from Sting's Coutts bank account with his sole signature. That sounded wrong to me, and Christopher was convinced that Keith had no solo signing ability, so that made a meeting with Coutts the first thing on the agenda.

Coutts was a well-respected bank, used by the queen of England herself. Very by the book, very British. A bank like that would have scrupulously gone by what the client's mandate said. It is, after all, a document that lets a bank know who is authorized to access an account. At Coutts in central London, I asked for an urgent meeting with the account manager for Sting. I brought an authority letter from Sting, giving me permission to see the mandate. The manager had no idea what was happening, so he obliged and produced Sting's bank mandate when I asked for it. After a quick look at the information, it was clear that Sting was the sole signatory; nowhere was there any mention of Keith Moore.

With that confirmation, I asked the manager, on what grounds did the bank allow Keith to sign checks? Now looking uncomfortable, he said it must have been an implied authority. I showed him the signature information on the mandate and asked, 'Where do you see any mention of an implied authority?' He saw none. 'Is this not the total signature information Coutts must act on?' He could only say yes. 'So, as you have paid out money on no authority from the account holder, I expect you will reimburse in full.'

The poor guy was stuck. He must have trusted Keith Moore, just as Sting did. It was a huge fuck-up that Coutts had no legitimate answer to, and the bank definitely did not want any sort of court battle with the wide public exposure that would bring. What would the queen say!? Coutts quickly agreed to reimburse Sting—and to top it off with interest.

The good news was that most of the money was retrieved from Coutts. The bad news was that it was not all of it. Those losses were small enough, however, that under the circumstances we all thought Sting should consider himself lucky. Which he did.

During the four-week trial a year later, we learned that, besides Sting, Keith also was the accountant for Queen and Big Country. I have no idea if they suffered any losses. Perhaps the funniest moment was when Sting was in the witness box and stated that the accounts were too many and confusing for him to get a proper 'handle on.' Keith's defense council retorted by trying to make something of Sting's A-level in economics and his previous employment with the Inland Revenue: 'You can't have somebody at the Inland Revenue who is horrified by financial documents.' There was laughter in court when Sting replied that this might have had some bearing on his short career as a taxman.

During the trial, most of the onlookers—and probably the jury too— had difficulty in understanding how anyone could not notice the theft of seven million pounds. Of course, the press made much of the lavish lifestyle of the successful pop star. The simple fact was that there were too many accounts, and Sting was not a big spender anyway. Some stars are into expensive art collections or throw money away on drugs and fancy cars, but Sting was not a wild spender, and he spent far less than he earned. That created the window for Keith Moore to do what he did.

As Sting's manager throughout the Keith Moore saga, I had gotten to know his lawyer, Christopher Burley, a lot better. He was of the old school that charged fees based on the length of time it took to do the work. In the USA, music lawyers like Allen Grubman had come to believe that their fees should be based on the size of the deal. They felt they were entitled to a percentage, so the bigger the deal, the bigger the fee, regardless of hours spent. Consequently, for the US lawyer, the thrust of any deal was to get as big an up-front payment as possible, as that would generate the biggest fee the lawyer could charge. The 'back end' and fine print did not really matter. As Allen said to me, 'If there's a problem, we'll deal with it when it comes up.'

I was never entirely happy with that idea. Allen once scolded me, saying, 'Elton just gave me a Rolls-Royce. He *appreciates* what I do for him.' The inference was that I didn't. Then there was Allen's oft-quoted motto: 'It's not about the money—it's about the money!'

My own view was more old school. My concern was that if a lawyer worked on a big fee, the temptation to get more up-front money on a deal versus better royalty and back end could skew any deal to the long-term detriment of the artist. Charging by the hour, that issue should not come up. In fact, the longer it took to work out the fine print and every last detail, the more the lawyer could charge.

I ended up with a compromise. For recording deals, which were really quite simple, Allen did the legal work for The Police, Sting, and IRS Records, and he got his big fees, though never as much as he asked for. For publishing deals, I looked to Christopher Burley. Publishing is a lot more complicated than recording, especially outside the USA. The fine print really does matter in a publishing deal.

Christopher was meticulous, sometimes painfully so. I used to get very irritated that he took so long to finish contracts, and how he dwelled on even the smallest detail. Before getting to know him, I will admit I would have been happy to see him fired. He was that pedantic. But the more I learned about the music-publishing world, the more I realized that this was exactly what a lawyer had to do, to squeeze every bit out of a worldwide deal. It was all about the pennies, and pennies add up.

Now that I have had time to ponder the best strategy for deal-making—Grubman versus Burley, or money up front versus money at the back end—my conclusion is this: It really depends on the level of success. For less successful acts, it would almost always be money up front; for superstar acts it is all about the back end.

When R.E.M. came to show me the Warner Bros deal, I advised them to go back to the company immediately and sign the deal before they changed their minds. I did not know at the time the huge success R.E.M. would soon have. Now that I do know, there is no question that R.E.M. ended up making more money than The Police and Sting put together—largely because all those huge albums reverted to the band. In effect, Warner Bros only 'rented' the albums for a limited period of time. Had R.E.M. done what I had wanted them to do—renegotiate their IRS deal to get bigger up-front advances and higher royalties in return for giving IRS several more albums—they would not have made as much money as they did.

❧

Zucchero Fornaciari, or as I called him *Il Grande Baboomba* (a name he hated), holds the record for the biggest-selling album of all time in Italy. In his country, he is a veritable superstar, but he has also achieved hit albums in France, Spain, Switzerland, and elsewhere throughout Europe. I was his manager from 1994 to 1997 with my partner, Henry Padovani.

In spite of the abrupt way our relationship ended, I will always have fond memories of Zucchero. I'm sure Henry would begrudgingly say the same. The essential point of understanding an artist like Zucchero must be his realization that he is an Italian, not fluent in English but essentially doing rock'n'roll in what is clearly an English-speaking music world. It's not like the Italian language is spoken in tons of other countries, like Spanish or even French. Was he ever going to make it with English-speaking audiences in the USA or England? Unlikely. Was he going to do an ABBA and effectively *be* an English-speaking artist? Also unlikely. So, one option would be to limit his horizons to becoming big in his own country, and perhaps some surrounding ones as well. But Zucchero wanted more than that.

What was most interesting about Zucchero was that, from the very start, he must have realized that *appearing* to be successful in America or England would help him become big in Italy as well. Perception is nine tenths of reality. To have real 'rock'n'roll' credibility in his own country, he had to make success in the 'Anglo' world seem a reality. That is, in effect, why I ended up as his manager for three years.

In May 1994, at my annual Printemps des Troubadours retreat in France, I already had Cher there, plus Jane Wiedlin and Charlotte Caffey from The Go-Go's, and a coterie of top writers from Nashville, the UK, and elsewhere. Tasked with inviting some major European artists, Henry, then head of the IRS Paris office, invited Zucchero. All I knew about him at this point was he was very big in Italy.

Zucchero showed up in his fancy Mercedes 500 convertible sports car with a passenger called Lorenzo who spoke no known language except Italian. Zucchero had apparently driven to the castle all the way from Carrara, near Pisa, in Italy—a twelve-hour drive. Neither Henry nor I had expected him to arrive with another person, and all the bedrooms were occupied, save for the one we had held for him, which had a single four-poster, king-size bed. I told Zucchero that if Lorenzo was planning to stay—which I hoped he wasn't—he would have to stay in Zucchero's room. That did not go down well. I suggested a nearby hotel but Lorenzo, when he figured out what was being suggested, started pleading with Henry, who luckily spoke fluent Italian: 'Please don't put me in a hotel, I know no one and don't speak French.'

Apparently, Zucchero had told Lorenzo to come along up the road to a songwriter thing, but he had not mentioned staying there or indeed very much else. Perhaps Zucchero had not known much about the facilities; Lorenzo certainly did not, and he was freaking out. He had brought no clothes, he could only speak Italian, and he had no idea what he was doing there. It was a pickle I could not solve, so in the end I had a mattress put in Zuc's room and told him we would figure it out in the morning. Lorenzo stayed in that room for the rest of the week.

Poor Lorenzo. For the next few days, he wandered around doing nothing, with no one to talk to except Henry and Zucchero; for the rest of us, it was a polite greeting and then quickly moving on. On the third day, probably out of sheer boredom, Lorenzo volunteered to do a pasta dinner for everyone. He must have known what he was doing, as he was very specific as to what he needed. It involved six kilos of tomatoes, an onion, and five garlic cloves, and he and our chef, Lucy, labored over it all afternoon. Together they created a quite fantastic, genuine Italian pasta dinner, and all of a sudden Lorenzo became a hero. I guess he felt the change in everyone and gained confidence, so during dinner he stood up and began singing—in *Italian*—what turned out to be Cher's big hit, 'Bang Bang (My Baby Shot Me Down).' Jane Wiedlin turned to Cher and said, 'Cher that's your song,' and everyone in the room joined in. From that point on, Lorenzo was the hit of the retreat. It turned out he had covered the Cher song when he was a young Italian pop star named Lorenzo de Penzo (Lorenzo, I am thinking of myself).

Meanwhile, Henry came to me and said Zucchero was looking to change his management setup, and what he really wanted was an 'international manager.' We would be the ideal team. Henry was keen to do it, and he promised me that he could handle the nuts and bolts of the job, especially where speaking Italian would count. He made a convincing argument, the main point of which was that Zucchero was already big in Italy, but he could also be big in France, Spain, and elsewhere in Europe. So, there was work to do, and we were well set up to help him do it.

By the end of the retreat we had an agreement, and I arranged to fly to Milan on June 1 to conclude the deal. When I got there, the first meeting was at the offices of Zucchero's record company, Polydor, to sign the management contract. Then Zucchero said, 'Let's go to the next room to make the announcement.' Not thinking much about it, we both went into the next room, and to my surprise there was a podium with microphones on a small stage with a room full of the Italian press. Zucchero wanted to make sure everyone in Italy knew that he now had a big-time international manager—the man behind The Police and Sting, etc. That was my confirmation that Zucchero knew his Italian market and the importance of the press to enhance his image as the top Italian music artist who was also accepted and revered in the rest of the world.

TWO STEPS FORWARD, ONE STEP BACK

In fairness, Henry was more important in the success we helped Zucchero achieve than I was. He spoke Italian, so I had to rely on that ability as well as the relationships he had built working with me as the IRS Records representative in Paris. As the original guitarist with The Police, Henry had media credibility as well as musical credibility. For me, he really was the perfect partner to work with in managing Zucchero.

I got Zucchero hooked up with musicians he wanted on his records, and booked onto shows he wanted to be on, like Woodstock '94 in the USA, plus Sting's Rainforest Foundation in New York, Net Aid, and a host of other examples of what Zucchero considered 'prestige' shows. In effect, I provided the icing, but Henry provided the cake. It was an effective team, and we delivered to Zucchero what he wanted. Henry worked with the French record company and media people, propelling Zucchero's first album, *Spirito De Vino*, to becoming a big chart hit in France and opening doors in Spain, Germany, and the rest of non-English speaking Europe. Then the *Blue Sugar* album was even bigger, selling over three million copies in Europe.

Zucchero was a fun artist to work with. One day, somewhere in Italy, he and I went to lunch with Pavarotti, who I remember ordered two pasta main courses. Another time it was Andrea Bocelli, who Zucchero had actually discovered, and who was now being managed by Zucchero's ex-manager. At his house in Carrara, we always had fantastic pasta. He used to joke onstage, 'Sorry, my English is like your pasta, not good.'

In London, Zucchero wanted me to get Jeff Beck to play on the *Spirito De Vino* album. Jeff came over to AIR Studios in London and over an hour or so did twelve takes of a guitar solo, each of which had bits of genius but then went out of tune. Zucchero, Henry and I kept looking at each other, not understanding how so great a player could go from pure genius to incompetence in the same solo. When we offered an auto-tuner, Jeff said, 'No, the ear mate; just the ear.' After several attempts but never quite getting one great solo from beginning to end, the engineer said he'd had enough; he could edit bits from each solo to come up with one that was in tune from beginning to end. We left the engineer to it but did not tell Jeff what the plan was. The Jeff Beck solo the engineer pieced together is one of the great guitar solos of all time—and certainly the greatest that never happened.

Recording in London, Zucchero called to ask me to book my brother Stewart to put drums on one of his tracks. A few hours into the session, Stewart called and said, 'Get me out of this.' Apparently, Zucchero knew exactly what he wanted the drums to do, so he should have hired a session musician. He didn't want Stewart's style of drumming—he wanted Stewart's name on the credits.

When I called Zucchero to kill the session, he asked if he could still put Stewart's name on the credits. 'He is not the drummer,' I replied, 'so the answer is no.'

Then there was the time at Sting's annual Rainforest Foundation concert at Carnegie Hall, New York, on April 30, 1997. Zucchero was happy to be there, especially because the bill also featured Aretha Franklin, one of Zucchero's all-time favorites. I introduced them, and all Aretha said was, 'Never heard of you.' Fortunately, I don't think Zucchero was unduly hurt by it. We had a laugh about it later.

As mentioned above, shortly after I became his manager, Zucchero pestered me about the second Woodstock festival, which was taking place on August 12, 1994. He *had* to be on that show, even though I told him it would not help him break the American market. Worst of all, I added, it was a one-off show that would cost a fortune, especially if he was to bring his entire band from Italy. He insisted, even promising that whatever it cost it would be his personal cost and would not affect any future management commission.

'Zucchero,' I said, 'they will put you on a side stage and few people will know you are there.'

Zucchero was undeterred. I contacted the promoter, Michael Lang, and got Zucchero on the show. And, as I predicted, he was to play on one of the small stages at the same time as a big act was playing on the main stage. There were no more than two thousand people there, out of the estimated three hundred thousand people that attended the festival, and most of them were Italians. Zucchero did bring his entire band from Italy, and it cost over $150,000. What about the promise that it would not show up on the accounts? Of course, it *was* on the accounts, which meant Henry and I paid our share, too.

Meanwhile, Zucchero was as happy as he could be, and he had no complaint about spending so much to perform for so few people in a market that he was unlikely to break. I thought it was stupid until I saw the Italian press, and how almost every newspaper and magazine of any note celebrated the fact that Zucchero was the only European act to be invited to Woodstock. The name 'Woodstock' was well known in Italy, and Zucchero being asked to participate in the 1994 version carried weight. And Zucchero wanted that weight as further confirmation that he was not just an Italian star but a worldwide one.

As Henry and I got to know him, we learned that he very much operated on this idea. Our problem ended up being that we had to contribute our management commission for it, even when he had committed to covering the costs personally.

As popular as he was, Zucchero was not able to escape controversy in Italy. One journalist accused him of plagiarism, and to some degree he was right. I actually looked at it as very clever, and, in a way, it was what we all do: being influenced by others and copying what they do in our own way. One afternoon in Carrara, where Zucchero had his office, he played me some songs from an Iron Butterfly album. Not the one with 'In-A-Gadda-Da-Vida' that everyone knew, but album four or five, which I never ever knew existed.

'Listen carefully,' he said. Sure enough, I heard a bass line and a bit of melody that Zucchero had adapted to be the main melody in one of his songs.

'So that's how you do it.'

Usually it was a small phrase—a bar or two—that I doubt even the musician who did it would recognize. Zucchero had a keen ear, and he made some great music because of it. One had to be impressed with such investigative skills, digging a song out of someone else's obscure album. Who would have thought little gems were lying there for someone like him to find?

Henry had a tougher time of it than I did, as he was the front-line, full-time person working with Zucchero. He had to deal with all the issues as they came up, whereas I was called in when needed, for major events, or when there was some fun for us all to have. Zucchero, like every artist, was not always reasonable, and he always had opinions, some of which he would not shake. What ended it for Henry and me was the accounting. The accounts got so confused that in the end we decided the only way to be sure we knew what was going on was to audit them. Zucchero considered that insulting: if we audited, he would fire us. We insisted on an audit. He fired us. But, like I said, I will always have a soft spot for Zucchero.

In 2014, my wife and I saw that Zucchero was performing at the five-thousand-seat Nokia Theatre in Los Angeles and decided to go. The promoter who set it up got us backstage passes. Adriana and I went back before the show, where there was a long line of people waiting to see Zucchero—Italian dignitaries and the like.

Zuc was in his dressing room, getting ready for the show. The tour manager, who I didn't know, asked us to wait along with everyone else. I said, 'Just tell Zucchero Miles and Adriana are here.' Within a minute we were ushered into the dressing room; Zucchero was in there alone, and the three of us hung out for the next fifteen minutes. When we went back to take our seats, I'll bet everyone was thinking, *Who the fuck are those people?*

∞

In 2011, Henry was made one of the three judges on France's version of *The X-Factor*, which became the #1 TV show in the country. Henry was famous, with billboards showing the three judges' faces all over the country. He got marriage proposals in the mail. He even talked me into letting *The X-Factor* film one show at the castle.

One night, Zucchero was playing a sold-out show in Paris, and Henry went along to say hello. Backstage, as fans came walking towards Zucchero and Henry talking, when they asked for an autograph, it was from Henry—not Zucchero.

In the early days with The Police, Henry was not much of a musician, but he always had *something*. It was great that later he became a really fine musician and songwriter, and an important cog that kept appearing in the machine of my life.

Henry went on to write a book about his time in The Police and after, *Secret Policeman*. He also started doing solo albums, and one day he sent one of them to me. All the songs were in French but they were so good that I said he had to let me release it in the USA, even though we both knew it probably would not sell. When filming started for the IRS documentary *We Were Once Rebels*, of course Henry was asked to contribute.

ଏ∾

By 1994, it was pretty apparent to me that IRS Records' days were numbered. I was not cut out to be a corporate guy, and what made IRS relevant in 1979 was no longer the case now. For the EMI deal, I had kicked myself upstairs, becoming chairman of IRS and making Jay henceforth the president of the label. So it was also becoming apparent that it made no sense to have two chief executives. It seemed obvious to me that one of us had to go. I discussed this with Jay Boberg and made the point that he was fifteen years younger than me, and would likely be more in demand than I would—he was also much more attuned to the workings of the corporate world than I was. He had actually taken off time from IRS Records one summer to study management at Harvard University. Whereas I would have a difficult time putting up with other people's stupid ideas, Jay knew how to go around them.

Perhaps it was his experience within the corporate world of EMI or the influence of his summer at Harvard, or perhaps just that we were all growing older, and IRS was not as carefree and fun as it once was. In the early 90s, there was also an unmistakable rift between the European part of IRS, under Steve Tannett in London and Henry Padovani in Paris, and Jay Boberg at the US company. This was partly due to the fact that pressure and diktats from EMI were delivered to the US company, and that gave a certain insulation to the European offices. But it was also due to a fundamentally different sensibility between the two camps. I have to admit that I had more fun with the Europeans than I did the US side.

The other point both of us had to face was, whether we liked it or not, the company was becoming divided. There were Jay's people and my people. I had some say, 'I work for you, not Jay,' and I am sure he heard the same thing from *his* people. In short, for all sorts of reasons, it was time for one of us to move on.

Jay left the company in 1994, and in February of 1995 he became president of MCA Records.

Following Jay's departure, I hired industry veteran Mike Bone to manage the label, as 1995 had me running around the globe with Sting, Zucchero, and others. In reality, I knew IRS was unlikely to survive the EMI structure and modus operandi. It was apparent not only to me but to the staff as well. As Mike later told me, he felt like he had become captain of the *Titanic*... after it had hit the iceberg.

With this in mind, I was in discussions with EMI on two fronts. First was an attempt to buy IRS Records, which took Mike Bone and me to meet various finance organizations like BlackRock in Boston and another in Nashville. Given the growing fears about internet piracy and the like, it was not a great time to be looking for financing for a record company that had no major acts on its books. To conservative financiers, IRS was too much of a risk, so I resorted to plan B, which was for EMI to give me a pure distribution deal to start a new label from scratch.

In April of 1996, IRS Records was terminated. Shortly thereafter, I launched a new label, Ark 21. I came up with the name thinking the label would be like Noah's ark saving all the animals, but in this case saving neglected acts that still had something to say, and taking them into the twenty-first century. In a sense, Ark 21 was the opposite of what IRS Records had been, but like IRS Records I was thinking of how to avoid going head-to-head with the major labels and all their money. I did sign new artists, but I also signed many who had been around a while and (as far as the recording business was concerned) were no longer financially interesting. My view was that if the price was right and they still made good music, then Ark 21 would be interested.

Over time, I signed acts like Alannah Myles, Steppenwolf, The Moody Blues, Waylon Jennings, and Leon Russell. The biggest problem was when the artists themselves considered themselves current and hated the idea that they were no longer the stars they had once been. Meanwhile, the only radio stations that were interested really wanted to play the old hits—none wanted to play the new albums, so of course the artists usually turned down a lot of the promotion we got them. Can't say I blame them.

The record business was changing too, with music free for the taking from places like Napster. CDs and physical product were becoming a thing of the past. The good old days of the record business were over. I was lucky to still be in the management side of the business.

CHAPTER 29

MERCURY
FALLING

. . . .

At one of my first retreats in France, one of the Nashville songwriters signed to my company, Doug Millett, said, 'My daddy always used to tell me, make sure the chorus comes in like a garlic milkshake.' I'll never forgot that advice because it was so right.

Nashville writers tended to work with well-established formulas that they'd seen work over a long period of time. Structure, hooks, and payoffs when one's brain expects them—these things were an ingrained discipline, to the point where, to the average Nashville writer, they were second nature.

All of Sting's biggest hits, like 'Roxanne,' 'Every Breath You Take,' 'Can't Stand Losing You,' and 'Walking On The Moon,' follow the basic hit song formula. But Sting seemed to have become bored with the formula—and I didn't find out until too late.

By the time I went in to listen to what became *Mercury Falling*, Sting had recorded and pretty much finished the songs. What I heard were songs that had all the makings of hits, but with no garlic milkshake. When I discussed what I was hearing with Sting, he was not sure what I meant, so we played one of the songs that I thought could be a hit. When the chorus came, he said, 'No, that's the middle eight.' I asked where the choruses were, and we played the song again. To Sting, there were two choruses before the middle eight, but they were at the same level as the verse that preceded them. To me, they sounded like a second part of the verse; the only chorus I heard was what he called the middle eight. He said he understood what I was saying, but he was happy with the song as it was, and he would pay the price himself if I was right. I knew he meant it, and our conversation ended.

When Sting left the room, I went to Hugh Padgham, the album's producer, and asked him what he thought about the songs and what I had said to Sting.

'You're right,' he said.

'If you know I'm right, why didn't you say something when it was being recorded?'

Hugh then said something that shook my faith in him as the producer that Sting needed: 'It's Sting, how can I tell him how to write a song?'

The good news was that Hugh knew the fundamentals of a hit song. The bad news was that he didn't think it was his place to advise Sting on what he should do. To me, that's what a producer is *supposed* to do. I decided at that moment that as good an engineer as Hugh was, he should not be the producer on the next album.

I also realized that I should have gone to the studio earlier. Sting listened, and maybe I could have made a difference.

I had always operated on the basis of instinct when it came to what makes a hit song, but those songwriting retreats allowed me to be able to verbalize the process. Carole King, Cathy Dennis, Sarah Hudson, and so many others—they all had their original tricks of the trade, but in essence there was a simple formula:

verse / CHORUS / verse / CHORUS / middle-eight / verse / CHORUS / out.

These days, that simple formula has often been replaced by throwing in a rap section, or putting two different songs together, or other ways of mixing it up. But the basic formula still works, just like the 'old grey whistle test.'

At almost every retreat, I asked writers if they knew what that 'test' was. Yes, it had been the title of a music show that aired for years on British TV, but what did it *mean*? It was an old saying at music publishing companies about how to choose a hit song. When a songwriter came into the publisher's office to pitch a song, the writer would be asked to wait while someone went out and stopped some random elderly pedestrians walking down the street and ushered them in; when they were seated, the publisher would ask the songwriter to play the song. Then the publisher would ask the old guys in grey suits to whistle what they had just heard. If they could whistle the melody, it could be a hit. If not, the song was rejected.

When one thinks about it, almost all hit songs have that one-listen 'hook' element, and that's what the old grey whistle test was all about. 'Walking On The Moon,' 'Roxanne,' 'Can't Stand Losing You,' 'Every Breath You Take'—all those songs have that simple formula. In my view, the songs on the *Mercury Falling* album should have used that formula, but they didn't. I was counting on the next Sting album to be different.

↢↣

I like India. I like the people, the art, the architecture, and especially the food. It's a great place to shop, a great place to sightsee, and, if you are careful, a great place to eat. But there are also a lot of things I don't like: the caste system, the way women are treated, the intentional maiming of children, the extreme poverty, the religious bigotry and perversions. I especially don't like Westerners who see none of that and want to 'be' Indian because they think it gives them some sort of spiritual superiority.

In early November 1998, Sting got an invitation from Channel V in India to come to New Delhi and receive an award for his 'Outstanding Contribution To Music.' The record company was supportive and promised to put out a best-of album that would make what they considered big sales. Sting was available, and a free trip to India sounded like fun.

Sting, his son Joe, and I left London on November 17 and headed for New Delhi. We stayed in a fancy Hilton Hotel somewhere in the center of the city, which also was next door to a serious slum. The difference in life for the rich and the poor was striking, and it was right there on the same block—right outside our window. But the tea in the morning was magical, and I made a point of buying bags of it before I left India a few days later.

The show itself was not so different from shows in Europe, other than the performance of 'Every Breath You Take' with the famed tabla player Talvin Singh and his duet partner, Shiamak Davar. The record company

271

was happy, though, and a recording of the duet was used as a bonus track on the best-of album they released after we left.

I spent the next morning shopping in the markets for trinkets, while Sting was making plans to go to the city of Benares, also known as Varanasi. A charter plane was booked, a hotel arranged, and Sting asked me if I wanted to come along. Neither of us had ever been to Benares, and it sounded like an adventure, so why not?

I can't remember the exact details, but we had somehow picked up a bit of an entourage to go with us. There was an Indian college professor who taught somewhere on the US East Coast and a guy who called himself Ram Dass but whose real name was Steve. He was an American from Woodstock, New York, who dressed like an Indian in a white robe and acted like he was a local. He even adopted Indian mannerisms when he spoke. I made a point of calling him Steve the entire time.

We took a taxi from the airport on a hair-raising ride into the city, dodging motorized rickshaws and cows all the way, and of course teaming crowds of people. The road was barely one lane each way, and the driving method was apparently: *Aim for the other vehicle and swerve just before you hit it.* I thought driving in Beirut was crazy, but this was at a whole new level. At least in Beirut you only had cars and people to deal with; here it was cows as well, and it was hard to predict what they would do. Meanwhile, everyone acted like all this bedlam was perfectly normal.

The hotel turned out to be more of a pension or two-story house. There were no frills to speak of, but it was clean, which was the most important thing—apparently, finding a clean place in Benares was not easy, so we should consider ourselves lucky. There were probably nicer hotels in the city, but the vibe of our trip seemed to be about experiencing the 'real' India (as much as we would dare).

My room was simple, with whitewashed walls and a single bed. Looking out of the window, I saw a large family of monkeys on the roof next door. In fact, there were monkeys all over the place. I could see the Ganges too, not even a block away, which was good, because we planned to walk to all the places we wanted to see.

The next morning, after breakfast, we walked along the riverbank toward the place where they do the ritual cremation ceremonies. The river had obviously receded; the way was littered with garbage and refuse of all kinds, and there was even a guy defecating, as if the bank was a public toilet. (I have always said, *If you think the Middle East is dirty, wait until you see India!* Beirut or even Cairo are like Switzerland compared to what we saw in Benares.)

At the cremation place there was a long flight of open-air stairs leading up to the main road, which had dilapidated palaces along its route. The palaces looked amazing from afar, but the closer one got one could see they were occupied by dirt and mud and no one was living in them. The steps themselves were covered in so much dirt that only the edges could be seen.

We walked up as best we could and sat down for a while to watch the proceedings down below by the water. The cremation process involved the body being delivered to some holy men who first dunked it into the Ganges in some sort of cleansing ceremony, then wrapped the body in white cloth, doused it with coconut oil, and placed it on a pile of wood. Then they set it alight. The smell permeated the whole area.

This was all part of a religious ceremony, but I could see nothing religious about it. It was all very matter of fact and primitive, and the filth everywhere was overpowering. I don't know what Sting was getting out of what we were seeing, but I assume his thoughts were far more benevolent than mine, and Steve and the college professor were no doubt totally into whatever the spiritual thing was that we were meant to experience. If there were criticisms, none were voiced.

After watching the cremations for a while, Sting decided we should rent a boat to go out into the Ganges and hold a ceremony honoring the death of Kenny Kirkland, the keyboard player from the *Dream Of The Blue Turtles* album and tour who had died a week earlier. He had been a friend and a valued musical colleague, so it made sense to do something.

The ceremony was called a *puja*. Steve and the college professor went to a group of holy men to negotiate what it would cost for one of them to administer it for us. Each holy man had a different price, and for some reason they chose the guy who charged the most. I don't know if it was the price, but our holy man definitely looked the part—he was older and balding, with bad teeth and nothing on his feet. I guess the worse you look, the more holy you must be.

The boat was more of a large rowboat—very simple, with seats around the side. Out we went into the sacred river, and before long a dead cow floated past, bloated and rotting and covered in flies. When the holy man started his thing, he dipped his finger in a jar of red paint and placed a red dot on everyone's forehead, until he got to mine. 'No dot on me, please,' I said. I was not trying to be a party-pooper, but I did not wish to pretend to believe in something I did not.

The *puja* also required water from the Ganges to be poured over our heads, but having just seen the dead cow float by, I didn't want any of that filthy water on me, so I passed the cup to the person sitting next to me. Kenny was honored in whatever that ceremony was, and, out of respect for him and for Sting, I kept my mouth shut.

The next day, we went to a temple to bless some sort of business transaction. In the center was a huge concrete elephant painted in gaudy colors, and apparently the tradition is that if you have an important business dealing, you give money to the elephant and thereby have your business blessed so you can be sure of success. How a concrete elephant is supposed to do that, I don't know—I had studied Hinduism and its monistic view of life in college, and the concrete elephant god did not fit my understanding. Another example of the perversion of a religion. It did seem like a good business, though, and if a merchandising stand had been set up to sell T-shirts, I'll bet it could have made a fortune.

As interesting and culturally illuminating as the trip had been, I could not resist saying what I thought when, on the last day, the college professor asked me, 'So, Miles, what do you think India can teach the West?'

I looked him right in the eye and said, as calmly and deliberately as I could, 'To be absolutely frank, NOT A GOD-DAMNED THING!'

'But don't you see how happy people look?' he asked.

'Ever been to the Beverly Center mall?' I replied. 'Do you see people moping around like their lives are shit? They look pretty happy to me, and a damned sight happier than I see around here! That guy we saw shitting in the river yesterday, how happy do you think he was? What about those fools giving money to a concrete elephant?

'I have been all over the world,' I continued, 'in the Middle East and other shitholes, and never have I experienced a country that has less spirituality than India. There is more spirituality in a Kansas outhouse.'

I probably went too far with the outhouse comment, but overall, I was right—all one has to do is look at the history books and turn on the television. One million people died when India went independent and Muslims and Hindus killed each other. People are killed all the time in India just because they are the 'wrong' religion. The caste system is an abomination.

Yes, the food is great and the tea exceptional. The art, architecture, workmanship, language, mathematics—India has given us so much. The tragedy is that for a smart, industrious nation, its people are fucked by a system and silly beliefs that hold them back. The same was true in China under Mao—look what happened when they dumped his bullshit communism.

This is not to say that Christianity or Islam or just about every other religion does not have its foolish or 'unfortunate' elements. Religion has been one of the great killers for thousands of years, and it is not limited to any one people or society. Tribalism, nationalism, racism, greed, and mankind's general propensity to fuck over the 'other' for whatever reason: I saw it growing up in Cairo and Beirut; I saw it in Birmingham, Alabama; and I was seeing it again now in India.

❧

That trip with Sting was not my first run-in with the perception that India has some kind of spiritual message for the West. It also occurred at the House Of Blues in Los Angeles.

From 1994, when it opened in Los Angeles on the Sunset Strip, to its closure in 2015, the club was a music institution, famous around the world. When my brother Ian died, we held a service there for him with all his music friends and associates. Its founders were the actor Dan Aykroyd, who gained his blues credentials from his work with John Belushi in *The Blues Brothers*, and Isaac Tigrett, who had started his restaurant career with the Hard Rock Café in London back in 1971. It was decorated to the hilt with rock'n'roll paraphernalia, Indian fabrics on the walls, and Indian wood carving. It was a spectacle for the eyes, but it also celebrated an Indian guru, Sathya Sai Baba, who I knew something about.

Isaac was an outspoken follower of Sai Baba, and portraits of him were all over the place. Way back in 1970, my best friend from high school in Beirut, Tal Brooke, had decided he needed to discover the truth and meaning of life, so he went off to India to get the spiritual guidance he thought he would find there. Every few months or so, I would receive a letter. At first, Tal studied with the Maharishi that The Beatles had championed. That did not give him what he was looking for. After a few more letters and a few more gurus, all of whom failed to answer his quest, I got one raving about a fantastic guru that had millions of followers and could create food out of thin air. Tal had apparently met 'the one,' and I thought he would end life as some sort of monk disciple, never to be seen in the West again.

The letters stopped, but then, to my complete surprise, Tal showed up at Marlborough Place in London with a tale to tell. After months of going to guru after guru, he ended up with Sai Baba, who he had become totally convinced was the real thing.

'So why are you back here?' I asked him.

It turned out that Tal had made it into the inner sanctum of the Sai Baba camp, along with a handful of other young Western boys, so he thought it was a great honor to be so chosen. Then, one day, Baba touched his genitals, which disturbed him, but Baba said it was about 'cleansing his pores.' This happened a few more times, and then Tal asked one of the other boys if this happened to them. It seems Sai Baba was doing regular 'cleaning of pores' on all those young boys. Tal realized Sai Baba was a pedophile, and he had come back to the West to expose him and warn everyone about this false prophet—which he did in a series of books.

I thought this would have been a great lesson for Tal, and perhaps now he had gotten all this spiritual quest stuff out of his system. A few months later, he contacted me again, this time from Virginia, and told me he had taken a triple dose of LSD, gone out into the woods, and discovered Jesus. His letter ended, 'God bless you.' Tal was now a Christian.

So, armed with all this information, I was not going to be taken in by all the spiritual mottos sprinkled around the House Of Blues. One night after a concert, the Sting entourage and I were invited by Isaac Tigrett to have dinner in one of the club's private rooms. There was a big picture of Sai Baba on the wall, so I took the opportunity to recount Tal's story with the punchline that Sai Baba was a fuckin' pedophile! It was probably impolite of me to say that in the man's club, but then again . . . Isaac was worshiping a fucking pedophile!

A couple of people told me to keep my voice down, but Isaac heard me, and was he pissed! Of course, it came out later that indeed Sai Baba was a pedophile, and Tal Brooke was right. Tal's first book, *Avatar Of Night*, exposes Baba's 'outward divinity concealed within a timeless, demonic presence.' Demolition of the House Of Blues began in 2017, to make way for the Sunset Time hotel.

ের

One day in 1998, I was riding a taxi through Paris. The radio was tuned to a station that was aimed at the Algerian immigrant community, and I asked the driver to turn it up. What piqued my interest was the Arabic-sounding music that also incorporated Western music elements. It was like the music I heard while growing up in Beirut had joined the music I was currently working with. I soon learned it was just that: music made by immigrants to France from Algeria. They used Arab instruments, like the qanun, oud, and darbuka, added Western guitar, bass, and drums, and called it *Raï*, which means 'opinion' in Algerian Arabic. And unlike most Arab music from Lebanon and Egypt, Raï had lyrics about social and political issues that dealt with everyday life, not just the standard love themes of most songs.

All of a sudden, I saw Arab music as a resource that could be drawn upon to supply new musical influences.

In Paris, I regularly visited the Polydor offices on matters relating to artists I represented, so I took the opportunity to see what Raï recordings they might have. There, I discovered that Cheb Khaled, Rachid Taha, Faudel, and Amina—top artists in the genre—were signed to that company. All of them lived in Paris. The more I looked into the subject, the more excited I got. I learned that Virgin Records had also signed some Raï artists, so I made a point of visiting the company and getting their Cheb Mami albums. Cheb Mami was also from Algeria but living in Paris. The more I listened, the more I thought there were ingredients here that might appeal to Sting.

277

Looking for off-the-beaten-track musical influences was nothing new to me. Spending as much time as I did in Los Angeles, I had also been looking to Latin music as another potential source of inspiration. Entering the punk music scene with no money, and later as a smaller record company with limited resources, I had been forced to look for musical styles that might be overlooked by the major companies. If a music was good and I liked it, and it was being missed by my competitors, that might create opportunities for me. Non-English-speaking records were rarely released by the front-line companies in America, and even Spanish-language ones were almost always in small, separate divisions.

I was not going to be able to compete in the mainstream of Latin music, but there was one niche developing that I might find some success in, and that was what was being called 'rock en español.' I had first been introduced to the genre in London by Phil Banfield, who I had teamed up with to form a European concert booking agency.

Phil had signed the Spanish group Heroes Del Silencio as early as 1988, and he got me interested enough to meet them at their hometown of Zaragoza, Spain, to come up with a plan to help them with EMI in the USA. The group had proved that there was a market for them outside Spain by selling half a million records in Germany. They were also beginning to sell in Latin America, in places like Argentina, Chile, and Venezuela. What's more, the genre was greatly influenced by The Police, so that gave me instant credibility.

Like the punks back in 1978, the rock en español artists also wanted to be taken seriously, but in their case that meant by mainstream or 'Anglo' American record companies. International acts had succeeded in the US market in the past, but only by singing in perfect English, like ABBA. Non-English-speaking acts rarely, if ever, made the mainstream music charts.

The Police had become a big influence by performing in countries like Argentina, Brazil, Chile, Venezuela, and Mexico, so one of my first projects in the genre was to do a Police tribute album called *Outlands D'Americas*, featuring the top rock en español artists of the day performing Police songs sung in Spanish.

At Virgin in Paris in 1998, when they gave me Manu Chao's *Clandestino* album, I assumed it was another *español* type of record. It was a lot more than that. Manu was French, sang in Spanish, and had a completely different approach to assembling an album. I started having visions of what a great stunt it would be to get some sort of collaboration going between Manu and Sting. Manu had fused musical elements just as The Police had done—and, just like Sting, Manu Chao was an influencer. The impact in Latin America, not to mention France and Spain, could be huge. Sting was already big in Latin America, but this could put serious icing on the cake.

☙

In the summer of 1998, Sting started writing songs for his next album at his new villa near Florence, Italy. He was now working with a new producer, who interestingly turned out to be Kipper, aka Mark Eldridge, who had been one of my IRS Records signings when he was the leader of the group One Nation. On one of my trips to see Sting, I decided to give him *Clandestino* and some of the Raï albums, to see if he might get inspired. I left them thinking it was unlikely he would listen to them, but what the hell.

To my amazement, when I returned a few weeks later, Sting told me he did listen to the albums, and he might even have an idea. He played music while he was doing his yoga practice every morning, and he liked what he'd heard. Unfortunately, he didn't really relate to *Clandestino*, but he did like the Raï stuff, and he wanted to see some shows.

Luckily, there was a huge Raï concert scheduled at the Bercy Arena in Paris on September 8, 1998, featuring three of the biggest Raï artists—Khaled, Rachid Taha, and Faudel—with a band of Arab, French, British, and American musicians. The show became famous as the 1, 2, 3 Soleils concert, and it would be a historic moment for the Raï genre. Interestingly, it was produced by Steve Hillage from Gong, with Geoffrey Richardson from Caravan doing string arrangements.

I organized tickets and went along to the show with Sting, Kipper, and tour manager Billy Francis, wisely choosing seats to the side high enough to see everything but not close enough to get mobbed. The sold-out venue was throbbing with thirteen thousand people, and the event stands as the biggest ever for the Raï scene in France. We went backstage after the show to meet everyone, chatting with Khaled, Faudel, and Steve Hillage, among others.

As much as we'd enjoyed the show, I said to Sting, 'Don't make any commitment yet, because I want you to see Cheb Mami first.' Mami was performing a concert a week or so later in the much more intimate setting of a small theater, making it easier to focus on the elements of the ensemble: violin, qanun, oud, guitar, drums, darbuka, bass, and Mami on vocals. There is no mistaking a killer voice and a unique style, even if you don't understand the vocals.

This time, Sting brought Trudie with us to the concert, and she said what we were all thinking: 'He's a real little star, isn't he?' Then Sting leaned over to me and said, 'That's the guy.'

Months later, Sting gave me a demo of the song that I was to give Mami, to see if he could come up with a duet part. When I heard back from Mami's manager, I arranged the studio time with Sting, then flew Mami with me to Italy to do the recording.

One of the first things I did was to explain to everyone that Cheb meant 'young' in Arabic, so they should call him Mami, not Cheb. Khaled had been called Cheb Khaled when he was young, but the Cheb was dropped when he became older. Calling him Cheb would be like calling someone 'Mister' as if that was his first name. I kept doing this, but to no avail. It didn't seem to register, and Mami went through his time with Sting with a new name: 'Young.'

At the studio, Mami sang his part and nailed it in the first take. We had been together for under an hour, so we could not very well say, 'OK, thanks, see you later.' Since Mami was there, it made sense to try other takes and versions, but the reality was that the first one was the keeper, so that was the one used. The song was 'Desert Rose.'

☙

Too bad Sting didn't take to *Clandestino*, but that didn't stop it going to #1 in the French charts—twice. It is rated as the most important album ever in the Latin rock field, selling over five million copies. I was lucky to release it in the USA on my Ark 21 label, where it was voted 'album of the year' by the Latin press, and I was given an award for releasing it. Of course, putting Sting and Manu together could just as easily have been a disaster as a success. Manu was not your average musical guy—perhaps he is better described for his political leanings.

When I released *Clandestino*, Virgin Records in Paris told me apologetically that Manu was somewhere in Chiapas, Mexico, with revolutionaries or indigenous people—I'm not sure which. I saw him only once during the entire promotion period for the album. Out of the blue one day, he called my office in Los Angeles and said, 'I'll be there in half an hour.' He had taken a bus from Mexico City. We scampered to try to set up some interviews and a photo session. He showed up, was as nice as he could be, and then half an hour later was gone. As far as I know, he went back to Chiapas.

The real pisser was that Virgin Records in the USA was so impressed with how well Ark 21 did with *Clandestino* that they lobbied the Paris division to let *them* release the second album. Of course, like me, they got no tour, no photos, no press interviews. Virgin was not the kind of company to work an album with no tools. If Manu didn't show up, they were on to the next thing. They lost the album in the first week.

Meanwhile, Sting finished recording his new album, *Brand New Day*, which this time seemed to have the necessary hit singles. Kipper's input helped, and Sting came up with the songs and a structure that this time worked for me. The obvious first single was also the album's title track, 'Brand New Day,' which was released in September 1999. It did reasonably well, got around fifteen Top 40 stations on it, but it never quite cracked the Hot 100 singles chart. Nevertheless, it helped move the album to sales of 900,000 copies in the USA.

At his age, Sting was no longer a shoo-in at Top 40 radio. That was an unfortunate reality of the record business. When I asked people to name their favorite track on the record, everyone, to a man, said 'Desert Rose.' So, when it came to the second single, both Sting and I thought 'Desert Rose' was the obvious choice, but the marketing people at the label didn't think so. They actually told me there was *no* second single on the album. Worse, I was told if I thought 'Desert Rose' was a single, I needed to take 'that Arab guy' off of it. The logic escaped me.

Fortunately, the Europeans—especially the French—liked 'Desert Rose' and agreed to put it out as the second single. Cheb Mami was well known in France, and the Europeans were generally less worried about language barriers. However, it was now an accepted fact that a single release required a video, so to satisfy the Europeans we had to make one.

A&M Records—which was really Interscope by now, with Jerry Moss long gone—provided a relatively small budget for the video. Unusually, the deals I had originally negotiated for The Police and Sting did not allow the record company to recoup video costs against royalties, so we were never given carte blanche to spend what we wanted. In the A&M days, this never was an issue, because of the huge sales we enjoyed, but now that Interscope was running the show, the budgets were tighter—and Sting was older, so sales might not be as great. In any case, the budget was adequate for a European video. The director had no great ideas other than to have Sting and Cheb Mami in a car to Las Vegas, driving across the desert. The car chosen was the new Jaguar, because it had a British look, in keeping with Sting's image.

When I saw the final cut of the video, my main thought was, *What a nice car that was.* By the end, I realized we had made a car commercial as much as a video for 'Desert Rose.' Even Sting's tour manager, Billy Francis, snickered, 'It's a fucking car commercial.'

For the first single release, the record company had gotten Compact Computers to participate in a joint promotion for the album. Though I didn't see any real relationship between Sting and Compact, I knew that any help should not be sneezed at. Sting was now over forty, and radio was aimed at the under-twenty-fives. The Sting/Compact deal gave me a useful contact in the US advertising agency world, which would now come in very handy. When I saw the 'Desert Rose' video, I called my contact and asked her to find out which ad agency handled Jaguar. Turned out it was a big firm in New York called Ogilvy & Mather. I called them the next day.

'This is a courtesy call,' I began. 'I wanted to inform you that, for the new Sting video, we used your new Jaguar S-Type, and it's going to be released around the world. I would like to send you a copy to see what you think.' The guy at the other end of the phone was dismissive—he must have thought I was a nut—but he gave me an address and I expressed him a copy. A few days later, he called me back with obvious reverence in his tone. I was now Mr. Copeland, and yes, Jaguar would be glad to do something with the video.

'I'm glad you like it,' I said, 'but here's the deal. That video has already sold your car. No need for you to add anything in that regard. My problem is, I need you to help me sell Sting's record. If you can make a commercial to do that, I will give you the rights to the video for free. But it has to look like an ad for "Desert Rose."'

When I got the first take of the proposed commercial, I showed it to Sting and got some more irritating snickers from some of the hangers-on. The old chestnut about 'selling out' came up. Old rules die hard with people with little imagination. But Sting knew that this might be the ticket to get the song into the market. He believed in that song—it was his baby, and he wanted it to have the best chance of success. We had to tweak the commercial a bit, but it did not take long to get it right. When Sting gave the go-ahead, I asked for Ogilvy's marketing plan, so I could show it to Interscope, since until now, no one at the record company was aware of any of these conversations.

When I got the budget, I was flabbergasted. It was the biggest budget I have ever seen for a single, and it still stands to this day as the biggest ever in the music business. It was over $18 million in TV ads for the USA only, including one during the Super Bowl. *Holy shit!*

I took that budget over to Interscope and met the head of marketing, Steve Berman, and announced that I had just given Jaguar the rights to the Sting 'Desert Rose' video for free.

'You did what!?' he replied. It would have been normal to charge a few million dollars for such rights.

'If you want me to hit them up for money, you will need to match this budget,' I said, and threw it down on his desk.

He looked at it and opened his eyes wide. 'That's the best money we never took,' he said.

I got the green light, but the company still did not consider releasing 'Desert Rose' as a single in the USA. When the ad started running, however, the strangest thing happened. It seems if you give people a chance to hear something great, they will respond. And they did. People began calling the radio stations, asking, 'Why aren't you playing the new Sting single?'

'What Sting single?'

'The one about the desert and the rose and stuff.'

The radio stations then called the record company: 'Why are you screwing our station? Why didn't we get the new Sting single?'

'*What* Sting single?'

'The one about the desert rose and the car.'

'Desert Rose' was rush-released and rose to #15 on the *Billboard* singles chart. That Arab guy's voice was still on it. The album took off and ended up selling nine million copies, and Sting's concert fees immediately doubled.

It was also a winner for Jaguar. What I didn't know until later was that, yes, Jaguar wanted to sell cars—but, even more, they wanted to lower the age of their average customer. Apparently, Jaguar was looked upon as an old person's car, with the average buyer aged over sixty-five. In not so many years, all of those customers would be dead. For Jaguar, it was a matter of survival to win over younger generations. Several years later, I was told by a Jaguar executive that had I not come up with the Sting/Jaguar tie-in, there would most likely be no Jaguar cars on the market today. The Sting commercial did exactly what the company needed: it lowered the age of the average Jaguar buyer to just over forty, *and* it sold lots of cars. It remains the most successful tie-in between a music star and a product ever.

Meanwhile, wouldn't you know it, there were still snickers from the hangers-on around Sting. But if there were any people who saw the commercial as 'selling out,' they were very few, and most likely people who never bought albums anyway. A huge radio hit and nine million sales should have proved something!

The problem for me was that the people who were prone to think small and work within the rules spent as much time with Sting as I did, and there was not much I could do about it. Sting lived in New York; I lived in Los Angeles. The first casualty was the print campaign for 'Desert Rose,' for which I got Ogilvy & Mather to agree to a spend of $3.5 million. Sting thought it might be a bridge too far. I did not agree, but why push it? 'Desert Rose' had already proved to be a big winner, so I had to go back to Ogilvy and say we couldn't do it, and apologize for suggesting it.

๛

That big win with 'Desert Rose' led the record company to decide to follow it with a third single, 'After The Rain'—a song I thought could have become even bigger. I managed to find another suitable company to back it with a $10 million ad campaign, which I proudly took to Sting. This time he said no. His actual words were, 'I guess we'll find out if I can have a hit without a commercial sponsor.'

We found out. The single disappeared from view within a week. For me, it was a disappointment, and a major lost opportunity. I had hoped that third single would have propelled the *Brand New Day* album to equal the big Police album sales. I will never feel good about that decision. But, in a way, it would soften the blow that came a year later, when Sting terminated my management, and I would no longer have to put up with those small-minded, rulebook-reading types that hovered around him ever again.

One would think that after the success of 'Desert Rose' I had insured my continued long-term relationship with Sting. Gil Friesen, the former president of A&M, called me on the phone to congratulate me after hearing about it. He considered it one of the biggest successes he had ever heard of in the music business.

'I guess you'll be managing Sting for a long time to come,' he said.

How little you know, I remember thinking.

There is an expression, 'No good deed goes unpunished.' And, true enough, in 2001, Sting fired me. I will admit it was a shock, but, in some ways, it was also a relief. I had never had a problem with Sting, never even had a heated argument, but I was becoming increasingly turned off by the hangers-on that surrounded him. There was the yoga master who insisted that *his* brand of yoga was the real one, and all the others were crap. Then there was the personal chef whose brief was everything organic and good for you. The spreads he put on looked amazing—until you tasted them. After lunch I would have to go to a nearby restaurant and order some real food.

285

And then there was Billy Francis, Sting's longtime tour manager, who seemed to hate everyone. He certainly hated Sting's wife, Trudie—and he *really* hated the lady who took over as manager from me. Worst of all, he hated my partner, Kim Turner, and he slowly undermined Kim to the point that Sting fired him. I could never forgive Billy for that. But, at the same time, part of me felt sorry for him. Perpetual cynicism wears thin, and I came to the conclusion that he probably hated himself more than anyone else.

Strangely enough, when I eventually got fired, I had phone calls from other managers, and they all said the same thing: 'I'll bet it was the wife.' I never had a problem with Trudie, though. I understood her predicament.

The most unfortunate thing was that it also ended things with Allen Grubman, the lawyer I had stuck with since 1974. On the day I got the letter from Sting, I called Allen. As usual, he was blunt and to the point.

'Miles, you know I'm going with the money. I'm Sting's lawyer now.'

It's like Kim Turner always said: 'If you want loyalty, get a dog.'

The one thing I will say for Allen is that he was always honest. 'It's not about the money—it's about the money.'

Meanwhile, 'Desert Rose' moved me more fully into the world of Arab music. From there, I fell into the dance world, bellydancers, Irish dance, tango shows . . . and eventually to advising the Pentagon on winning over hearts and minds in the Middle East. Who would have thought it?

CHAPTER 30

BREAKBEATS AND BELLYDANCERS

. . . .

'Desert Rose' opened up my eyes to the potential of Arab fusion music in the USA market. It was another overlooked market. From Polydor France I'd picked up Khaled, Rachid Taha, and Faudel, and a recording of the 1, 2, 3 Soleil concert. From Virgin France I'd picked up Manu Chao's *Clandestino* and Cheb Mami. I guess the word got out, because I started getting calls from record companies in Egypt and Lebanon, and, when I started hearing more music from those regions, I liked what I heard. As *Billboard* reported in 2001, I became the main (non-Arab) purveyor of Arab music in America.

On one hand, I had once again tapped into a newsworthy niche where few others were, but on the other hand I realized that touring large bands from the Middle East as a way to promote records in America was going to cost too much money, and there were too many obstacles in front of me. Visas, airfares, language issues; touring such artists was not like working with The Police and Squeeze. Of course, the 9/11 attacks on New York's World Trade Center did not help either. The word 'Arab' now had a lot of negative baggage attached to it.

I did organize one tour for Khaled and the Egyptian artist Hakim, and it got tons of press. But front covers of world music magazines were not going to be enough to change things. Besides, most of the Arab artists I was dealing with were huge stars in their own region, and they were not about to come to the USA and play for peanuts.

One strategy was to look for smaller bands that fused East and West, as Sting had done on 'Desert Rose.' Steve Tannett in the London office found Oojami, a UK-based band fronted by Necmi Cavli, a Turkish musician who had created a band with Brits and Arabs doing East/West fusions with modern techno beats. Next came Zohar, fronted by Erran Baron Cohen (brother of the comedian Sacha Baron Cohen, aka Ali G), who blended mystical Middle Eastern sounds with modern technology and dance grooves.

I am sure most people thought I was crazy, but the strange thing was, the albums actually sold—not in large numbers, by any means, but these were actual sales, sort of like the early days of the punk releases. There was no radio play, though, so who was buying these records? At first, it was a mystery. Then Oojami delivered an album with a title whose significance I did not realize at the time, but which was to set my next decade in motion. *Bellydancing Breakbeats*. It was a worldwide deal, and the label had a contractual commitment to the band, so I had to do something. To bring them over for a tour of America seemed risky, and probably too expensive, so we looked for another way.

ↄ

Around this time, I had my most serious issue with my inability to tell an artist what they wanted to hear. During the early 80s, Duran Duran had become one of the most successful English bands on the circuit. They were all about glamor and cool videos, and they had hit singles around the world, so they had the elements that usually appealed to me. I never knew them personally, but I liked their music. Like me, they were quick to realize the importance of MTV in building an image.

As the decade progressed, the band went through member changes, leaving only two constants, singer Simon Le Bon and keyboardist Nick Rhodes. By early 2001, the albums were no longer big winners, and the concerts were OK but not what they had been in the band's heyday.

In September of 2001, Duran's accountant, David Ravden, called me at my home in St John's Wood with the news that the original five members of Duran Duran—Simon, Nick, John Taylor, Andy Taylor, and Roger Taylor—were going to re-form, and that would be a big deal. And they wanted me to manage them. As I was no longer managing Sting, and as I had always liked Duran Duran, I was immediately into the idea. I did not have to be talked into it.

I met the four band members who were in London, and later met with John Taylor in Los Angeles. Things moved quickly, and within a month a management agreement had been drawn up and even signed by all of us. I was the official manager of Duran Duran. Helping me was Steve Tannett from my London office.

To celebrate, I took the band to dinner in London, joined by Steve, and all went well until one of them asked how much money I thought I could get as a record advance. It was a moment when I knew that the truth was not going to fly. For once in my life I needed to tell a lie, and a pretty big one.

Steve and I had already been to see EMI Records A&R head Tony Wadsworth, who had worked on the previous Duran albums. He made it pretty clear the new band was not that exciting a prospect. EMI had released the previous albums with Simon and Nick, and, as far as the company was concerned, there was no reason for the new band to sell much more than they did. He suggested record stores would place their orders based on sales of the last album, *not* the one from when the original five members were together, six or so years earlier. When he said he might consider an advance of £500,000 but might not even want to do that, both Steve and I were shocked.

We got similar hesitation from the several other labels we approached. Our conclusion was that the real business would be the concerts, and record sales would really depend on how great the album was—and, even then, it was unlikely to be as huge as the band might be thinking.

Both Steve and I had had the chance to visit the recording studio, where the band had already started recording with their own money. What we heard did not fill us with excitement. It was good, but not enough to be a game-changer. No slam dunk album or hit single, so once again the thought was, *It's all about the concerts.*

So, when I had to answer the question at dinner that night, I knew that an advance of around £500,000 was likely, but I bit my tongue and told the big lie.

'Two million pounds.'

The table went quiet, and a kind of darkness descended. I left the dinner thinking they might have smelled a rat—that I was another bullshitter telling them what they wanted to hear.

The next day, David Ravdon called me and said simply, 'The band thinks they made a mistake, and you are not the right manager.'

I assumed they had seen through what I said about the advance, but when I started to explain that I knew I had exaggerated, David stopped me.

'No, they think you don't believe in them.'

'What? You mean I should have said more?'

They were expecting the answer to be *five* million. My big lie was not big enough!

'David,' I said, 'you know that is impossible—even God can't do that.'

'That's not what the band thinks.'

All I could do is say, 'Let's have another meeting together ASAP and see if we can sort this out.'

Steve and I went to the meeting the next afternoon, and it was obvious from the start that their minds were already made up. I told them even two million was not easy, and if they really thought they could find a manager to get them five million then they were right: I was the wrong guy.

'So, it's over then?' I asked. I took out the contract we had all signed, tore it in half right in front of them, and Steve and I left the studio. It was the shortest management deal of my career—less than a month.

When I got home, I called John Taylor in Los Angeles to tell him what had happened. He already knew, and he also knew that a five-million advance was pie in the sky.

'Miles, they shot the messenger.'

I am not sure John cared one way or another. His wife, Gia, was the owner/founder of the Juicy Couture clothing brand, and she was doing huge business. (A few years later, she would sell the brand for $42 million while remaining president of the company.)

I never met up with the band again, but I came to learn that they spent something like £800,000 on the album out of their own money and when they finally got a record deal it was the £500,000 Tony said he might pay.

That was the rumor, anyway. But the concerts did very well, just as I'd predicted.

෨

Meanwhile, we were beginning to find out who was buying those Arab albums Ark 21 was releasing. It was American women, with no ancestral relationship with any Arab country, who had gotten into bellydancing. Bellydance in North America had apparently morphed into a health exercise method, as well as a women's empowerment movement. There were little groups and teachers all over the country. There were even a couple of annual festivals that attracted a few thousand people each time. There was an under-the-radar underground scene all over the place, even in Alabama. Who knew?

Then I had a bright idea: let's do a launch of the Oojami record by holding a contest in a Los Angeles club for bellydancers—give a prize to the best dancer, and they all have to dance to one of the songs on the Oojami record. Invite the press and voilà: we have a cool launch for the *Bellydancing Breakbeats* album.

The Knitting Factory on Hollywood Boulevard was booked for March 1, 2002, and we put the word out on the internet and through some bellydancers my staff had contacted. Before we knew it, we had 160 applicants from all across the country. After days of auditions, we reduced the numbers down to twenty dancers, and then I had to make the final judgment. We ended up with thirteen dancers. My choices were made purely on what I saw. I did not bother to read any résumés, which was why they were all reasonably young and attractive—and, from what I saw, the most talented.

By the middle of the show, I started getting the idea that this was almost like MTV—a visual version of each song, just like a video. It was entertaining, as well as easy to put on. All one needed was a CD, a sound system—which every venue had—and the dancers. From that germ of an idea, I thought, *Why not create a Riverdance-style show of dancers; travel it across the country, dancing to the CDs we were releasing, and the show could work as a vehicle to sell the records?* Even better, it might also work as a moneymaking show, just like *Riverdance*.

291

Riverdance was represented by the William Morris agency, which was lucky, because my brother Ian's star booker from FBI, Brent Smith, was now working there. He connected me with Clint Mitchel, the *Riverdance* agent, who would make no commitment but was at least encouraging. That set me off to think seriously about building a show.

I was no expert in the art of dance. I only knew what I could see, but that meant I could be honest with what I liked. I had a simple view: if I was prepared to pay to see a dancer then I had to assume others would as well. That is pretty much what I did to choose music. And if it worked for music, why not dance?

I had the makings of a troupe from the dancers I had met at the Knitting Factory, but now I started looking for others. Brent Smith called one day, feigning interest, to ask how my show was coming, so I told him it was going great and he was going to be sorry he didn't take it on. He then told me that Clint Mitchel was too busy and not interested in my show anyway, implying I was wasting my time. Brent was being honest, but that left me pretty much dead in the water.

A few weeks later, Brent called me again and said, 'Miles, you need to come over to the William Morris office immediately and kiss my ass.'

What!?

'Believe me,' he said. 'When you hear what I have to say, you will *want* to kiss my ass. Come now, my pants are down, my ass is waiting!'

Then he told me the story of Perry Farrell of the band Jane's Addiction at a William Morris meeting to settle on the bill for the upcoming 2003 Lollapalooza tour. This was a festival-type tour with a main stage and several smaller stages, and they were trying to fill out the entire bill. There would be twenty thousand people at every show, and even thirty thousand at some of them. The agents had put forward every act they had, and they'd even started offering acts from other agencies. Perry liked none of them.

Finally, Brent raised his hand and said, 'Miles Copeland has this bellydance show thing.' To his surprise, and that of everyone else in the room, Perry said, '*That's* what I want!' and the next half hour was spent talking about my bellydance show (that did not yet exist).

I did not know what to say other than, 'Brent, get serious, bellydancers on Lollapalooza? What are we going to get, dance in a tent at two in the afternoon in the heat to a few hundred curious onlookers? Not our audience!'

Brent had a simple answer. 'If you do Lollapalooza, promoters across the world will take your show seriously. It puts you on the map.'

I could not argue with that. We talked some more, and finally I said, 'OK, since the dancers can dance to a CD, there is no equipment to set up. If we can do a set on the main stage between the last two acts, even for fifteen minutes, I will do it. Just pull the curtain, and the changeover can be happening as we are dancing in front of the curtain.'

Performing in front of the main audience was the only thing that made sense to me. Performing in a side tent in the afternoon made no sense. We discussed it a bit more, and he agreed to see if that could happen. In the end, a compromise was agreed. We would do an afternoon show for one hour in one of the tents and a fifteen-minute show on the main stage in front of the headline act in the evening. When it came to the fee, it was half of what I estimated it would cost, but Brent said, 'This puts you into the game, you can make up the loss later.' Somewhat reluctantly, I agreed.

I now had to hire the dancers and pull a show together. And hire a team to help me. And work out the transportation. And figure out what it would cost. From the Knitting Factory show I had four or five dancers, and I had met a bellydance choreographer called Jillina, who was prepared to work out group pieces. To fill out the troupe, I went to an annual bellydance festival in San Francisco and looked for dancers there. One stood out: her name was Rachel Brice. She was a style they called 'tribal,' and when I saw her dance I was sold—she was not only great but different from all the others. Sort of the dark side of bellydance: tattoos, black leather, rough tribal jewelry from Afghanistan and Southern Morocco. The other dancers were in the Egyptian tradition: sparkly, beautiful dresses, feminine. I figured the contrast would be great for the show that I was creating.

A big rock'n'roll traveling festival and a troupe of bellydancers trying to make something out of what had never existed before should make a unique story, so I thought, *In for a penny in for a pound, let's make a documentary film*. It had worked for The Police—why not for my bellydance show?

I called a friend of mine working at Fuse TV who I knew worked with small budgets, thinking he might know the right type of affordable director. He recommended Jonathan Brandeis. Jon was actually a good choice. He explained that even a documentary has to have a storyline—something to hook you at the beginning, so you want to see how it turns out in the end. What that storyline would be, neither of us knew at the start, but we figured with all those visuals, bellydancers, rock'n'roll bands, there had to be one in there somewhere. Jonathan was in.

Then, out of the blue, I was approached by the promoter Matt Taylor to help book bands for the World Peace Music Awards, which were to be held in Bali in June, just under six weeks from the start of the Lollapalooza tour. His idea was to highlight Bali after the terrorist bombings of October 2002. He wanted a cultural mix, not just the usual superstars, who he couldn't afford anyway. I put forward some names I thought I could attract and added some artists I was working with. There was no money in it, and it sounded like a big idea that would not be as big as projected without superstar names.

Matt said he expected an audience of thirty thousand (it ended up being ten thousand) and planned to broadcast the show to sixty countries. I have no way of knowing if that actually happened. But he seemed to have the money and the will, so I said yes, on the condition I could add my new bellydance show to the bill—and bring a crew to film them. Matt agreed. I remained skeptical until he handed me all the return plane tickets to Bali and back to LA, and the confirmed hotel booking in Bali. At that point, I figured, worst case, we will get some great footage for the documentary.

I can't say that the Bali show was any sort of game-changer for any of the acts that performed there, but it was in Bali, in the summer, and that alone made it a worthwhile experience. It definitely gave Jon Brandeis some good footage he could use in the *American Bellydancer* documentary. It had the glamor and exotic elements I liked, which would need to be part of the promotion of the bellydance show, just as those elements had been part of the promotions that worked for The Police.

Around this time, I had arrived at the name Bellydance Superstars in an attempt to focus on the fact that the dancers were, in my opinion, the best of the best. The name was aimed at the kind of mainstream audience that would likely go to see *Riverdance* or a tango show. Little did I know the furor it would create within the bellydance community itself. They were incensed that I, a man who knew nothing, would have the balls to say who was a superstar or not. In fact, there was no such thing as a bellydance superstar, and those that thought they were stars were stars largely in their own minds.

Meanwhile, back in Los Angeles, we hurriedly pulled together the show for Lollapalooza. As soon as it started, there were quickly two views of the tour. Mine, and the dancers. They loved it. For them, it was the big time at last. For me, it quickly became a financial nightmare. The merchandise was not selling. Worse, the press was not interested. They focused on the main acts and hardly covered the smaller acts, and we were the bottom of that barrel.

By the third week, Jon had filmed everything he needed, and more of the same would just mean more footage on the cutting-room floor. By week four, I was down $50,000 and looking to lose more than that on the final leg of the tour. I called Brent at William Morris and asked if there was any way to get more money. He laughed and said, 'You have a better chance of bringing Elvis back.' He gave me the number of Adam Schneider, Perry Farrell's manager, and said, 'Call him and see if he will let you off the tour.'

I made the call and pleaded my case. We were full of appreciation for the opportunity—I thanked him profusely, but it was killing me more than I thought it would. Adam was remarkably understanding and said it was unlikely they would pay any more, 'But, just in case, what are we talking about?'

I said another $50,000 and I would continue. He would get back to me. A day later, he called and said, 'OK, you got it: $50,000.'

I was shocked. He explained that when he brought up the idea of the bellydancers leaving the tour, the road crew all revolted: 'If they go, so do we.' Apparently, the ladies had so brightened the backstage area with their feminine charm that if they left, all that would remain would be smelly roadies, and the whole vibe of the tour would evaporate. The dancers' happiness to be on that tour was apparently infectious

I immediately called Brent.

'Hey, Brent, Elvis Presley is back!'

From that strange beginning, the Bellydance Superstars spent the next few years doing eight hundred shows in twenty-five countries, including China, Taiwan, Japan, six months in Monte Carlo, Dubai, Morocco, England, France, Germany, Spain, Switzerland, Ireland, Italy, and all over the USA and Canada. Jillina created a new show for each new US tour, and we filmed them all, eventually releasing five show DVDs, including one shot at the Folies Bergère in Paris. I created a series of *Bellydance Superstars* compilation CDs using songs from all the acts we signed, which ran all the way to *BDSS 12*.

We added two more tribal dancers to the show and spread that version of the dance to Europe and around the world, then added another dancer from Cirque du Soleil's *O* show in Las Vegas. The show got tons of press all over the world, including the front page of the *Sunday Times* in London. It was the most successful professional dance show using bellydance. It upped the game for every bellydancer, and it was widely copied. But, in the end, everyone made money except me.

෴

The *American Bellydancer* film aired on PBS in February 2005. One review captured the idea well: 'With wardrobe malfunctions, quarreling musicians at a world peace festival, *American Bellydancer*, the new film documentary by director Jonathan Brandeis, presents cultural history, human drama, sardonic humor, and a reason to view the art and commerce of bellydancing in a new light.' All in all, it was a fun experience, and I learned a lot. In Japan, Taiwan, and China, we sold out shows of two and three thousand people; in Europe it was half of that, and in the USA it went from several thousand to a few hundred, so it was hard to budget what was needed. In Morocco, the stage was huge, and twelve dancers were not enough to fill it; in Monte Carlo, it was small, so we had less dancers.

There were telling moments all the time. In Dubai, during the show, I had a guy come up to me and say, 'Which of the dancers are Arabs?' I said none. He was stunned. 'None? But Americans can't dance like that!' In Morocco, an elderly lady pulled me aside and whispered, 'Keep doing what you are doing—it's important!' The US Ambassador came to the show too, with all the embassy staff, and loved it.

The most moving was a letter I got from a woman in Georgia. She wanted to thank me for giving her back her husband. She explained that she was a bellydancer, took lessons, and loved it, but her husband always snickered and didn't get it. It hurt their relationship. When she took her husband to the BDSS show, he was so impressed that he said, 'OK, now I get it, and I see what you see in it.' Apparently, the show had totally changed his attitude.

That was all very well and rewarding, but in the end it was eating away at the company finances. One day, my team sat me down and said, 'You've tried it this way and that. If you do the same thing over and over and always get the same result, one more time and you will get the same result again.'

I hated to give up but one can only fight reality so often. Then something happened out of the blue that gave a whole other dimension to what we had been doing. It was a call from Donald Rumsfeld's office at the Pentagon.

CHAPTER 31

HEARTS AND MINDS

. . . .

In 2003, in one of the stupidest blunders in the history of American foreign policy, the USA invaded Iraq. As the problems in the country were mounting, the Pentagon was looking to figure out a way to win 'hearts and minds' in the region. They cooked up various plans, then contacted Hilary Rosen, president of the Recording Industry Association of America (RIAA), to see if she knew anyone in the entertainment business that could help vet the plans. Hilary said there was only one person—it was me.

I had met Hilary several times in the never-ending battle between the recording industry and artists to get more laws passed to protect their rights. The RIAA was basically a lobby group for the music industry. Through our meetings she had gotten to know of my activities with Arab artists and bellydance, and that I grew up in the Middle East.

My secretary put her hand over the mouthpiece of the phone and called to me: 'Miles, it's Donald Rumsfeld at the Pentagon—he wants to speak to you.'

My response was, 'Fuck off.'

'No, it's really the Pentagon!'

I took the phone and it was the deputy secretary of defense, Torie Clarke. She explained that she was heading the Rumsfeld team, looking for ways to win over Arabs in general and Iraqis in particular. Would I vet the programs they were looking to do?

Of course, I agreed.

When I went over the proposed programs, I knew they would fall flat and maybe do more harm than good. As politely as I could, I explained this to Torie when I got her back on the phone.

'OK,' she said, 'will you come to the Pentagon and tell us what to do?'

That would be a hard invite to ignore. Within a few days I had arrived in Washington, rented a car, and driven to the Pentagon for the meeting. I showed up at the entrance I was told to go to, went through the metal detector, and was met by my marine escort and a golf cart. We went up the corridor of war and down the next one to Donald Rumsfeld's section. I was ushered into a large meeting room with huge oval table in the center and placed at the far end. Torie sat at the opposite end. There were twelve other people in the room, from the State Department, White House, and the Pentagon. Each of them introduced themselves, and then all eyes turned to me.

What I said should have been obvious. It was a bit like the *My Britain* program I had done in England. I was speaking what I thought would be common sense, but it sounded like news to the people I was talking to. These people were obviously very smart and keen to do the right thing, but they had little understanding of what they were dealing with. None of them had grown up in the Middle East, as I had, and they knew little about how that part of the world thinks.

I was there an hour or so, and then I left. Torie's office set me up with a meeting at the State Department, but in the end I don't think anyone was in a position to listen—or, if they were, they had no way of acting on any of my suggestions. There were more conversations after I returned to Los Angeles, but Iraq proved to be more than anyone in Washington could deal with, and things kept changing anyway.

Of course, there is a touch of irony that I should have been the one to be asked to advise the Pentagon about Iraq. My father had been one of the key CIA operatives involved in installing Saddam Hussein there and having him overthrow the communist-leaning prime minister, al-Bakr. Saddam had been a US ally for most of his time as leader of that country. As my father used to say, 'He is a bad guy, but he is *our* bad guy.'

Torie Clarke later published a book called *Lipstick On A Pig* that chronicled the meeting I had at the Pentagon. It was quite flattering. I had arrived in a Brooks Brothers suit, as straight as I could be. It was the Pentagon after all. Torie used a bit of poetic license, describing me as arriving like Clint Eastwood in *A Fistful Of Dollars*. Her version is much better than mine, and the one I am going to adopt as the 'true description.'

⟐

In another out-of-the-blue phone call in early 2006, I heard from the actor Steven Seagal. He was embarking on his dream of a musical career and he wanted me to manage him. From the call it was clear he fancied himself as a pretty hot blues guitar player; he had formed a blues band and he wanted to tour. He had also recorded an album and wanted to get it released.

I thought I could do all that, so I agreed to meet him. To be honest, it was probably more out of curiosity that I went along. At his house in Beverly Hills, I first noticed statues of various Indian deities in the garden, so I assumed he had taken up Buddhism or some other Eastern religion, which would make sense, as he was well known as a martial arts master. When he came to the door, my first thought was about how big he was. Probably six four or six five. In person, I didn't see much sign of Eastern religion—every third word was a swearword. Then he played me the fuckin' great album and played some cool shit on his fuckin' large guitar collection, and, to my surprise, he was a pretty fuckin' good guitar player. I guess it was just nutty enough that I agreed to work with him.

The next day, I was having lunch with a friend at Cheebo on Sunset Boulevard, just down from my house on Hillside Avenue, when the owner of Guitar Center came in and sat down at the table next to us. Both of us knew him, and my friend said, 'Guess who Miles is going to manage? He's known as the biggest shit in Hollywood.'

The response, in a second, was, 'Oh, you mean Steven Seagal?'

What? How come I am the only one that doesn't know that?

It was not long before I got an idea of how Steven had acquired his reputation. He was not a warm and fuzzy guy. Political correctness was not in his vocabulary. At one of the first meetings at his house, he brought in a lawyer who was Jewish and kept saying things like, 'You're OK, for a Jew.'

I don't think the lawyer took it badly because Steven seemed to have abuse for every ethnic group. Steven was an equal-opportunity shit.

He also didn't seem to care about money. I told him I could book fifteen or twenty club dates up the West Coast, but the way he wanted to travel—first class hotels, limos, and the like—it would lose money. He didn't care. Most of the promoters were willing to take a shot—also probably out of curiosity—and many of the people that came to the shows were coming out of curiosity as well. Nevertheless, he was a good player, and his band was not bad either. I'm sure a lot of people were surprised. But I don't think Steven knew what it was really like to travel like a rock band playing clubs.

Next, he wanted to play bigger shows. When I told him I could get him to open for Sammy Hagar at a big 'shed' show in Phoenix, in front of ten thousand people, but it wouldn't pay much, he said, 'Book it.' Like Steven, Sammy had once asked me to manage him out of the blue, and though it didn't work out we became friends.

When I called Sammy about an opening slot, he was as intrigued about Steven as I had been. 'If he'll take $1,000, sure, put him on.'

In typical Seagal fashion, on the day of the show, June 4, 2006, we went to Van Nuys airport, caught a Learjet he had rented, and flew the band to the gig. The short flight cost was something like $9,000, plus there was the cost of the truck to drive the equipment to Phoenix and the fees to the band. When we got there, a limo was waiting to take us to the venue, and Steven held court backstage until it was time to go on.

Just as he was announced, Steven turned to me and handed me two .45 revolvers from the back of his pants. 'Here, hold these—careful, they're loaded.' I must have looked shocked as a roadie next to us said, 'I'll hold them.' As Steven walked offstage, he retrieved the revolvers and stuck them back in his pants. He looked at me as if to say, *Gotta protect myself.* Apparently, Steven was a marked man and had had some issue with a mafia boss—he didn't want to go into detail. I started thinking, *Do I really want to be traveling with this guy?*

For the show, Steven insisted I get a thousand copies of his CD delivered to the venue so he could sign them for buyers. He insisted he could do that many, but in fact he signed no more than a hundred before he got tired and we went back to the airport. Of course, when I went to get a check for the thousand copies, he stiffed me.

One day, Steven called me to say I should go with him to New Orleans for dinner at Emeril Lagasse's famous restaurant. Once again, we would fly by Learjet from Van Nuys. A limo was waiting at the airport to take us to the dinner. It was in a private room, and as I walked in the place was full of high-ranking policeman in dress uniform. They all knew Steven, and they sat him at the head of the table next to the chief of police. I sat next to him on the other side. It was obvious no one *there* thought he was a shit, and I learned that he had been the martial arts instructor for the Louisiana police force. He was a big deal in New Orleans.

Steven was also a big deal in Europe, and especially in Asia. When he went to France, a photographer friend of mine went with him and called me the next day to tell me what was happening. Steven was mobbed and had to be snuck into the hotel. He needed four bodyguards everywhere he went. It was insane.

It ended up pretty insane for me, too, and after no more than five months I resigned. He never did pay me for those CDs, or for the T-shirts I made for him. Luckily, I sold enough through my Universal distribution deal to break even. However, I did donate a trunk-load of Steven Seagal shirts I got stuck with to an orphanage in Kenya, Africa. All the kids lined up to take a photo with those shirts on. I guess Steven would be huge somewhere in the bush of Kenya, too, if he ever chooses to go there.

⌘

A few years later, after Torie Clarke had moved on from the Pentagon and President Obama was in the White House, she called me again to tell me about a series of programs that America's Public Broadcasting Service (PBS) was working on called *America At A Crossroads: Twenty Films About America Since September 11*. She thought one of the ideas I had pitched at that Pentagon meeting would be perfect for PBS and asked if she could suggest it to them.

'By all means,' I said.

A few days later, one of the top producers at PBS in Washington called me and said they wanted to come to LA to meet me to discuss how I would make the film idea I had given the Pentagon. What could I say but yes? Normally, a producer would be lobbying PBS to get *them* to commit to doing a film. Now *they* were lobbying *me*. Torie must have done a hell of a pitch.

My basic idea was to take Arab musicians and put them together with American musicians and watch the appreciation grow between the two camps—mutual respect. Arab or American, we are really all the same—we all have something to contribute. Great talent is not just American, it is Arab as well. Show you appreciate them, and they are more likely to appreciate you. To me, it was simple Dale Carnegie. As Torie Clarke said, 'I like people who like me.'

PBS commissioned the program, and I asked Jon Brandeis to direct the film. We were given an initial budget to establish the outline of the film and a final budget to make the actual documentary. I brought in Issam Houshan, who had been key to helping me with the Bellydance Superstars, as the drummer for the drum solo part of the show. He was born in Syria and spoke fluent Arabic, so he was an important cog in our machine.

Our first trip to the Middle East was to find and vet the artists we wanted to film. It was a fact-finding mission, to help us home in on what the final story would look like, and it took us to Lebanon, Dubai, Jordan, and Egypt. The second trip was to film additional elements and to finally choose and sign up the artists we wanted to bring to Los Angeles for the final part of the film: Arab artists collaborating with American artists, culminating in a show at the Roxy in Los Angeles.

The artists ranged from Tareq Al Nasser in Jordan, to singer/songwriter Tania Saleh in Lebanon, who spoke English well and was quite brilliant at lyrics in both Arabic and English, to artists who spoke no English but represented the music of their culture. There was a rapper called Rayess Bek who wrote political lyrics about life in Lebanon. There was Mohamed Mounir, a grand old man of the *Nubian* style of Arabic music. From Iraq, we met another icon of the region, Ilham al-Madfai, who had escaped Saddam Hussein's regime and was now living in Beirut. He also spoke English and was well versed in how to explain his craft, and would we thought be perfect to work with the American musicians on camera. We met a famous Tunisian singer, Latifa, in Cairo, and were very tempted to bring her to America, but in the end we had to work within our budget, and that meant tough choices.

Part of the brief was to get a cross-section of Arab artists, to show the range of the music and the culture. I had toured the Egyptian singer Hakim in the USA and released several of his albums, so for selfish reasons I wanted to get him involved. He was very popular with the American bellydancers, but he had become sensitive to the political pressures of Islamic fundamentalists, so he declined to participate. A similar Egyptian artist who did respond turned out to be a real superstar: funny, socially aware, and a real man of the people. That was Saad al Soghrier (Saad The Little). He, like Hakim, was part of what was called the Shaabi field of music. Shaabi means 'street people,' not the elite. I had heard Saad on the radio and soon realized that not only was he good fun, his music would be great for bellydancers, so I was keen to film him *and* make a deal for his albums in the USA.

Meanwhile, in Cairo, Jon had found a local film 'fixer,' Ramy Romany, who he used to call the Pharaoh of All Media. He was one of the ten percent of Egyptians who were Coptic Christians, and he spoke perfect English. He was a real hustler who knew how to get things done. Working for foreign film companies was his business.

When I said we wanted to film Saad, Ramy told me he was not sure it was possible. Saad lived in Shubra, a really rough part of Cairo where foreigners never went—hell, few 'upmarket' Egyptians went there either. Ramy somehow managed to set it up, but only if we agreed to a police escort—the government did not want to take the chance of an American film crew being murdered in Cairo. We agreed and set out with Ramy, thinking our escort would be a few policemen. When we arrived at the spot outside Shubra to pick up the escort, it turned out to be two trucks carrying an army colonel, twenty-four machine-gun-toting police officers, and several more cops on motorcycles. There was a fucking army going with us!

Our first thought was that this Shubra place must be much more dangerous than we thought, but we were here, we had the troops, and Saad was waiting, so let's do it. We entered Shubra down dirt roads, dodging donkeys, carts, and men in djellabas who were looking at us like, *Who the fuck are these people?*

When we got to Saad's address, he said we had to go upstairs to meet his mother and take tea. Obligingly, we did. I was trying to resurrect my Arabic, and thankfully Ramy was with us to make sure the translations were correct. We had tea, and finally Saad said, in Arabic, 'We'd better go downstairs and tell all the people gathering that it's all OK and I am not being arrested—or there will be a riot.'

We went downstairs to a street full of highly agitated Saad supporters. They did think something was happening to Saad, until he yelled out 'Koullo quais: it's OK, this is a film crew from Los Angeles, and they are here to film us for American TV.'

The people went wild. 'America good' was the instant chant. I was a hero, Jon was a hero, 'America Good.' It was exactly like my message to Torie Clarke: show the people you respect them and like what they like, and they will like you.

Saad agreed to come to Los Angeles and do the film, and we left it to Ramy to set things up. I later learned that we were the first film crew that had ever been to Shubra. Even Egyptian TV had never gone there. No wonder we were heroes!

The final filming of the documentary took place in Los Angeles, at the SIR rehearsal rooms on Sunset Boulevard, and finished at the Roxy on Sunset Strip. It featured US artists like Nile Rogers, Jack Blades from Night Ranger, Charlotte Caffey from The Go-Go's, and RZA from The Wu-Tang Clan, working with Arab artists we had flown over like Ilham al-Madfai, Tania Saleh, and of course Saad Al Soghrier. The final title was *Dissonance And Harmony: Arab Music Goes West*.

At one point, Saad wanted to film a quick video outside the Roxy along Sunset Strip, so we hurriedly rented a convertible. I called my cousin, Courtney Cox, and asked her if she could spare a few minutes to appear in the video. She agreed, and we gave Saad his video, which must have done something for his image back in Cairo.

A few months after filming the video, I went to see Saad in Cairo, this time with no escort and no film crew. I met him at his house in Shubra and saw, parked outside, a huge bright yellow Hummer. I asked him how he, being a man of the people, could be seen with so flashy a car in that poor neighborhood?

'My people know I am rich and can afford to live in a nice neighborhood,' he explained, 'but I choose to live in the same poor neighborhood with them. *But* if I drove a cheap car, they would think I choose to live with them only because I am so cheap. The big car proves I am *not* cheap, so my living in Shubra is because I *want* to be with them.' Saad knew his audience.

The PBS film showing of the *Dissonance And Harmony* documentary in the USA turned out to be limited, due I think to hostility at the time towards anything that showed Arabs in a good light. There was leadership trouble at PBS, and the people who commissioned my show were either fired or resigned—I don't know which. PBS has always been under pressure from the Republicans who want to close it down—something Donald Trump would still be going on about years later.

Meanwhile, Al Jazeera bought the film for the entire Middle East and aired it many times over two years, so in fact it did do what Torie Clarke and I had originally intended it to do. In that respect, it was a great success. It did not do much to help sell records in the USA, however, which was my other intention. You can't win them all.

ↄﾟ

From hearing Raï music on the radio in Paris to becoming an advisor to the Pentagon was a pretty strange confluence of events. The final happening added a SWATU to the mix.

What the hell is a SWATU, you might ask? Well, it was an accounting entry I first heard at the annual meeting of label presidents at EMI. When IRS was sold to EMI, part of the deal was that I would attend the annual corporate meeting of label heads. (It was at that time that I elevated Jay Boberg to become president of the label.) This was where we'd tell the corporate heads what IRS Records expected to do for the year coming, and where EMI presented the financial target IRS Records had to meet—if, of course, we expected to get a Christmas bonus.

Towards the end of the meeting, all of the attendees were given a full EMI company projection for the year. In the income column were all the expected categories of catalogue sales, superstar upcoming releases, new act sales, and various other income streams, and at the bottom was SWATU.

'What the hell is *Swatu*?' I asked.

The answer was, 'Something Will Always Turn Up.' There was an actual income figure attached to it for something like several million dollars. It was a realization that in the record business there is normally an unexpected success that one can't accurately predict; like a new act breaks, or a license happens, or some other big win occurs.

In 2014, one of our top Bellydance Superstars tribal dancers, Zoe Jakes, called me to ask if I would give a record deal to her boyfriend's band. Zoe was from San Francisco, which is where the tribal dance style had started, and she with her friends Rachel Brice and Sharon Kihara were the most famous of the genre. Between the three of them I had filmed and released six instructional DVDs, and they were featured on the many full-show as well as solo-performance DVDs we released. Her pitch was similar to the ones I had used myself to sign The Police and IRS Records: the music was good, and she could guarantee that she and all the tribal dancers around the world would buy the CDs to dance to. And if they danced to the songs, there was a ready market there for the taking. Plus it was cheap: all the band needed was $2,500 for the album. It was a 'can't lose' argument.

The band turned out to be two guys who made the CD in their bedroom using the modern technology of the day. Zoe was one of our best dancers, so the deal was hard to say no to. Terms were quickly agreed, and Beats Antique were signed to the company. When I got the LP, I was glad I had said yes. In fact, it was a two-album deal, and if I could do it all over again, I would have made it for more. The two albums were *Tribal Derivations*, released in 2007, and *Collide*, released in 2008.

Zoe was right: both albums sold very well to the bellydance community, with relatively little promotion necessary other than the touring and relationship we had built with that community. The music was all-instrumental, with no direct connection to traditional Arab music, but it worked for the tribal dancers, who did not automatically go for Arab music influences. The sales crossed over to a wider, non-bellydance audience as well.

Then I got a call from the advertising agency who handled Audi cars in Germany. They wanted to use a Beats Antique song in a commercial. The fee was $400,000. From that little $2,500 deal, the band and I split the fee. Beats Antique went on to become a successful act, performing at Coachella and across the country. They ended up creating a stage show, too, with Zoe a central part of it.

I imagine 'Walk Like An Egyptian' would have been a SWATU for CBS, and 'Desert Rose' one for Interscope. Now I had one, too.

POSTSCRIPT

I get invited from time to time to give lectures, mostly relating to what people imagine I have learned, pointers I can give, ideas I can impart, and stories that may serve to inspire others towards success or even just to entertain. Fifty years in business and seventy-five years of life give one various thoughts and truths one might think to have learned over those years. For me, like I said at the beginning of this book, I never liked the idea of a pure autobiography to tell what I did. Surely what I learned is most interesting. If those lessons can apply to others, all the better. So, here are some thoughts.

As a marketer/salesman/promoter, as well as someone with a keen interest in politics, my favorite saying has to be Lincoln's: 'You can fool some of the people all of the time, and all the people some of the time, but you cannot fool all the people all of the time.' However, my life has shown me that one rarely, if ever, has to 'fool all the people.' In a democracy, it need only be fifty percent plus one vote, and in some systems it can be less, provided you fool the *right* people. So to Lincoln's words of wisdom I add my own caveat: 'The trick therefore, whether one is promoting an idea or a product, is to focus on the some of the people you can fool all of the time.' To make my point, one only has to look at the Fox 'news' network in the USA, and indeed the presidency of Donald Trump.

It was probably always so, but over the past few years, particularly in the Trump era, the whole idea of 'truth' has lost its meaning. In the words of Trump advisor Kellyanne Conway, we are in an era of 'alternative facts.' So, the first rule of today must be, 'Don't believe everything you read.' With the computer's ability to manipulate visuals, we can add, 'Don't believe anything you see.' Or, as some pundits like to say, 'Don't believe your lying eyes.'

As I have seen in so many books and articles, even the most scrupulous writers tend to take in other people's laundry, and once it's in print it tends to be repeated, even if it's not true. As we have seen on the internet, stories can take on a life of their own and be exaggerated and expanded with each telling, until the end story bears little resemblance to the original one. It's like a game of whispers, where the first person whispers a line in the ear of the person next to him, then that person repeats the line to the next person, and so on until it comes back around to the first person, by which time the line has markedly changed. I fear this is one of the greatest dilemmas society faces for the future. To this, I would have to add another aspect of the Trump era: 'Tell a lie enough times and people start to believe it's true.' A great lesson for any marketeer.

Another unfortunate reality is that it's in the interests of the media to exaggerate and make an event seem more significant than it actually is. Remember the rule, 'If it bleeds, it leads.' It makes a better story that The Police hated each other than that they loved each other. When I pitched a *Behind The Music* story on The Moody Blues to VH1, I was told clearly there was no story: no one killed anyone, stole someone else's wife, turned into a drug freak, or went to jail. They were nice guys who had hit records. Where is the story in that? Would the Elton John movie have been the same had Elton not been in rehab and had serious life issues? Probably not.

Writing this book brought me face-to-face with the old adage, 'A success has many fathers, but a failure is an orphan.' So true of the IRS Records story. I have read that IRS was co-founded by Jay Boberg, while some add Carlos Grasso as a co-founder. Bob Laul claims he was a co-founder. The reality is the label was started as an extension of what I was doing in London. If there was a co-founder, it would have to be Jerry Moss. If he had not agreed to my proposal, there would not have been an IRS Records. It was my concept, I came up with the name, I pitched the deal, and I funded it entirely. But so what? It was definitely co-built. I could not have done it alone. Jay Boberg, Carlos Grasso, Michael Plen, Barbara Bolan, Bob Laul, Paul Orescan, John Guarnieri, Steve Tannett, Henry Padovani, and so many others were key players in building the label. But would IRS have existed without me? No. Would IRS have existed without them? Yes. If I had not hired them, I would have hired someone else.

Then there is my father's oft-quoted rule, 'Never let the truth stand in the way of a good story.' I often see books and articles that stray so far from the truth they are nearly pure fiction. In Chris Difford's book on Squeeze, he describes being at a songwriters' retreat when Cher was there. She was there two years after he was. Then there was an acquaintance of my father, who wrote a book telling of his exploits being trained by my father in London to be a CIA agent—thirty years after my father had resigned from the agency. Pure fabrication. What gets into people? Forgetting is one thing, but page upon page of pure invention? You have gotta have some gall. Apparently, lots of people do—which will surely be the story of Donald Trump.

Finally, for those who have known me for many years, there is my motto: 'People are shit.' Close friends have said that is a very negative way at looking at life, but I have always disagreed, saying that in fact it is just the opposite. If one expects good and gets bad, that is depressing. But if one expects bad but gets good, one is pleasantly surprised. I would rather go through life with the occasional pleasant surprise than with the inevitable disappointments.

Writing this book and talking to past employees, some of them reminded me of other rather flippant mottos I apparently foisted on my staff from time to time. One was 'Never trust a man with a ponytail.' If you are so vain about your hair getting in your eyes, cut your fucking hair! Then there was 'Never hire someone who owns a Ferrari.' Why buy a car that goes 150 miles an hour when the speed limit is 55? A person had a better chance being hired by me driving a Volvo than some fancy sports car.

I asked my longtime secretary, Alletta Kriak, for her recollections of her time with me. I first met her when she was manager of the Cleveland Opera Company, when my brother Stewart performed his first opera, *Holy Blood And Crescent Moon*, there in October 1989. She was super-efficient and cool-headed—just what I needed. I hired her to join me in Los Angeles, and she started on January 1, 1991. She left the company ten years later. This is what she said:

My fave is the bird you found at Marouatte that you tried to nurse to health while you were fixing away at the castle. You made it a sweet nest in a box to keep it warm and gave it food and water. That was a side that most folks didn't get to see. I felt super-lucky to watch it happen, and it showed me your true heart.

I still giggle at an incident back at Universal, when you had a day of meetings separately with a DiBlasio, a DiStefano, and a DiFranco, all within hours of each other. Names not being your strong suit, you ended up calling each one by the wrong name all day long, but no one stopped you. When you finally realized it, you asked one of them why he never corrected you. He was so afraid of you—or at least the image everyone had of you—he blurted, 'Miles, you can call me any name you want!'

In a similar vein, I loved how you would casually mosey out of a meeting to my desk. The meeting folks had no idea what was going on and thought you had lost interest in the conversation. A look would come over your face, and you would lean in and quietly ask me, 'What's this guy's name?' If they only knew!

And you worked hard. Very hard. You worked from the moment you woke in the morning until you went to bed. Truth—I would 'hide' from you in the morning in London until I was ready to work. I knew once you saw me, we hit the ground running, and we wouldn't stop.

⳥

Going over all the acts I worked with over the years, I could think that IRS Records was a very unlucky record label, and that might be true, except for one fact. For all of us in the music business, there has been one often-stated 'truth.' One out of ten signings leads to success. Or, to put it another way, nine out of ten fail—and that is on a *good* day. One has a better chance at winning at the roulette table. In that regard, IRS Records did pretty well.

IRS, however, was not all about the artists. Many came through the doors on the business side and went on to populate the entertainment business. IRS contributed executives to Virgin Records, MCA Records, Warner Bros, Universal, and so many others that the legacy and lessons we

312

learned still live on. The documentary *We Were Once Rebels*, to be released in 2021, attests to that fact.

Meanwhile, when I think back, I can't help being reminded of what my father said back in 1982: 'Flexibility.' Being open to the unexpected or unplanned tangent. Starting down one road, coming to a dead end, only to see another that looks more promising. That certainly seems to be part of my story. Out of Silas Loader came Greg Wells the songwriter/producer; out of Squeeze came Jools Holland; out of Torch Song came William Orbit; out of Cat Iron came Kim Turner and Tony Brinsley; out of Menace came Steve Tannett; out of the Lords came Nick Turner; out of Wishbone Ash came Steve Upton; and so on. From bandleader to record producer, from band member to TV host, tour manager, company executive, or whatever. Yes, 'flexibility' seems to have been a very real if unwitting part in my life, and indeed the lives of many that I worked with.

As a final dedication, I should tip my hat to all those managers, promotion people, publicists, and other behind-the-scenes people that were instrumental in the success of an artist or company or a product or an invention but, when history was written, they were forgotten. Glory comes to the people on the stage in the spotlight. C'est la vie. However, there are some of us who know the truth that what you see on the stage is usually more like the tip of the iceberg rather than the iceberg itself. You know the truth, and in the end that is what counts.

Thanks to John Bevilacqua for all his help in pulling this together; Danny Quatrochi, Jill Furmanovsky, my wife Adriana, John Brandeis, and Carlos Grasso for photos; Lawrence Porter for his IRS documentary work that reminded me of so many things I had forgotten about; and Dietmar Cloes for checking facts. I should also tip my hat to my editor, Tom Seabrook, who had the good sense to publish this book and helped me structure it while interfering little in what and how I wrote. So if there are any mistakes, omissions, or other faux pas, they are all mine—Tom is not to blame. Finally, thanks to COVID-19 for locking me down long enough to write this book.

Miles A. Copeland III
January 2021

INDEX

PHOTO CREDITS

Unless otherwise noted, the photographs in this book are from the author's collection. Additional sources are as follows, and we are grateful for their help. If you feel there has been a mistaken attribution, please contact the publisher. **Photo insert** *The Cortinas*, Peter Swan; *Sniffin' Glue, Star Truckin' line-up, Gene October, Billy Idol, Squeeze, Miles and Ian*, Jill Furmanovsky via rockarchive.com; *IRS logo*, Carlos Grasso; *IRS team 1983*, Edward Colver; *poolside with Sting, singing with Sting, Cheb Mami, Ilham al-Madfai*, Daniel Quatrochi. **Cover** *The Police*, Gijsbert Hanekroot/Getty Images; *Bellydance Superstars, portraits of Miles*, Aaron Stipkovich.

ALSO AVAILABLE IN PRINT AND EBOOK EDITIONS FROM JAWBONE